Abstracts of the
TESTAMENTARY PROCEEDINGS
of the
PREROGATIVE COURT OF MARYLAND

Volume XV: 1719–1721

Liber: 24, 25 (pp. 1–87)

by
V. L. Skinner, Jr.

CLEARFIELD

Printed for
Clearfield Company by
Genealogical Publishing Co.
Baltimore, Maryland
2008

ISBN-13: 978-0-8063-5376-0
ISBN-10: 0-8063-5376-7

Made in the United States of America

INTRODUCTION

Purpose of the Prerogative Court.

The Prerogative Court was the central point for probate for Provincial Maryland. It was mirrored after the Prerogative Court of Canterbury. There was a judge as well as clerk(s) of the court. Initially, all probate was brought directly to the Prerogative Court, located in the Provincial Capital. As the Province became more populous, all documents were still to be filed with the Prerogative Court; however, administration of probate was delegated to the various county courts. Even so, there are documents only in the Prerogative Court and not in the appropriate county, and vice versa.

Documents filed in the Prerogative Court.

The following documents were filed in the Prerogative Court: administration bond, will, inventory, administration accounts, and final balances. The testamentary proceedings contain the administration bond and the docket for the court. If the administrator is lax in filing documents, then a summons is also recorded.

Equity Court

The Prerogative Court was also the court for equity cases--resolution of disputes over the settlement and distribution of an estate. The case was brought before the judge and could take several years to resolve. Often depositions were taken and recorded in the minutes.

Notes on the Abstraction.

1. The left hand column contains the liber/folio number. The folio numbers are presented just as they appear in the actual document, e.g., 32a, 78½.

2. The right hand column contains the abstraction text.

3. Various libers specify a particular session for the Prerogative Court, e.g., 1678; or, September Court 1742. This information is presented as "Court Session:" followed by the

appropriate session. Should no session have
been specified, then the phrase "no date" is
used.

4. An ellipsis (...) is used to indicate a
continuation of the previous information, but no
relevant genealogical information is present.

5. The following symbols are used in the
abstraction:

?   difficult to read.
\#   pounds of tobacco.
!   [sic].

Abbreviations.

The following abbreviations have been used
throughout this abstraction:

AA - Anne Arundel Co.   administration
ACC - Accomac Co.   LoD - list of debts
BA - Baltimore Co.   MA - Massachusetts
CE - Cecil Co.   MD - Maryland
CH - Charles Co.   MO - Montgomery Co.
CR - Caroline Co.   NE - New England or
CV - Calvert Co.   "non est"
dbn - de bonis non   NEI - "non est
DE - Delaware   inventar" (not
DO - Dorchester Co.   found)
ENG - England   NY - New York
FR - Frederick Co.   NYC - New York City
g - gentleman   p - planter
HA - Harford Co.   PA - Pennsylvania
IRE - Ireland   PG - Prince George's
JP - justice of the   Co.
    peace   PoA - power of
KE - Kent Co. MD   attorney
KEDE - Kent Co. DE   QA - Queen Anne's Co.
LaC - letters ad   SM - St. Mary's Co.
    colligendum (for   SMC - St. Mary's City
    temporary   SO - Somerset Co.
    collection &   TA - Talbot Co.
    preservation of   VA - Virginia
    assets)   WA - Washington Co.
LoA - letters of   WO - Worcester Co.

This volume is a continuation of the series,
covering 1719 to 1721. The Deputy Commissaries
in the various counties are now responsible for
appointing the appraisers, and approving the
administration accounts. The Court is meeting
every 2 months to review the docket, and to take
appropriate actions.

24:1   19 June. Exhibited from AA:
- accounts of Ruth Warfield
  administratrix of John Warfield.
- inventory of Richard Powell.

23 June. Fran. Holland (BA) exhibited:
- bond of Honour Arden administratrix
  of Samuel Arden. Sureties: Jonas
  Bowen, Edward Mahey. Date: 23 April
  1719.
- bond of John Lowe administrator of
  William Lowe. Sureties: John Lowe,
  William Lowe, Thomas Norris. Date:
  15 June 1719.

Deputy Commissary (BA) to examine
accounts of:
- John Sumers & his wife
  administratrix of Andrew Berry.

24:2   24 June. Mr. Alexander Contee (CH) to
examine accounts of:
- George Brett executor of William
  Brett.
- Elinor Philpott & John Philpott
  executors of Edward Philpott.
- Anne Freeman executrix of Nathaniel
  Freeman.
- Thomas King & John Cooper executors
  of William Muncester.
- John Maning executor of Joseph
  Maning.
- Issabella Dryden executrix of George
  Dryden.

William Smith executor of William Fisher
was granted continuance.

James Harris (KE) exhibited:
- will of Thomas Medford, constituting
  Rachell Medford executrix. Said
  Rachell was granted administration.
  Sureties: Abraham Redgrave, Richard
  Kennard. Date: 24 June 1719.
24:3   - bond of Theodolia Roberts
  administratrix of John Peters.
  Sureties: John Clark, Roger Hix.
  Date: 18 June 1719.
- inventory of William Harcum.

Alexander Contee (CH) exhibited:
- renunciation of Margarett Miller on

estate of Jacob Miller. John Courts was granted administration. Sureties: Ledstone Smallwood, James Maddox. Date: 18 May 1719.

- bond of Charles Musgrave administrator of William Musgrave. Surety: John Miller. Date: 3 June 1719.
- inventory of James Neale the younger.
- inventory of John Compton

24:4
- inventory of William Munkister.
- inventory of Hannah Wilson.
- inventory of Edward Philpott.
- inventory of Joseph Harrison.
- accounts of Thomas Morris administrator of Stephen Morris.
- accounts of Mary Perry executrix of Thomas Perry.
- additional accounts of Jane Brooke administratrix of John Brooke.
- accounts of John Barker & his wife Frances administratrix of Mathew Ferrell.
- accounts of John Chandler administrator of Joseph Lewin.
- accounts of John Crackson administrator of Thomas Crackson.
- additional accounts of Elisabeth Haley administratrix of John Haley.
- accounts of John Causeen & Thomas Reaves administrators of William Causeen.

26 June. Dr. Patrick Hepburne (PG) exhibited:
- will of William Head, constituting Anne Head executrix. Said Anne was granted administration. Sureties: Patrick Andrews, Bernard White. Date: 6 June 1719.

24:5
- inventory of Nicholas Davis.
- inventory of John Prather.
- inventory of Stephen Johnson.
- final accounts of Patrick Andrews administrator of Rebecca Becraft.
- 5th additional accounts of Thomas & James Grienfield executors of Col. Thomas Grienfield.
- additional accounts of John Jones & his wife Anne executrix of Henry Gutridge.

- accounts of Edm. Major administrator of Nicholas Davis.
- bond of Elisabeth Foster administratrix of John Foster. Sureties: Philip Green, Thomas Holland. Date: 20 June 1719.
- accounts of Edm. Major administrator of Mathew Day.

30 June. Exhibited:
- accounts of John Woodall administrator of Edward Plestoe (KE). Also additional inventory.

24:6 1 July. Exhibited from QA:
- bond of Robert Jones administrator of William Sweatnam, during minority of Hester & Sarah children of said William. Sureties: Thomas Hynson Wright, John Wright. Date: 24 June 1719.
- inventory of George Mather.

2 July. Alexander Contee (CH) exhibited:
- accounts of George Brett executor of William Brett.
- accounts of Thomas Michell & Archibald Johnstone executors of Richard Coleman.
- accounts of John Maning executor of Joseph Manning.

24:7 3 July. Exhibited:
- accounts of Elisabeth Warfield executrix of Benjamin Warfield (AA). Also additional inventory.

4 July. Exhibited:
- accounts of William Young executor of George Young (CV).

8 July. Exhibited:
- accounts of John Gray administrator of Zachry Gray (AA).

10 July. Exhibited:
- will of John Harwood.

12 July. Exhibited:
- bond of Anne Smith executrix of William Smith. Sureties: Henry

Court Session: 1719

Attwood, Abell Hill. Date: 12 July
1719.

Court Session: 14 July 1719

24:8   Docket:
       • J.B. for John Burle vs. Hugh
         Merikin. Struck off.
24:9   • E.J. for Thomas Gray vs. T.L. for
         John Gray. Libel & answer.
       • T.L. for Jacob & Thomas Holland vs.
         John Harris. Agreed.
24:10 • Attachment issued to Anne Bladen
         widow of William Bladen, Esq. (AA).
         Stephen Warman (sheriff, AA)
         returned: NEI.
       • Woolman Gibson & his wife
         administratrix of Lambert Clements
         vs. Henry Bullen. Charles Ungle
         (sheriff, TA) to summon defendant to
         show cause why inventory may not be
         received.
24:11 Said Henry Bullen, age 36, deposed.
24:12 ...
24:13 Letter of breach of duty to said
       Ungle.
       • Richard Trensam admitted as proctor
         to court.
24:14 • Thomas Hamond vs. Carpenter
         Lillingstone (QA). Edward Wright
         (sheriff, QA) to summon defendant to
         render perfect accounts on estate of
         Richard Macklin & on estate of
         Joseph Lambert.
24:15 • Letter from Benjamin Tasker:
         Mrs. Bladen awaits appraisal of
         certain items. Date: 15 July 1719.
24:16 ...
24:17 Exhibited inventory of goods in AA,
       SM, & QA.
24:18 ...

24:19 Deputy Commissary (PG) to examine
       accounts of:
       • Cathrine Prather executrix of John
         Prather.
       • William Diggs executor of Edward
         Diggs.

       Jonathon Hopkins for John Brookes vs.
       Hermanus Schee (mariner, KE) & his wife
       Johanna executrix of Philip Hopkins

Court Session: 14 July 1719

(KE). Said Brooks is a legatee on said estate. Summons to defendants.

24:20   Mr. Robert Tyler was granted continuance on estate of:
- James Mullikin.
- John Reaves.

Deputy Commissary (SM) to examine accounts of:
- John Taney & Robert Hutchins on estate of William Huthins.

Deputy Commissary (SO) to examine accounts of:
- John Hampton who married Mary widow & executrix of John Henry (SO).

Per Henry Bayly, letter to Mr. Turbutt (TA) exhibited:
- Lambert Clements has been dec'd many years & no LoA were granted. If Henry Bayly & his wife Elisabeth do not apply for LoA, then LoA is to be granted to John Clements, as next-of-kin. Date: 26 June 1719.

24:21   Exhibited:
- Accounts of Thomas & Joseph Wellman executors of Michell Wellman (SM).
Elisabeth Wellman executrix of Michaell Wellman (AA) was granted continuance.

Philip Hamond (AA) exhibited:
- final accounts of John Merikin executor of Joshua Merikin.
- additional accounts of Daniel Carter & his wife Ruth administratrix of John Warfield.
- inventory of William Fisher.

24:22   Exhibited:
- additional accounts of Mary Weeks executrix of Benjamin Weeks (QA).
- accounts of John Cornelius & his wife Sarah administratrix of Stephen White (QA).
- additional accounts of Francis Dorsey executrix of Nicholas Dorsey.
- accounts of Gideon Pierce executor of Maj. William Potts (KE).
- accounts of Nicholas Hyland administrator of Philip Howell (CE).

24:23 • will of William Husband (CE).

Foster Turbott (TA) exhibited:
- bond of Elisabeth Martindale administratrix of Henry Martindale. Sureties: Robert Hopkins, Stephen Richant. Date: 17 May 1719.
- bond of Hannah Parrott administratrix of Issaiah Parrott. Sureties: Edward Clarke, Sr., Joshua Clark. Date: 23 June 1719.
- bond of Henry Bayly & his wife Elisabeth administratrix of Lambert Clements. Sureties: Thomas Hopkins, Franc. Armstrong. Date: 17 July 1719.
- inventory of John Newman.
- inventory of Margarett Raglass.
- accounts of Elinor Crowley executrix of Daniel Crowley.
- accounts of John Wilson & his wife administratrix of Francis Kinimont.
- accounts of Thomas Hampton & his wife administratrix of Richard Hall.

24:24 • accounts of Thomas Banyard executor of William Thompson.
- accounts of Robert Willin administrator of Darby Macmallawn.

24 July. Exhibited:
- additional accounts of Gideon Pierce executor of Maj. William Potts (KE).

25 July. Alexander Contee (CH) exhibited:
- will of Issabella Dryden, constituting Susanna Yopp executrix. Said Yopp was granted administration. Sureties: Thomas Mathews, Richard Chapman. Date: 1 July 1719.
- inventory of William Smith.
- inventory of John Denegoe.
- inventory of Charles Yopp.

John Baker (SM) exhibited:
- inventory of William Aisquith.

24:25 • will of Kennelmn Cheseldyne, constituting Mary Cheseldyne (alias Mary Phippard) executrix. Said Mary was granted administration.

Court Session: 14 July 1719

    Sureties: John Baptista Carbery,
Thomas Guybert, Gerrard Jourdaine,
Philip Tippett. Date: 29 May 1719.
- will of Adam Bell, constituting Anne
Bell executrix. Said Anne was
granted administration. Sureties:
Richard Hopewell, Charles King.
Date: 19 June 1719.

28 July. Phil. Hamond (AA) exhibited:
- accounts of Margarett Todd executrix
of Richard Todd.
- accounts of Joseph Jones who married
Mary administratrix of Richard
Harwood.
- accounts of Thomas Cockey acting
administrator of John Ingram.
- accounts of John Nicholson executor
of Robert Moss.
- additional inventory of John Ingram.

24:26   31 July. Exhibited from SM:
- additional accounts of Cornelius
Maning administrator of John Maning.
- accounts of William Brewer
administrator of Thomas Davis.

Exhibited:
- accounts of John Buck administrator
of John Martin (BA).
- accounts of John Eager & Luke
Trotten executors of John Downes
(BA).
- accounts of Luke Trotten
administrator of Samuel Heathcoate
(BA).

4 August. Exhibited:
- additional accounts of James Crouch
& his wife Anne administrators of
Samuel Skidmore (AA).
- LoD of Elisabeth Wellman executrix
of Michael Welman (AA).
24:27 - accounts of Anne Renshaw widow &
administratrix of Francis Roberts
(SO).

6 August. Exhibited:
- accounts of Philemon Hemsley
administrator of Thomas Waples (CH).
Also LoD.
- inventory of Thomas Williamson (BA).

Court Session: 14 July 1719

- accounts of George Dent executor of William Herbert (CH).
- additional inventory of William Herbert (CH).
- inventory of William Bladen, Esq. (KI, SM, AA).

24:28

Alexander Contee (CH) exhibited:
- accounts of Thomas Stoddert administrator of James Saffron.
- additional accounts of William Sander executor of Robert Sander.
- accounts of Anne Freeman administratrix of Nathaniel Freeman.

George Douglas executor of Sarah Herbert (CH) was granted continuance.

10 August. Exhibited:
- additional accounts of John Standforth executor of Abraham Fisher (AA).

Exhibited from KE:
- bond of Thomas Ares administrator of Daniel Dunsey. Sureties: John Davis, Richard Davis. Date: 27 November 1718.

24:29
- bond of Abraham Taylor administrator of Henry Brooke. Sureties: Josias Lanham, Griffith Jones. Date: 10 October 1718.
- bond of Mary Wilkinson administratrix of Anthony Wilkinson. Surety: William Deane. Date: 11 March 1717.
- inventory of Edward Browsbank.
- additional inventory of William Welsh.
- inventory of Henry Brook.
- inventory of Daniel Dunsey.
- inventory of Anthony Wilkinson.
- inventory of John Clerk.
- accounts of Rachell Browsbanks administratrix of Edward Browsbanks.
- accounts of Abraham Taylor administrator of Henry Brook.
- accounts of Thomas Ares administrator of Daniel Dunsey.
- additional accounts of Richard Fulston. administrator of William Scott.

Page 8

Court Session: 14 July 1719
- accounts of Edward Davis executor of Thomas Harding.
- accounts of Francis Lewis administrator of James Lewis.

24:30   Deputy Commissary (KE) to grant LoA to:
- Thomas Eubank on estate of William Eubank.

Deputy Commissary (KE) to examine accounts of:
- Samuel Clark & his wife administratrix of Dennis Clarke.

Deputy Commissary (PG) to examine accounts of:
- Joseph Belt executor of John Lashly.

Court Session: 11 August 1719

24:31   Docket:
- E.J. for Thomas Gray vs. T.L. for John Gray. Libel.
- R.T. for Jonathon Hopkins vs. J.B. for Hermanus Schee & his wife. Libel. Simon Wilmore (sheriff, KE) to summon defendants.

Court Session: August 1719

24:32   James Frisby for Richard Smithers & John Stokes vs. William Marshall & his wife administratrix of George Wells. Edward Hall (sheriff, BA) to summon defendants.

Edward Wright (sheriff, QA) to render attachment to Carpenter Lillingstone to render accounts on estate of Richard Maclin & on estate of Joseph Lambert.

24:33   Stephen Warman (sheriff, AA) to serve Proclamation of Rebellion against Anne Bladen widow of William Bladen, Esq. (AA).

24:34   She is not found.

Col. Richard Tilghman executor of Dorothy Colt was granted continuance.

John Nicholson for Rebecca Nicholson administratrix of John Nicholson (AA) was granted continuance.

Court Session: August 1719

Cathrine White administratrix of Timothy White (AA) was granted continuance.

Woolman Gibson who married administratrix of Lambert Clements (TA) was granted continuance.

24:35 Phil. Feddeman (sheriff, DO) to summon:
- Moses Lecompt executor of Moses Lecompt to render inventory.
- Mary Warner administratrix of Stephen Warner to render accounts.
- John Rix & William Thomas administrators of Martha Woolman to render accounts.
- Nehemiah Becwith administrator of Henry Becwith to render accounts.
- Jennett Oneale administratrix of Mathew Oneale to render accounts.
- Edward Alford administrator of Cesely Bourk to render accounts.
- George Fee administrator of William Vaughan to render accounts.
- Richard Pritchard administrator of Richard Stanford to render accounts.
- Elisabeth Wetherall executrix of William Wetherall to render accounts.
- Benjamin Woodward administrator of James Woodward to render accounts.
- Rachel Vicars executrix of John Vicars to render accounts.
- Edward Newton administrator of Edward Paule to render inventory.
- Cathrine Bruff administratrix of Thomas Bruff to render inventory.
- Henry Trip administrator of Austin Parker to render inventory.
- John Flower administrator of William Burnell to render inventory.
- Elisabeth Mattig administratrix of Godfrey Mattig to render inventory.
- Anne Maudsley executrix of James Maudsley to render inventory.
- Elisabeth Hargesson administratrix of George Hargesson to render inventory.
- Elisabeth Ennalls executrix of Thomas Ennalls to render inventory.

24:36 Henry Bullen vs. Woolman Gibson & his wife. Charles Ungle (sheriff, TA) to

Court Session: August 1719

summon defendants to render inventory on estate of Lambert Clements.

24:37   12 August. Exhibited from AA:
- inventory of John Cread.

18 August. Exhibited from CH:
- additional inventory of Lydia Yates.

19 August. Foster Turbott exhibited:
- bond of Risdon Bosman & his wife Frances executrix of Philip Sherwood. Sureties: Thomas Bosman, James Dawson. Date: 6 August 1719.
- bond of Anne Turner administratrix of Edward Turner, Sr. Sureties: William Turner, Edward Turner. Date: 21 July 1719.
- bond of Robert Ungle administrator of Thomas Collier. Sureties: David Robinson, William Ayres. Date: 27 July 1719.
- bond of Michael Fletcher administrator dbn of Thomas Smithson, unadministered by executrix. Sureties: William Clayland, Edmond Fish. Date: 28 July 1719.
- accounts of Perry Benson & his wife executrix of Michael Russell.
- accounts of William Vickers & his wife executrix of John Keld.

24:38   20 August. Dr. Patrick Hepburne (PG) exhibited:
- will of Andrew Hamilton, constituting his widow executrix. Also renunciation of said widow. Col. Thomas Addison was granted administration. Sureties: Thomas Cleggatt, Basell Waren. Date: 8 August 1719.
- inventory of Thomas Wells, Sr.
- inventory of William Head.
- additional inventory of James Shaw.
- accounts of Samuel Thacker administrator of William Howell.

Adderton Skinner (CV) exhibited:
- will of David Bowen. Also bond by James Deavers & his wife Elisabeth executrix. Sureties: William

Wilmott, John Brooke. Date: 27 June
1719.
- will of Elisha Sedgwick. Also bond
by James Murrain & his wife Grace
executrix. Sureties: Henry Chew,
Daniel Emry. Date: 26 June 1719.
- bond of Cornelius Dwyer
administrator of Daniell Spencer.
Surety: Daniell Sullivan.

24:39
- Date: 18 July 1719.
- deed from Elisabeth Griffith to
Samuel Griffith.
- inventory of David Bowen.
- inventory of Charles Nash.
- additional inventory of James
Paskall.
- inventory of John Owen.
- inventory of Samuel Wallis.
- inventory of Elisabeth Paskall.

24 August. Raphaell Neale executor of
Leonard Brooks (CH) was granted
continuance.

Elisabeth Brook administratrix of Roger
Brooke (PG) was granted continuance.

Henry Satyr administrator of Edward
Stevenson (BA) was granted continuance,
as Commissary General is indisposed.

24:40 Exhibited from PG:
- inventory of John Reaves.
- inventory of James Mullikin.

26 August. Exhibited from CH:
- bond of John Browne & Edward
Anderson administrators of Richard
Morris. Sureties: George Goodrick,
Percivall Ferson. Date: 8 August
1719.
- bond of Margarett Yopp
administratrix of Roger Yopp.
Sureties: Richard Chapman, John
Glasson. Date: 15 August 1719.

31 August. Exhibited:
- additional accounts of George Ogg
administrator of William Talbott
(BA).
- 2nd additional inventory of John
Warfield (AA).

Court Session: August 1719

24:41   Exhibited from AA:
- 8 September. additional inventory of Morgan Jones.
- 4 September. accounts of William Jones administrator of Morgan Jones.
- 7 September. additional accounts of William Jones administrator of Morgan Jones.
- 7 September. additional accounts of William Mead executor of Francis Mead.

Mr. Adderton Skinner (CV) to examine accounts of:
- John Dickinson executor of Edward Dickinson.
- James Roberts executor of Robert Dixon.
- Amy Doring executrix of Edward Doring.

Court Session: 8 September 1719

24:42   Docket:
- E.J. for Thomas Gray vs. T.L. for John Gray. Libel.
- R.T. for Jonathon Hopkins vs. Hermanus Schee & his wife. Libel.

Commissary General is very indisposed.

Court Session: September 1719

24:43   Richard Willis (coroner, DO) to render attachment to Philip Fedeman (sheriff, DO) for contempt.

Summons to Anne Dixon to prove will of Thomas Dixon (CH).

24:44   Thomas Brannock & Henry Becwith vs. Nehemiah Becwith administrator of Henry Becwith. Philip Fedeman (sheriff, DO) to summon defendant.

Richard Tilghman, Esq. executor of Dorothy Coult to be no more summoned. Said estate "is a very small one", given to one of said Tilghman's children.

Richard Tilghman, Esq. administrator of George Lillingstone summoned to render inventory. Said Tilghman exhibited that he only took LoA in order to recover a debt.

24:45   Deputy Commissary to examine accounts of:
- Sarah Truman executrix of Thomas Truman (PG).

Deputy Commissary (TA) to examine accounts of:
- Rebecca Bromwell executrix of Thomas Beswick (TA).

Samuel Hopkins (SO) exhibited:
- will of Walter Read, constituting Pierce Read executor. Said Pierce was granted administration. Sureties: Francis Joce, Joseph Filleman. Date: 8 August 1719.
- will of Abraham Fall, constituting Mary Fall executrix. Said Mary was granted administration. Sureties: John Holland, William Walton. Date: 3 July 1719.
- will of John Brown, constituting Mary Fountaine. executrix. Said Fountaine was granted administration. Surety: John Fountaine. Date: 17 June 1719.

24:46
- bond of Naomy Shiles administratrix of Thomas Shiles. Sureties: Benjamin Cottman, Adam Heath. Date: 19 June 1719.
- bond of Sarah Wheatly administratrix of William Wheatly. Sureties: Stephen Horsey, Thomas Potter. Date: 17 June 1719.
- bond of Henry Philips administrator of Charles Philips. Sureties: William Denson, Samuel Marchment. Date: 22 August 1719.
- bond of Richard Holland administrator of Charles Shewell. Sureties: Walter Evans, Jones Richards. Date: 22 August 1719.
- inventory of Warren Hader.
- inventory of Thomas Holbrook.
- inventory of John Gray.
- inventory of John Bratten.
- inventory of Joseph Austin.
- inventory of Joseph Wouldhave.

Court Session: September 1719

- inventory of Benjamin Wouldhave.
- inventory of Abraham Richards.
- inventory of William White.

24:47
- inventory of Daniel Lary.
- inventory of William Round.
- inventory of Thomas Browne.
- accounts of Sarah Hayman administratrix of James Hayman.
- accounts of Priscilla Mezeck administratrix of Julin Mezeck.
- accounts of Margaret White administratrix of William White.
- accounts of Tabitha Clark administratrix of John Clark.
- accounts of Anne Dukes administratrix of John Dukes.
- accounts of Anne More administratrix of John More.
- accounts of James Bound administratrix of William Bound.
- accounts of Anne Layfield administratrix of Robert Layfield.

Exhibited from CV:
- inventory of Nathaniell Miles.
- accounts of Mary Newgin administratrix of Thomas Newgin.

Exhibited from DO:
- will of Jacob Paul

24:48
- inventory of William Marrett.
- inventory of Austin Parker.
- inventory of James Canon.
- inventory of William Insley.
- inventory of Anne Dawson.
- accounts of John Pullen & his wife executrix of John Noele.
- accounts of Benjamin Woodward administratrix of James Woodward.
- accounts of Edward Newton administrator of Edward Paule.
- accounts of Rachel Vicars executrix of John Vicars.

Exhibited from KE:
- will of Col. Thomas Smith, constituting Matha Smith executrix. Said Matha was granted administration. Sureties: James Smith, William Thomas. Date: 5 August 1719.
- bond of Cathrine Maddin

administratrix of John Maddin.
Sureties: Richard Fullston, Daniel
Cooly. Date: 12 August 1719.
- bond of William Spearman
administrator of Michael Gaughagan.
Sureties: James Kelly, Vivian Black.
Date: 2 September 1719.

24:49 Exhibited from SM:
- will of Peter Watts, constituting
Elisabeth Watts executrix.
Sureties: Thomas Wauhop, George
Clarke. Date: 27 July 1719.
- will of Richard Brooke, constituting
Leonard Brooke executor. Said
Leonard was granted administration.
Sureties: Clement Gardiner, William
Spalding. Date: 4 August 1719.
- bond of Frances Howell
administratrix of Evan Howell.
Sureties: Stephen Watts, John Welsh.
Date: 22 August 1719.
- bond of Cathrine Hammett
administratrix of Robert Hammett.
Sureties: Joseph Laurence, James
Baker. Date: 27 July 1719.
- bond of Richard Keene administrator
of William Creatchett. Sureties:
Charles King, Thomas Aisquith.
Date: 19 May 1719.

24:50
- will of Edward Barrett.
- inventory of William Creatchett.
- inventory of Robert Hamett.
- inventory of John King.
- inventory of Thomas Kendeloe.
- inventory of William Hazle.
- inventory of Guilbert Turbefield.
- inventory of Joshua Turner.
- accounts of Henry Colby & his wife
administratrix of Simon Comb.
- accounts of Michael Branson
administrator of Philip Harney.
- accounts of John Heard administrator
of John Dowagan.
- accounts of James Biscoe
administrator of Thomas Grace.
- Thomas Kirby administrator of Thomas
Vaughan.
- accounts of Elisabeth Brady
executrix of Owen Brady.
- accounts of Peter Peake
administrator of Richard Walker.

Court Session: September 1719

- accounts of Dorothy Racey
  administratrix of Thomas Racey.
- accounts of Moor Langley
  administratrix of John Langley.
- accounts of John Tarlton
  administrator of William Wherrett.

24:51   Exhibited from PG:
- inventory of William Nicholls.
- inventory of John Hambleton.
- inventory of Thomas Clarke.
- inventory of Thomas Harvey.
- inventory of Thomas Robin.
- accounts of Joseph Belt executor of
  John Lashly.

Exhibited:
- inventory of William Ridgley (AA),
  by administratrix.
- inventory of Thomas Lewis (TA).
- accounts of James Porter executor of
  Francis Porter (TA).

24:52   9 September. Mr. James Harris (KE)
exhibited:
- final accounts of John Glory
  administrator of John Smith.
- final accounts of Samuel Clarke
  executor of William Lewis.
- accounts of Samuel Clark who married
  executrix of Dennis Clark.

10 September. Exhibited:
- additional accounts of Mary
  Wrightson executrix of John
  Wrightson (TA).
- accounts of John Oldham
  administrator of Thomas Lewis (TA).
- accounts of Cathrine Severson
  administratrix of Thomas Severson
  (CE).
- accounts of Daniel Jenifer & his
  wife executrix of John Rogers (CH).
24:53 - accounts of John Flowers executor of
  David Rogers (TA).
- inventory of Mary Ganyott (SM).
- accounts of Thomas Hynson Wright &
  his wife executrix of John Coursey
  (QA).

11 September. Phil. Hammond (AA)
exhibited:

Page 17

Court Session: September 1719

- nuncupative will of Richard Bickerdike, constituting Anne Bickerdike executrix. Said Anne was granted administration. Sureties: Thomas Williams, Daniel Larke. Date: 11 September 1719.
- bond of William Yiealdhall administrator of John Stephens. Sureties: Joseph Hall, Charles Stephens. Date: 10 September 1719.
- renunciation of Sarah Stephens on estate of John Stephens, recommending William Yiealdhall.

24:54
- bond of Margarett Macnemara administratrix of Thomas Macnemara ("a most turbulent & seditious person". Sureties: Daniel Dullany, Thomas Larkins. Date: 10 September 1719.

12 September. Deputy Commissary (CH) to examine accounts of:
- Joseph Harrison administrator of Elisabeth Hague.
- Susanna Yopp executrix of Charles Yopp.
- Susanna Yopp executrix of Issabella Dryden.
- Thomas King & John Cooper executors of William Muncester.

Exhibited:
- inventory of Thomas Eager (PG).

14 September. Mr. Foster Turbott to examine witnesses, per Robert Grundy who married Margarett widow & executrix of John Pemberton (TA):

24:55
Enion Williams et.al., in the presence of Mr. Benjamin Pemberton.

16 September. Phil. Hammond (AA) exhibited:
- renunciation of John & Mary Docwra on estate of Thomas Docwra. Also bond of Charles Carroll, Esq. Sureties: John Baldwin, Daniel Carroll. Date: 16 September 1719.
- bond of Samuel Peele administrator of John Ward. Surety: John Beard. Date: 14 September 1719.
- additional inventory of William

Court Session: September 1719

Catton.

Bernard White administrator of Jonathon White was granted continuance.

24:56 Exhibited:
- receipt of Mary Murlow from her father-in-law Henry Acton for all that was left her by her father Richard Gambrill. Date: 15 April 1719. Signed: William Murlow, Mary Murlow. Witnesses: Thomas Purvis, John Taylor. Attested on 5 September 1719 before James Stoddert.

24:57 On an attachment to Patrick Andrews (g, CV) administrator of Rebecca Becraft (PG) to render accounts, said Andrews exhibited that accounts have already been filed.

24 September. Francis Holland (BA) exhibited:
- will of Abraham Taylor.
- inventory of Richard Freeborn.
- inventory of Samuel Arden.
- inventory of John Boon.
- accounts of Fran. Street administrator of William Sumers.

24:58 30 September. Phil. Hammond (AA) exhibited:
- accounts of Alexander Warfield executor of Amos Pierpoint.
- 3rd accounts of Daniel Carter & his wife administratrix of John Warfield.
- accounts of William Phelps administrator of John Keys.
- accounts of Elinor Chinton executrix of George Valentine.
- accounts of John Gray administrator of Zachry Gray.
- inventory of William Smith.

2 October. Exhibited:
- accounts of Robert Yates administrator of Lydia Yates (CH).

6 October. Aderton Skinner (CV) exhibited:

Page 19

Court Session: September 1719

- bond of James Brown administrator of Joanna Thompson. Sureties: Daniel Sulivan, Thomas Ireland. Date: 19 September 1719.
- accounts of Mary Newgin administratrix of Thomas Newgin.

24:59
- accounts of Naomi Doring administratrix of Edward Doring.
- accounts of Kensey Johns administrator of Elisabeth Paskall.

9 October. Mathias Vanderheyden (CE) exhibited:
- will of William Dare, constituting Mary Thompson executrix. Said Thompson was granted administration. Sureties: John Dowdall, Richard Thompson. Date: 6 May 1719.
- bond of Adam Brown administrator of Michaell Coulter. Sureties: Stephen Knight, John Campbell. Date: 14 July 1719.
- inventory of Jonathon Beck.
- inventory of John Thompson.
- inventory of Thomas Eddrington.
- inventory of Andrew Rosenquist.
- inventory of John Hidckcock.
- inventory of George Truddletstone.
- accounts of William Price & his wife administratrix of Olive Wallice.

24:60 Alexander Contee (CH) exhibited:
- will of John Barron, constituting Anne Barron executrix. Said Anne was granted administration. Sureties: Mathew Barnes, Daniel Macdonald. Date: 26 August 1719.
- will of John Boye, constituting Pigeon Boye executrix. Said Pigeon was granted administration. Sureties: Richard Price, William Groves. Date: 21 September 1719.
- inventory of Benjamin Hanson.
- inventory of Issabella Dryden.
- inventory of William Musgrave.
- accounts of Elinor & John Philpott executors of Edward Philpott.
- accounts of John Barker & his wife executrix of Mathew Ferrell.
- accounts of Richard Harison administrator of Joseph Harrison.
- additional accounts of Mat. Stone

administrator of John Killingsworth.

24:61 Samuel Hopkins (SO) exhibited:
- inventory of John Jones.
- inventory of Walter Reed.
- accounts of Jane Rich administratrix of Henry Rich.
- accounts of William Aiers & his wife administratrix of Denum Olandum.

12 October. Exhibited from DO:
- bond of Mary Barnes administratrix of Mathew Barnes. Sureties: Peter Ross, David Mackall. Date: 11 August 1719.
- inventory of Thomas Woodward.
- accounts of John Meekins executor of Richard Meekins.

10 October. Deputy Commissary (KE) to examine accounts of:
- Benjamin Pearce & his wife on estate of Edward Cooper (KE).

24:62 John Jones (g, SO) to examine accounts of:
- George Dashiell administrator of John Clarke (SO).

Deputy Commissary (CH) to examine additional accounts of:
- Daniel Jenifer & his wife executrix of John Rogers (CH).

14 October. Deputy Commissary (SO) to examine accounts of:
- Sarah Dashiell executrix of Robert Dashiell.

Dr. Patrick Hepburne (PG) exhibited:
- will of James Gardiner. Also bond of Samuel Magruder. Sureties: Ninian & John Magruder. Date: 14 October 1719.

24:63
- will of John Smith.
- inventory of John Foster.
- 15 October. additional inventory of Thomas Truman.
- accounts of Robert Tyler administrator of John Reave.
- accounts of Robert Tyler administrator of James Mullikin.

Court Session: September 1719

- accounts of John Norris & his wife
  administrators of Thomas Windon.

Robert Jones (QA) exhibited:
- bond of Edward Cockey administrator
  dbn of Issaac Harris. Sureties:
  Francis Barnes, Joseph Sadler.
  Date: 4 June 1719.
- inventory of Winifret Vincent.
- inventory of Ralph Distance.
- inventory of Newton Barber.
- inventory of Christopher Goule.
- inventory of William Montsier.
- inventory of John Baimon.
- inventory of Thomas Rouse.
- inventory of Thomas Willotson.
- inventory of Renatus Smith.
- inventory of Morte Bryant.
- inventory of William Wilson.
- additional accounts of Richard
  Bennit executor of John Hunt.

Exhibited:
- additional accounts of Jane Vandever
  administratrix of John Giles.

Exhibited from BA:
- bond of John Taylor executor of
  Abraham Taylor. Sureties: Francis
  Dollarhide, Mat. Hall. Date: 11
  August 1718.
- renunciation of Ann Hopkins widow of
  John Hopkins, recommending Capt.
  Francis Dollarhide.
- renunciation of William Low on
  estate of his father William Low,
  recommending John Low.
- will of John Willmott, constituting
  John Willmott executor. Said
  executor was granted administration.
  Sureties: John Arthuron, John
  Cromwell. Date: 13 November 1719.
- LoD on estate of George Wells.

Exhibited from SO:
- accounts of John Jones executor of
  Luke Valentine.
- accounts of Alexander Carlyle
  administrator of Robert Lawson.
- accounts of John Caldwell
  administrator of Charles Wharton.
- accounts of Mary Shaw executrix of

24:64

24:65

Thomas Shaw.
- accounts of John Hampton & his wife administratrix of John Henry.
- bond of Abigall Newbold administratrix of William Newbold. Sureties: William Handy, Solomon Coulbourne. Date: 30 September 1719.

24:66 19 October. Deputy Commissary (DO) to examine accounts of:
- Elisabeth Ferguson administratrix of George Ferguson.
- Henry Bradley & his wife administratrix of Thomas Woodward.

22 October. Exhibited:
- accounts of John Dickinson executor of Edward Dickinson.
- accounts of Thomas Talbott administrator of James Paskall.

23 October. James Harris (KE) exhibited:
- bond of John Attwick administrator of William Lowkock. Sureties: Guybertus Comegeys, Frances Read. Date: 9 October 1719.
- inventory of John Madden.
24:67
- additional accounts of Edward Davis executor Thomas Hardin.
- additional accounts of Herm. Schee & his wife executrix of Phil. Hopkins.

26 October. Foster Turbott (TA) exhibited:
- will of John Tyler, constituting Edward Turner executor. Said Turner was granted administration. Sureties: Thomas Scokwell, William Barker. Date: 7 August 1719.
- will of Sarah Stephens, constituting John Stevens & name Webb Sarah executors. Said executors were granted administration. Sureties: Henry King, William Warner. Date: 24 September 1719.
- bond of Elisabeth Rippith administratrix of James Rippith. Sureties: Philip Horney, George Shannahawn. Date: 10 November 1719.

Court Session: September 1719

- bond of Christo. Arrington administrator of Prudence Woolman. Sureties: Silvester Abbot, James Tucker. Date: 1 October 1719.
- inventory of Thomas Beswik.
- inventory of Lambert Clement.
- inventory of John Love.
- additional inventory of Michael Russell.
- inventory of Thomas Beswick (p).
- inventory of Richard Webb.
- inventory of James Taylor.
- inventory of Thomas Jenkins.
- inventory of Jonathon Neale.
- accounts of Sarah Webb administratrix of Peter Webb.
- accounts of John Mullikin executor of Anne Wall.
- accounts of Frances Holstien administratrix of Andrew Holstien.
- accounts of Peter Sanders & Philip Casey executors of David Fairbank.
- accounts of John Smith administrator of Elisabeth Worrell.

24:68

28 October. Phil. Hamond (AA) exhibited:
- bond of James Mouat, Stephen Warman, John Beale, & James Nicholson executors of William Nicholson. Sureties: John Watkins, William Chapman, John Baldwin. Date: 19 October 1719.
- bond of Albert Grinin administrator of John Arnoldy. Sureties: Hugh Keneday, Moses Adney. Date: 8 October 1719.
- will of William Peirse.
- inventory of John Ward.
- additional accounts of Rebecca Nicholson administratrix of John Nicholson.
- inventory of Edward Mariartee.
- accounts of Sarah Aldridge executrix of Thomas Aldridge.

24:69

Deputy Commissary (TA) to examine witnesses regarding will of John Pemberton, at request of Robert Grundy.

Thomas Cross vs. estate of Elinor Cross (AA). Caveat exhibited.

Court Session: September 1719

John Jones (g, SO) to examine accounts of:
- George Dashiell on estate of John Clarke.

Deputy Commissary (SO) to examine accounts of:
- James Dashiell & Jane Handy on estate of John Winder.

Sheriff (KE) to summon John Inch & his wife widow of William Jones to take LoA or render renunciation on his estate.

24:70 29 October. Exhibited:
- accounts of Mr. Laurence Lant who married administratrix of Joseph Edwards administrator of David White. Said accounts were not accepted.

Elisabeth Brooke administratrix of Roger Brooke was granted continuance.

Deputy Commissary (CV) to examine accounts of:
- Susan & David Hellen executors of David Hellen.
- James Roberts executor of Robert Dixon.

2 November. Exhibited from AA:
- inventory of Richard Bickerdike.
24:71 - 7 November. will of Jonathon Jones, constituting Mary Jones executrix. Said Mary was granted administration. Sureties: John Norris, John Jones. Date: 7 November 1719.
- 9 November. accounts of John Norris & his wife executrix of Mary Watkins.

Robert Jones (QA) exhibited:
- will of Charles Ereckson, constituting Elisheba Ereckson executrix. Said Elisheba was granted administration. Sureties: George Comerford, Henry Weeden. Date: 27 May 1719.
- inventory of Charles Ereckson.
- will of Renatus Smith. Also bond of

Richard Cole administrator.
Sureties: Richard Iago, Charles
McLoyd. Date: 25 June 1719.

- bond of Geor Philips administrator
  of Elisabeth Cavenah. Sureties:
  Robert Kent, Christo. Philips.
  Date: 9 October 1719.
- bond of Elisabeth Blangey executrix
  of Jacob Blangey. Sureties:
  Nathaniel Conner, Francis Barnes.
  Date: 27 August 1719.
- inventory of William Sweatnam.
- inventory of Nathaniel Wright.

24:72

- inventory of Juliana King.
- inventory of Jeramah Barraclough.
- inventory of Richard Moore.
- additional inventory of William
  Denton.
- additional inventory of Solomon
  Wright.
- inventory of Margarett Woolahand.
- inventory of Jacob Brandt.
- accounts of Sarah Denney
  administratrix of Peter Deney.
- accounts of Peter Forcum executor of
  Peter Forcum.
- accounts of John Winchester & his
  wife administratrix of Thomas Rouse.
- accounts of John West administrator
  of Robert Farrow.
- accounts of Anne Chapman executrix
  of George Powell.
- accounts of Christo. Granger
  administrator of Juliana Darnall.
- accounts of Peter Wiles & his wife
  executrix of Richard Moore.
- accounts of Sarah Gold executrix of
  William Bolton.
- accounts of John Welsh administrator
  of William Denton.
- accounts of John Durden
  administrator of Thomas How.
- accounts of Christo. Graven
  administrator of Ralph Distance.
- accounts of Margarett Montsier
  administratrix of William Montsier.
- accounts of Mathew Williams
  administrator of Henry Williams.
- accounts of Solomon Clayton
  administrator of Robert Munday.
- accounts of Thomas Harvey
  administrator of Winifret Vincent.

Court Session: 10 November 1719

24:73   Docket:
- E.J. for Thomas Gray vs. John Gray. Libel exhibited.
- R.T. for Jonathon Hopkins vs. Hermanus Schee & his wife. Libel; order for answer.

Court Session: November 1719

24:74   John Stephens vs. Daniel Maccambly administrator of John Donahoe (QA). Sheriff (QA) to summon defendant to render accounts.

Robert Jones (coroner, QA) summoned Edward Wright administrator of James Hepburne (QA) to render inventory.

24:75   Daniel of St. Thomas Jenifer (sheriff, SM) summoned Martha Wellman widow & administratrix of Michael Wellman. Said Martha refused to take the oath. She was remanded to the custody of sheriff (AA). On 11 November, she took the oath.

24:76   She delivered to Thomas Wellman an account of sundry papers. LoD delivered to John Shanks (subsheriff, SM).

Samuel Hanson (sheriff, CH) to summon:
- Joseph Harrison administrator of Elisabeth Hague to render perfect accounts.

24:77   Attachments issued against:
- John Norris administrator of Thomas Windon (PG) to answer contempt.
- Sarah Truman executrix of Thomas Truman (PG) to answer contempt.

Summons issued to:
- Timothy Hepburne & his wife Elisabeth executrix of John Smith
- widow of Thomas Burton
to show cause why LoA not given.

Deputy Commissary (CE) to examine accounts of:
- Anne Bristor administratrix of John Bristor (CE).

24:78 Sheriff (SM) summoned William Jameson & his wife Mary widow & executrix of Thomas Barber to render inventory. Said Jameson exhibited certificate from Samuel Williamson that inventory was delivered to Mr. Aisquith. Mr. Baker to examine accounts.

Mr. William Cumin is admitted as proctor to Prerogative Court.

Deputy Commissary (TA) to examine accounts of:
- John Green & William Clayton administrators of Mary Smytly (TA).

John Baker (SM) to examine accounts of:
- Joseph Hardin & his wife on estate of John Welsh.

24:79 Sheriff (PG) summoned William Harris administrator of William Ransom to answer contempt to render inventory. Said Harris exhibited that he couldn't render an inventory until the accounts were done on the estate of George Ransome. Said William was heir & executor. Continuance was granted.

Attachment issued to:
- Thomas Morris administrator of Stephen Morris to render accounts. Said Thomas exhibited that accounts were rendered. Case discharged.

24:80 Sheriff (QA) rendered attachment to:
- George Comerford administrator of Margarett Woolahan to render inventory. Continuance was granted.

Daniel of St. Thomas Jenifer (sheriff, SM) rendered attachment to:
- Richard Griffin administrator of Thomas Singer to render accounts.
- Thomas Dillan administrator of Mary Ganyott to render inventory.
- Jone Welsh administratrix of John Welsh to render accounts.
- Joseph Vansweringen administrator of John Kelly to render accounts.
- Anne Taylor executrix of Thomas Taylor to render accounts.

Court Session: November 1719

- John Borroughs administrator of John Borroughs to render accounts.
- Robert Scot administrator of William Gutherick to render inventory.

24:81
- Mary Barber administratrix of Thomas Barber to render inventory.
- Thomas Sumers administrator of Vincent Langford to render inventory.
- Charles King executor of Edward Hall to render inventory.

James Vanbeber (sheriff, CE) rendered attachment to:
- Elisabeth Hitchcock executrix of John Hitchcock to render inventory.
- Benjamin Cox administrator of George Truddlestone to render inventory.
- Elisabeth Hitherington administratrix of Thomas Hitherington to render inventory.
- Anne Bristoe administratrix of John Bristoe to render inventory.
- Johanna Dampier administratrix of Daniel Dampier to render accounts.
- Jos. Young administrator of Thomas Corne to render inventory.
- Mary Thompson administratrix of John Thompson to render inventory.
- Mary Beck administratrix of Jonathon Beck to render inventory.

24:82   Sheriff (TA) rendered attachment to:
- Rebecca Pitts executrix of John Pitts to render accounts.
- Thomas Emerson, Jr. executor of Anne Emerson to render accounts.
- Cathrine Githins executrix of Benjamin Githins to render inventory.
- Samuel Dickinson executor of Matthew Picket to render accounts.
- Mary Newman administratrix of John Newman to render accounts.
- Mary Newman administratrix of John Sumers to render inventory.
- Cor. Dwyer administrator of William Dwyer to render inventory.
- John Kemble administrator of Peter Housekin to render inventory.
- William Clayton administrator of Darby Ryon to render inventory.

Court Session: November 1719

- Elisabeth Hopkins executrix of Turlo Higgins to render inventory.
- Elisabeth Hopkins executrix of Robert Hopkins to render inventory.
- Henrietta Crump administratrix of Walter Crump to render inventory.
- Elinor Cotner administratrix of Alexander Cotner to render inventory.
- John Sprignall executor of Anthony Wise to render inventory.
- Mary Welsh administratrix of Pierce Welsh to render inventory.
- John Fisher administrator of Edward Brinney to render inventory.
- Elisabeth Field administratrix of Christopher Field to render inventory.
- Henry Martindale administrator of Samuel Martindale to render inventory.

Thomas Clegett (sheriff, PG) rendered attachment to:
- Joseph Edwards executor of Robert Mansell to render accounts. Dead.
- Thomas Robins executor of Henry Robins to render accounts. Dead.

24:83
- Sarah Truman executrix of Thomas Truman to render accounts.
- Susanna Windon executrix of Thomas Windon to render accounts.
- Joseph Belt executor of John Lashley to render accounts.
- William Harris executor of William Ransom to render inventory.
- Richard Lancaster administrator of Luke Ray to render inventory.
- Ruth Miller administratrix of George Miller to render inventory. Dead.

Sheriff (DO) to render attachment to:
- John Rix & William Thomas administrators of Martha Woolman to render accounts.
- Mary Warner administratrix of Stephen Warner to render accounts.
- Nehemiah Beckwith executor of Henry Beckwith to render accounts.
- Jennet Oneale administratrix of Mat. Oneale to render accounts.
- George Fee administrator of William

Vaughan to render accounts.
- Richard Pritchard administrator of Mary Stanford to render accounts.
- richard Pritchard administrator of James Walker to render accounts.
- Elisabeth Wetherall executrix of William Wetherall to render accounts.
- Cathrine Bruff administratrix of Thomas Bruff to render inventory.
- Henry Tripp administrator of Austin Parker to render inventory.
- Elisabeth Mattiggs administratrix of Godfrey Mattiggs to render inventory.

24:84   Sheriff (QA) to render attachment to:
- Peter Falcom executor of Peter Falcom to render accounts.
- Anne Powell executrix of George Powell to render accounts.
- Anne Kirby executrix of William Kirby to render accounts.
- Ernault Hawkins executor of John Hawkins to render accounts.
- Elisabeth Wood administratrix of John Wood to render inventory.
- Joanna Impey administratrix of William Impey to render inventory.
- George Comerford administrator of Margarett Woolahan to render inventory.
- Samuel Hunter administrator of John Hays to render inventory.
- Ernault Hawkins administrator of John Spry to render inventory.
- Richard Tilghman administrator of George Lillingstone to render inventory.
- John Wilson administrator of William Wilson to render inventory.
- Susanna Rouse administratrix of Thomas Rouse to render inventory.
- Barbara Jackson administratrix of William Draper to render inventory.
- Sarah Deney administratrix of Peter Deney to render inventory.
- Elinor Prat administratrix of William Prat to render inventory.
- Sarah Tool administratrix of Timothy Tool to render inventory.
- Judith Moore executrix of Richard

Moore to render inventory.
- Frances Nicholson executrix of John Nicholson to render inventory.
- Joseph West administrator of Robert Farrow to render inventory.
- Hanah Bryon administratrix of Cor. Bryon to render inventory.
- John Dahley administrator of Ralph Distance to render inventory.
- John Gibbs executor of Ralph Arnault to render inventory.
- Margaret Montsiere administratrix of William Montsiere to render inventory.
- Neriah Wright administratrix of Nathaniel Wright to render inventory.
- Sarah Gold administratrix of Christo. Gold to render inventory.
- John Wright administrator of Thomas Willotson to render inventory.
- Thomas Harvey administrator of Winifret Vincent to render inventory.

24:85   Samuel Hanson (sheriff, CH) to render attachment to:
- Joseph Harrison administrator of Robert Kerr to render accounts. NEI.
- Thomas Morris administrator of Stephen Morris to render accounts.
- Frances Loften administratrix of John Loften to render inventory.
- Thomas Howard administrator of Jacob Brandt to render inventory.

Abm. Downe (sheriff, CV) rendered attachment to:
- Richard Bond executor of John Rankin to render inventory. "Mort est".

Stephen Warman (sheriff, AA) rendered attachment to:
- Charles Carroll, Esq. administrator of Just Englehert Rychin to render accounts.
- Charles Carroll, Esq. administrator of Richard Pawson to render accounts.
- Charles Carroll, Esq. administrator of John Dodd to render accounts.

Court Session: November 1719

- Daniel Mariartee administrator of Edward Mariartee to render inventory.

24:86 Exhibited from CE:
- inventory of William Dare.
- inventory of John Bristow.
- accounts of James Galloway & his wife administratrix of Jonathon Beck.
- accounts of Mary Thompson administratrix of John Thompson.
- accounts of Benjamin Cox administrator of George Huddlestone.
- accounts of Elisabeth Hitchcock executrix of John Hitchcock.

Exhibited from DO:
- inventory of Thomas Bruff.
- accounts of John Rix & William Thomas on estate of Martha Woolman.
- accounts of John Samuels & his wife administratrix of Mathew Oneale.

Exhibited from PG:
- accounts of William Harris executor of George Ransom.
- accounts of Sarah Truman executrix of Thomas Truman.

24:87 Exhibited from KE:
- renunciation of Thomas Pinar executor of William Glanvill. Date 21 October 1719. Witnesses: David McBride, James Harris.
- inventory of Edward Lappidge.
- additional inventory of John Clark.
- accounts of George Reed administrator of John Clark.

24:88 Exhibited:
- 2 additional inventories of Sarah Herbert (CH), by Joseph Douglas executor.
- accounts of Thomas Howard administrator of Jacob Brandt (CH).
- accounts of Carpenter Lillingstone administrator of Joseph Lambert (QA).

Exhibited from SM:
- will of Francis Hutchins,

constituting Robert Hutchins executor. Said Robert was granted administration. Sureties: William Wilkinson, Robert Clarke. Date: 25 September 1719.

- bond of Sarah Barrett executrix of Edward Barrett. Sureties: Richard Poore, William Bayley. Date: 14 September 1719.

24:89
- bond of Elinor Heardman administratrix of James Heardman. Sureties: James Thompson, Oswald Dash. Date: 5 November 1719.
- bond of Anne Reed administratrix of James Meekins. Sureties: John Reead, Robert Clarke. Date: 11 September 1719.
- bond of Kathrine Schurlock administratrix of Richard Schurlock. Sureties: James Thompson, Thomas Cooper. Date: 5 November 1719.
- inventory of William Gutherie.
- inventory of James Meekins.
- inventory of Kenelmn Cheseldyne. Administration granted to (N) Phippard.
- inventory of Peter Watts.
- inventory of Adam Bell.
- inventory of Thomas Norman.
- inventory of Richard Brooks.
- accounts of Thomas Sumers administrator of Vincent Langford.
- additional accounts of Raphaell Neale executor of Leonard Brooks.
- accounts of Anne Brooksbank administratrix of Abraham Brooksbank.
- accounts of John Tawney & Robert Hutchins executors of William Hutchins.
- accounts of John Berroughs executor of John Berroughs.
- accounts of Henry Wharton executor of George Cusack.

24:90
- accounts of Charles King on estate of Edward Hall.
- accounts of Anne Coode executrix of John Cood.
- accounts of Elias Hennington administratrix of Daniel Conally.
- accounts of Mat. Mason executor of John Mason.

- accounts of Ann Laurence administratrix of Henry Laurence.
- accounts of Mary Jessop executrix of Joseph Jessop.
- additional accounts of Charles Neale executor of James Cecill.
- accounts of Fran. Heathman executrix of Alexander Heathman.
- accounts of John Cermichell & his wife administratrix of William Merrill.
- accounts of Jane Buterworth executrix of Michael Butterworth.
- inventory of Franc. Hutchin.
- inventory of Daniel Conally.

Exhibited:
- inventory of John Henry (SO).

Exhibited from TA:

24:91
- inventory of William Dwyer.
- inventory of Turlo Higgins.
- inventory of Edward Pinar.
- inventory of Mary Smythson.
- inventory of Robert Hopkins.
- inventory of Darby Ryon.
- inventory of Robert Register.
- inventory of Edward Briney.
- inventory of William Dickinson.
- inventory of Philip Sherwood.
- accounts of William Clayton administrator of Darby Ryon.
- accounts of Cornelius Dwyer administrator of William Dwyer.

19 November. Exhibited:
- accounts of Woolman Gibson & his wife administratrix of Lambert Clements.
- 3rd accounts of Edward Cockey administrator of Issaac Harris (QA).

24:92 21 November. Exhibited from BA:
- renunciation of John Street (BA) son of Francis Street (dec'd), recommending Richard Gist (merchant, BA). Date: 31 August 1719. Witness: Christopher Caval.
- bond of Richard Gist administrator of Francis Street. Sureties: Luke Stansbury, Josephus Murrey. Date: 29 October 1719.

- bond of William Todd executor of Thomas Todd. Sureties: James Philips, John Cromwell. Date: 12 October 1719.
- bond of Stephen Gill administrator of John Leckin. Sureties: Alexander Macomus, William Macomus. Date: 5 November 1719.
- inventory of William Low.

24:93 24 November. Exhibited from PG:
- inventory of William Ransom.
- inventory of Andrew Hambleton.
- accounts of Anne Head executrix of William Head.

1 December. Exhibited from DO:
- bond of Anne Hooper administratrix of Richard Hooper. Sureties: John Robson, John Sare. Date: 13 November 1719.
- inventory of Mathew Barnes.
- accounts of James Insley administrator of William Insley.
- accounts of Richard Pritchard administrator of Mary Stanford.
- accounts of Richard Pritchard administrator of James Walkes.
- accounts of John Flowers administrator of William Bennitt.

Exhibited from TA:
- will of Elisabeth Low.
- inventory of Thomas Tyler.
- accounts of John Fisher administrator of Edward Briney.
- accounts of Elisabeth Stevens administratrix of William Stevens.
- accounts of John & William Harrison executors of Robert Harrison.

24:94 7 December. Exhibited from CV:
- will of Richard Bond, constituting Elisabeth Bond executrix. Said Elisabeth was granted administration. Sureties: Kensey Johns, Samuel Chew. Date: 16 November 1719.
- bond of Mary Tonge administratrix of Thomas Tonge. Sureties: James Heighe, Robert Heighe. Date: 18 November 1719.

- bond of William Young administrator of Francis Young. Surety: John Brome. Date: 18 November 1719.
- bond of Sarah Wilson administratrix of John Wilson. Sureties: Samuel Galloway, Jeremiah Cox. Date: 5 December 1719.
- bond of Elisabeth Mauldin administratrix of Mary Boyl. Surety: William Mauldin. Date: 2 December 1719.
- inventory of Elisha Sedgwick.
- inventory of John Rankin.
- inventory of Daniel Spencer.
- accounts of Thomas Boyston & his wife administratrix of John Shehon.
- accounts of Cornelius Dwyer & his wife administratrix of Daniel Spencer.
- accounts of Robert Lee administrator of Nathaniel Miles.
- accounts of Marjory Mackdaniell administratrix of Enos Mackdaniell.

24:95 Exhibited from CH:
- bond of John Butt & James Maddox administrators of Thomas Gooly. Sureties: John Goodrick, John Hopewell. Date: 14 October 1719.
- bond of Edward Gardiner administrator of Thomas Smoott. Sureties: Douglas Gifford, John Serogin. Date: 9 November 1719.
- bond of John Suttle administrator of thomas Waterman. Sureties: Richard Chapman, John Ragon. Date: 31 October 1719.
- inventory of John Barrow.
- inventory of Roger Yopp.

15 December. Exhibited from TA:
- will of Henry King, constituting Sarah Webb executrix. Said Webb was granted administration. Sureties: Thomas Taylor, Foster Turbutt. Date: 12 December 1719.
- will of Mary Githin, constituting Edward Hardin executor. Said Hardin was granted administration. Sureties: James Hurlock, John Reynoulds. Date: 8 December 1719.
- bond of Anne Dodd administratrix of

Edmond Dodd. Sureties: David
Robinson, john Gaskin. Date: 4
October 1719.

24:96
- inventory of Issaiah Parrott.
- accounts of Elisabeth Skinner
  executrix of Andrew Skinner.

20 December. Exhibited from AA:
- will of Peter Forrester,
  constituting Mary Forrester
  executrix. Said Mary was granted
  administration. Sureties: John
  Elder, Leonard Wayman. Date: 14
  December 1719.
- bond of Mary Cross administratrix of
  Elinor Cross. Sureties: Stephen
  West, Thomas Howard. Date: 19
  November 1719.
- bond of Mary Packett administratrix
  of Daniel Packitt. Sureties: Thomas
  Holmes, Edward Smith. Date: 5
  December 1719.
- bond of Thomas Larkins administrator
  of John Leckie. Sureties: Benjamin
  Tasker, John Baldwin. Date: 9
  December 1719.
- inventory of John Stephens.
- inventory of John Ware.
- accounts of Thomas Worthington
  administrator of William Catton.
- will of John Preston.
- additional accounts of Thomas
  Bordley, Esq. administrator of Elias
  Poleman.

24:97 Exhibited:
- 4th additional accounts of George
  Comerford & his wife executrix of
  Thomas Marsh (QA).
- bond of Mary Rawley administratrix
  of Samuel Rawley (DO). Sureties:
  John Cullen, John Ecclestone. Date:
  9 December 1719.
- additional accounts of Daniel
  Mullikin executor of James Barber
  (KE).

23 December. Exhibited:
- accounts of Hugh Merikin & his wife
  executrix of George Westall (BA).
- will of Patrick Ogelvie, exhibited
  by Richard Bennitt (g, QA).

Original to be sent to NE.
- bond of William Loch administrator of Alexander Watts. Surety: William Cuming. Date: 23 December 1719.

24:98 Mr. Phillip Hammond (late Register) has left his Lordship's service. Thomas Bordley, Esq. appointed Vachel Denton (Annapolis) as Clerk & Register.

24:99 Date: 28 December 1719. Bond of said Denton. Sureties (g): John Beale, Thomas Larkin.

John Beale, Esq. was appointed Deputy Commissary (AA). Sureties: Stephen Warman, Vachel Denton. Date: 28 December 1719.

24:100 28 December. Mr. Bernard White was granted administration on his father's estate.

31 December. Mr. John Baker (SM) exhibited:
- bond of Thomas Holland administrator of William Holland. Sureties: John Hammond, Herbert Thomas. Date: 24 November 1719.
- bond of John Johnson Southeron executor of Mary Rose. Sureties: Michael Branson, John Branson. Date: 18 December 1719.
- bond of Mary Clark administratrix of Thomas Clark. Sureties: Roswell Neale, John Black. Date: 26 November 1719. Also deposition of John Clark (brother of dec'd) regarding will.
- accounts of Robert Laurance administrator of John Beans.
- accounts of Joseph Vansweringen administrator of John Kelly.
- accounts of Rachel Woodward executrix of Thomas Woodward.
- accounts of Henry Horne executor of Philip Ragon.
- accounts of Mary Cox (alias Mary Dean) executrix of Philip Cox.
- accounts of Mary Barber (alias Mary Jameston) executrix of Thomas Barber.

24:101 - accounts of Mathew Mason executor of

John Mason.
- inventory of William Holland.
- inventory of Vincent Langford.
- will of Mary Rose, constituting John Southern executor.

17 January. Exhibited from AA:
- inventory of Daniel Packet.
- will of Elinor Cross.
- will of Philemon Hemsley.
- nuncupative will of John Lackey, insinuated by Frances Campbell.

20 January. Dr. Patrick Hepburne (PG) exhibited:
- bond of James Haddock & Weldon Jefferson executors of Robert Hall. Sureties: Thomas Sprigg, Jr., John Docwra. Date: 18 December 1719.
- will of Robert Hall.

24:102
- inventory of James Gardner.
- inventory of Dr. William Fisher, of medicines.
- accounts of Grove Tomlin & his wife executors of John Burk.
- accounts of Sarah Busey executrix of Paul Busey.

2 February. James Harris, Esq. (KE) exhibited:
- will of William Glanvill.
- bond of William Glanvill & Nathaniel Hynson administrators of William Glanvill. Sureties: Frederick Hanson, Thomas Riccaud. Date: 11 November 1719.
- bond of Mathew Pinar administrator of William Hunt. Sureties: Thomas Pinar, John Fanning. Date: 4 November 1719.
- bond of Simon Wilmer administrator of John Buley. Sureties: Charles Hynson, Thomas Piner. Date: 21 December 1719.

24:103
- inventory of John Hancok.
- accounts of Edward Mitchell administrator of John Hancock.
- accounts of Abraham Redgrave, Jr. who married Elisabeth executrix of Philip Reason.
- will of Dennis Sullivan.
- additional inventory of Hugh Perry.

Court Session: November 1719

- inventory of Thomas Medford.

Mrs. Jane Wilmote (BA) widow of John
Wilmote, Sr. (BA) repudiated his will &
chose her 1/3rds. Date: 2 December
1719. Witnesses: William Cumming,
George Walker.

24:104 Said John died on 24 October 1719.

9 February. Exhibited:
- bond of Peter Bond, unsigned by
relations per Hill Savage who
married the widow Elinor executrix
of said Peter. Summons to said
Savage & William Bond & John Bond
(kindred of dec'd).

James Harris, Esq. (KE) to examine
accounts of:
- Samuel Clark & his wife Mary
executrix of Dennis Clark.

Mrs. Margaret Macnemara administratrix
of Thomas Macnemara, Esq. was granted
continuance.

Court Session: 10 February 1719

24:105 Docket:
- E.J. for Thomas Gray vs. John Gray.
Libel & answer.
- R.T. for Jonathon Hopkins vs.
Harmanus Schee & his wife. Libel &
answer.
- Michael Fletcher administrator of
(N) Smithson vs. J. Green & William
Clayton. Libel to be filed.

Court Session: 1719

24:106 10 February. Exhibited from QA:
- accounts of John Gibb executor of
Ralph Arnold.

Exhibited from AA:
- accounts of James Powell & his wife
Elisabeth executrix of Edward
Talbott.

12 December. Exhibited:
- accounts of Darby Callahon & his
wife Mary administratrix of Daniel

Packett.

Mr. John Baker (SM) to examine accounts of:
- William Thompson administrator of (N) Herbert.
- Anne Bell executrix of Adam Bell.
- Richard Keen administrator of William Cretchet.
- Elisabeth Watts executrix of Peter Watts.
- Katherine Hammott executrix of Robert Hammott.
- Bridget Richardson executrix of Nicholas Richardson.
- James Baker administrator of William Hebb.
- Anne Biscoe executrix of Anne Biscoe.
- Thomas Turner administrator of Joshua Turner.

Sheriff (BA) to summon:
- Francis Dollahide administrator of John Hopkins
- John Taylor administrator of Abraham Taylor
to render security.

24:107 Foster Turbutt (TA) to examine accounts of:
- Thomas Sander & his wife Rebecca executrix of Henry Frith.
- Charles Stevens executor of John Start.
- James & John Pemberton executors of Thomas Beswick.
- Sarah White administratrix of Rowland White.
- Rebecca Webb executrix of Richard Webb.
- Issabell Taylor executrix of James Taylor.
- Elisabeth Hopkins executrix of Robert Hopkins.

Summons to (N) Rattenbury widow of John Rattenbury (BA) to take LoA on his estate, per Mr. Richard Trensam (Annapolis).

15 February. Mr. Alexander Contee (CH)
exhibited:
- will of Henry Brett, constituting
  Sarah Brett executrix. Said Sarah
  was granted administration.
  Sureties: Richard Harrison, Thomas
  Price. Date: 8 December 1719.
- bond of Joseph Harrison
  administrator of Richard Harrison.
  Sureties: Henry Barnes, William
  Stone, Jr. Date: 14 November 1719.
- bond of Laurance Anders
  administrator of Henry Franklin.
  Sureties: David Hopper, David
  Parsons. Date: 12 January 1719.

24:108 - bond of Thomas Jameson executor of
  Winifred Lee. Surety: Alexander
  Hawkins. Date: 7 December 1719.
- nuncupative will of Winifred Lee.
- bond of Anne Dixon administratrix of
  Thomas Dixon. Sureties: Walter
  Story, Douglass Gifford. Date: 24
  November 1719.
- bond of Dorothy Parry administratrix
  of John Parry. Sureties: Robert
  Hanson, Daniel Jenifer, Bernard
  White, Luke Barber. Date: 11
  November 1719.
- accounts of Elisabeth Martin
  executrix of James Martin.

Mr. Adderton Skinner (CV) to examine
accounts of:
- Jonathon Holliday administrator of
  John Owen.

17 February. Mr. Robert Jones (QA) to
examine accounts of:
- Kathe. & John Chares executors of
  John Chares (QA).

Mr. Bernard White was granted
continuance on estate of his father.

22 February. Exhibited:
- 3rd accounts of George Ogg surviving
  executor of William Talbot.

24:109 Mordecai Hammond & his wife Frances vs.
Carpenter Lillingston (g, QA) executor
of Joseph Lambert (QA) executor of Mr.
John Lillingston (QA), said John &

Edward Chetham (dec'd) executors of Richard Macklin (QA). Summons to answer libel.

Exhibited:
- accounts of John Smith & his wife Dorothy administratrix of Thomas Williamson (BA).

Mary Cockey vs. estate of her husband William Cockey. Caveat exhibited. She is not well, or are her children. Date: 29 January 1719 at Patapsco.

25 February. Capt. Thomas Cockey administrator of John Ingram was granted continuance.

Exhibited:
- will of Philemon Hemsley, Esq., which was sent to Mr. Robert Jones (QA) with instructions to grant LoA to Mr. William Hemsley (son of dec'd).

24:110 Hugh Merekin who married executrix of George Westall was granted continuance.

26 February. Exhibited:
- inventory of John Brown (g, BA). Also a notice from Richard Burrough who married Elisabeth executrix of said Brown, that he gave notice to Anthony Drew & his wife Margaret, being nearest of kin. Also, no known creditors. Date: 25 February 1719.

At request of Philemon Lloyd, Esq., summons issued:
- for such persons necessary in relation to estate of Col. Edward Lloyd.
- widow & executrix of said Edward.

24:111 Exhibited from PG:
- accounts of Charles Beall administrator of Ninian Beall.
- accounts of Elisabeth Johnston executrix of Stephen Johnston.
- will of Joseph Jeans.
- will of Benjamin Berry, constituting

Mary Berry executrix Said Mary was granted administration. Sureties: Edward Willott, Baruch Williams, Thomas Williams. Date: 20 February 1719.

- bond of John Bradford administrator of David MackDaniel. Sureties: Thomas Johnston, William Renshaw. Date: 5 February 1719.
- bond of Daniel Delliose & his wife Mary (formerly Mary Brauner) administratrix of William Brauner. Sureties: William Ellott, John Brauner. Date: 19 February 1719.

Exhibited:
- accounts of John Brewer (AA) administrator of Joseph Brewer.

27 February. Mr. Alexander Contee (CH) exhibited:
- accounts of Edward Gardner administrator of Thomas Smoot.
- additional accounts of William Sanders surviving executor of Robert Sanders.
- inventory of Mr. John Parry.
- inventory of Thomas Smoot.
- inventory of Thomas Waterman.
- inventory of Thomas Dixon.

24:112

Deputy Commissary (CH) to examine accounts of:
- Anne Dixon administratrix of Thomas Dixon.

Mr. Adderton Skinner (CV) exhibited:
- will of Richard Johns, constituting Priscilla Johns executrix. Said Priscilla was granted administration. Sureties: Kensey Johns, Isaac Johns. Date: 14 December 1719.
- will of Samuel Cluley, constituting Thomas Marshall executor. Said Marshall was granted administration. Surety: Martin Wells. Date: 4 February 1719.
- bond of Thomas King administrator of Charles King. Sureties: Abraham Cocke, Jacob Jones. Date: 4 January 1719.

24:113
- bond of William Willmott administrator of James Willmott. Surety: Jeremiah Sheredine. Date: 9 January 1719.
- bond of Elisabeth Peacock administratrix of William Peacock. Surety: Roger Wheeler, Date: 2 January 1719.
- bond of Alexander Parran administrator of John Kennyman. Surety: John Wilkinson. Date: 16 January 1719.
- inventory of Peter Madrin.
- accounts of Elisabeth Rankin executrix of John Rankin.
- accounts of Elisabeth Nash administratrix of Charles Nash.

29 February. Mr. Foster Turbutt (TA) to alter summons issued at the request of Philemon Lloyd, Esq. in relation to estate of Edward Lloyd, Esq. Mentions: widow.

Alexander Contee (CH) to examine accounts of:
- Anne Dixon administratrix of Thomas Dixon.

James Harris, Esq. (KE) to examine accounts of:
- James Tibbott administrator of William Harcom.

24:114 Mr. Adderton Skinner (CV) to examine accounts of:
- Grace Brook administratrix of Robert Brook.

Phillip Feddeman (DO) to examine accounts of:
- Katharine Bruff administratrix of Thomas Bruff.

James Harris, Esq. (KE) exhibited:
- will of Phillip Hissitt.
- will of Elinor Hissitt.
- inventory of John Buly.
- accounts of Simon Wilmore administrator of John Buly.
- bond of Mathew Pope administrator of William Pope. Sureties: Thomas

Court Session: 1719

Pinar, William Graves. Date: 12
February 1719.
- bond of Thomas Browning
administrator of Noah Laurence.
Sureties: John Limorn, John Harris.
Date: 8 February 1719.

1 March. Foster Turbutt (TA) to examine
accounts of:
- Ann Cockayn administratrix of Samuel
Cockayne.

2 March. Samuel Hopkins (SO) to examine
accounts of:
- Katherine Mackneel executrix of Hugh
Mackneel.

24:115 <blank>

Court Session: 1 March 1719

24:116 Docket:
- E.J. for Thomas Gray vs. T.L. for
John Gray. Libel & answer.
- R.T. for Jonathon Hopkins vs.
Harmanus Schee. Libel & answer.
- Michael Fletcher administrator of
William Smithson vs. W.C. for J.
Green & William Clayton. Order for
libel.
- renewed summons to (N) Rattenberry
widow of John Rattenberry, at
request of Richard Trensam (g).
- summons to John Taylor executor of
Abraham Taylor to give new security.
- summons to Francis Dollahide
administratrix of John Hopkins to
give new security.
24:117 - W.C. for Mordecai Hammond & his wife
vs. Carpenter Lillingston executor
of John Lillingston, etc. Libel;
order for answer.

Court Session: March 1719

Mr. Foster Turbutt to alter summons in
relation to estate of Col. Loyd, as
agreed to by Mr. Phile. Loyd &
executrix of said Edward.

Summons to Hill Savage & his wife
executrix of Peter Bond, William, & John

24:118 Bond regarding inventory of said Peter. Said William & John signed the inventory on 1 March 1719.

3 March. Exhibited:
* inventory of Anne Thornberry (AA).

8 March. Mr. Samuel Chew executor of Samuel Chew was granted continuance.

Elisabeth Chew administratrix of John Chew was granted continuance.

Exhibited from BA:
* inventory of John Wilmott.

24:119 9 March. Exhibited from AA:
* inventory of William Pearce, by Elisabeth Pearce executrix. Mentions (relations who refused to sign): Sarah Harris, Thomas Harris.
* additional inventory of John Marriott. Also accounts of Joseph & Augustine Marriott executors.

John Baker (SM) to examine accounts of:
* Bridget Richardson executrix of Nathaniel Richardson.

Mrs. Elisabeth Cole executrix of Robert Cole (SM) was granted continuance.

Thomas Brannock vs. Nehemiah Beckwith. Summons to defendant.

Foster Turbutt (TA) to summon Madam Loyd executrix of Col. Loyd.

24:120 12 March. Exhibited:
* inventory of Peter Forrester (AA).
* additional accounts of John Burroughs, Jr. administrator of John Burroughs (SM).

14 March. Exhibited:
* distribution of estate of Christopher Goodhand (equally): widow, Marmaduke, Elisabeth wife of Saladine Eagle.
* additional accounts of Edward Parish attorney for executor of Isabell Capell.

Court Session: March 1719

Robert Jones (QA) exhibited:
- bond of Edward Jones executor of William Arland. Sureties: John Swift, John Long. Date: 26 November 1719.

24:121
- bond of Judith Brown administratrix of John Brown. Sureties: George Holladay, James Dobson. Date: 9 December 1719.
- bond of Richard Bennett administrator of Norton Knatchbull. Surety: Robert Jones. Date: 14 January 1719.
- bond of James Couden administrator of Augustin Finn. Sureties: John Welsh, Richard Moore. Date: 25 November 1719.
- will of Barbary Jackson, constituting Francis Jackson & Joseph Jackson executors. Said Francis & Joseph were granted administration. Sureties: John Emory, William Mason. Date: 28 January 1719.
- bond of Nicholas Marsey administrator of James Bennett. Sureties: Daniel Newnam, Charles Lowdes. Date: 5 December 1719.
- accounts of Nathaniel Wright executor of Solomon Wright.
- inventory of Ralph Arland, by John Gibb executor.
- inventory of James Hepburn, by Edward Wright administrator.
- bond of David Young administrator of Edward Payn. Sureties: Otho Coursey, George Jackson. Date: 10 March 1719.

24:122 15 March. Richard Tilghman, Esq. to examine accounts of:
- Thomas Hynson Wright & his wife Mary executrix of John Coursey (QA).

21 March. Mordecai Hammond & his wife vs. Carpenter Lillingston. Summons issued to defendant.

Samuel Hopkins (SO) exhibited:
- bond of Samuel Tarr administrator of Ambros Archer. Surety: Johnson Hill. Date: 4 December 1719.

Court Session: March 1719

- bond of Esau Boston administrator of Esau Boston. Sureties: Isaac Boston, Jonathon Noble. Date: 20 November 1719.
- bond of Robert Martin administrator of James Manuell. Sureties: John Devorecks, Ebenezar Franklyn, James Dayle. Date: 10 November 1719.

24:123
- inventory of John Jones, by Elisabeth Jones administratrix.
- inventory of Charles Showell, by Richard Holland administrator.
- accounts of Edward Beacham administrator of John Heath.
- accounts of Thomas Bellin & his wife administratrix of Samuel Collins.

23 March. Richard Trensam (G) vs. Margaret Rattenberry widow of John Rattenberry (BA). Summons to defendant.

Summons to Richard Burroughs & his wife Elisabeth executrix of John Brown to show cause why they have not taken LoA.

Mr. Patrick Hepburn (PG) exhibited:
- bond of Elisabeth Jeans executrix of Joseph Jeans. Sureties: Thomas Addison, James Haddock, Esq. Date: 24 February 1719.

24:124
- bond of Robert Gorden administrator of William Downes. Sureties: James Stoddert, John Queen. Date: 4 March 1719.
- accounts of William Digges executor of Edward Diggs.

24 March. Patrick Hepburn (PG) to examine accounts of:
- Johanna Edgar administratrix of Richard Edgar.
- John Docwra & his wife administratrix of James Robinson.

Exhibited:
- bond of Sarah Smart administratrix of John Smart. Surety: John Davison. Date: 2 March 1719.

Court Session: 1720

25 March. Exhibited:

Page 50

Court Session: 1720

- bond of Margaret Rattenberry widow of John Rattenberry on his estate. Sureties: John Cromwell, William Slayde.

24:125 Appraisers: John Orrick, John Ashman, Lancellott Todd to administer oath.

28 March. Bond of Daniel of St. Thomas Jenifer on estate of Thomas Johnson (CV) is assigned to Daniell Dulany attorney for William Whittington, Esq.

31 March. Katherine Crade executrix of John Crade (AA) was granted continuance.

Samuel Harrison was granted continuance on estate of his father.

4 April. Mr. John Baker (SM) exhibited:
- bond of Henry Cunliffe administrator of Samuel Corbesly. Sureties: Joseph Vansweringen, Richard Lewellin. Date: 27 November 1719.
- will of Thomas Reeves, constituting Ubgatt Reeves executor. Said Ubgatt was granted administration. Sureties: Samuel Maddox, Sr., Thomas Scott. Date: 7 January 1719.

24:126
- bond of Agnus Penny administratrix of John Penny. Sureties: William Johnson, John Griggs. Date: 6 February 1720.
- bond of Mary Miller administratrix of Edward Miller, Jr. Sureties: Owen Smithson, John Biscoe. Date: 22 December 1719.
- bond of John Medley administrator of John Tubbs. Sureties: John Young, Esq., Vitus Herbert. Date: 21 March 1720.
- bond of Pheby Harwood administratrix of William Harwood. Sureties: Thomas Richardson, John Batson. Date: 27 February 1720.
- additional inventory of William Hebb.
- inventory of Richard Scurlock.
- inventory of William Harwood.
- inventory of Thomas Clarke.
- inventory of Edward Miller.

Page 51

- inventory of James Heardman.
- inventory of Mary Rose.
- inventory of Samuel Corbesly.

24:127
- additional inventory of William Herbert.
- accounts of Richard Griffin administrator of Thomas Singer.
- accounts of Joseph Hardyne & Joan Welch (alias Joan Hardyne) administratrix of John Welch.
- accounts of Barbary Feilder (alias Barbary Johnson) executrix of William Feilder.
- additional accounts of Ann Lawrence (alias Ann Baily) administratrix of Henry Lawrence.
- accounts of Ann Taylor executrix of Thomas Taylor.
- additional accounts of Robert & Elisabeth Cole executors of Edward Cole.
- accounts of John Mackellvie & Kathrine Mackellvie (alias Cathrine Hammett) administratrix of Robert Hamett.
- accounts of William Coode administrator of John Shank.
- accounts of Owin Smithson & his wife Ann (alias Ann Briscoe) executrix of John Briscoe.
- accounts of Owen Smithson executor of Mary Guyther.
- accounts of Steph Nottingham administrator of Francis Miles.
- accounts of James Poaker (alias James Heb) executor of William Hebb.
- accounts of William Thompson & Elinor Thompson (alias Elinor Herbett) administrators of William Herbett.

24:128
- accounts of George Gallaspie & Mr. John Cay executors of Rev. George Irvin.
- accounts of Ann Bell executrix of Adam Bell.
- accounts of Nathaniel Cooper administrator of Henry Spinkes.

John Baker (SM) to examine accounts of:
- John Haines administrator of Joyce Haines.
- Hugh Hopewell executor of John King.

- William Jameston & his wife administratrix of Thomas Barber.
- Mary Miller administratrix of Edward Miller.
- Elisabeth Aisquith executrix of Col. William Aisquith.

Mr. Foster Turbutt (TA) exhibited:
- bond of John Mackerly & his wife Elisabeth administratrix of Thomas Taylor. Sureties: Dennis Hopkins, Joseph Hopkins. Date: 9 February 1719.
- bond of Peter Harwood administrator of David Whitcharly. Sureties: Thomas Atkinson, Foster Turbutt. Date: 20 March 1720.
- **24:129** bond of Thomas Atkinson & John Bartlet administrators of Timothy MacDaniel. Sureties: James Ratcliff, Thomas Sanders. Date: 29 March 1720.
- bond of Jane Ford administratrix of Ambrose Ford. Sureties: Arthur Conner, Thomas Brown. Date: 26 March 1720.
- bond of Jean MacDaniel administratrix of Laughlin MacDaniel. Sureties: Chrismas Jones, George Cooley. Date: 22 March 1719.
- bond of Sarah Harrison administratrix of John Harrison. Sureties: Nicholas Lowe, John Pattison. Date: 5 February 1719.
- bond of Sarah Moore administratrix of Joseph More. Sureties: George Watt, Lotan West. Date: 22 February 1719.
- bond of Elisabeth Smith administratrix of Daniel Smith. Sureties: Thomas Smith, Patrick Mullikin. Date: 27 January 1718/9.
- bond of William White, James White, & Elisabeth White executors of Richard White. Sureties: John Sherwood, John Burnyatt. Date: 23 February 1719.
- **24:130** bond of Nicholas Lowe & David Robinson executors of Elisbeth Low. Sureties: Thomas Taylor, Foster Turbutt. Date: 1 February 1719.

- bond of William Harrison & Francis Harrison executors of William Harrison. Sureties: Samuel Dickenson, Peter Sharp. Date: 2 February 1719.
- bond of Anne Dawson executrix of John Dawson. Sureties: John Carslake, Woolman Gibson. Date: 22 March 1719.
- will of John Dawson.
- will of Richard White.
- will of William Harrison.
- inventory of Edmond Dodd.
- inventory of Edward Turner.
- inventory of Anthony Wise.
- inventory of Thomas Martin.
- inventory of Prudence Woolman.
- inventory of Pierce Welsh.
- inventory of Christ. Field.
- inventory of James Rippeth.
- inventory of Mary Githin.

24:131
- accounts of Robert Morton & his wife Ann executrix of John Davis.
- accounts of Mary Newnam administratrix of John Newnam.
- accounts of Mary Newnam administratrix of Edward Pinner.
- accounts of Hannah Tate administratrix of Thomas Tate.
- accounts of Charles Stevens executor of John Start.
- accounts of Thomas Sanders & his wife executrix of Henry Frith.
- additional accounts of William Elbert & his wife Frances administratrix of Andrew Holsteen.
- accounts of Rebecca Brumwell executrix of Thomas Beswick.
- additional accounts of Peter Harwood surviving administrator of Thomas Scantlebury.

6 April. Nehemiah Beckwith executor of Henry Beckwith (DO) was granted continuance.

Exhibited:
- additional inventory of Thomas Holdsworth (CV).
- accounts of Nehemiah Beckwith executor of Henry Beckwith.

Court Session: 1720

24:132 <u>7 April</u>. Exhibited:
- final accounts on estate of Joseph Hopkins (KE).

MM Henry & Bennet Lowe were granted continuance on estate of Henry Lowe.

Deputy Commissary (TA) to examine accounts of:
- John Herbert (TA) & his wife on estate of Joseph Bullock.

Alexander Contee (g, CH) exhibited:
- bond of Mary Roch administratrix of Charles Roch. Sureties: John Leverett, John Shaw. Date: 12 March 1719.
- bond of William Milstead administrator of Henry Blanksheets. Sureties: Edward Milstead, William Warden. Date: 19 March 1719.
- bond of Anne Short executrix of George Short. Sureties: John Bucknam, John Cadell. Date: 14 March 1719.
- bond of Elenor Sanders executrix of Mathew Sanders. Sureties: John Sanders, William Sanders. Date: 24 March 1719.

24:133
- will of George Short.
- will of Mathew Sanders.
- inventory of Richard Harrison.
- inventory of Henry Brett.
- inventory of Jane Boy.
- inventory of Richard Morris.
- inventory of Elisabeth Hague.
- inventory of Winifred Lee.
- accounts of Joseph Harrison administrator of Elisabeth Hague.
- accounts of Mathew Cumbton surviving executor of John Cumbton.
- accounts of Thomas King & John Cooper executors of William Moncaster.
- accounts of Robert Hanson administrator of Benjamin Hanson.

<u>9 April</u>. Mr. John Dorsey to examine additional accounts of:
- William Marshall & his wife Mary on estate of George Wells.

Exhibited:
- accounts on estate of George Wells.

24:134 12 April. Mr. Samuel Hopkins (SO) exhibited:
- bond of Lewis Jones executor of Samuel Jones. Sureties: Robert Laws, Thomas Laws. Date: 1 March 1719/20.
- bond of Robert Ponton who married executrix of Isaac Luke. Sureties: Richard Longwood, William Ennis. Date: 10 December 1719.
- bond of James Perry administrator of Mary Lary. Surety: James Mumford. Date: 19 December 1719.
- bond of Frances Erwing administratrix of John Erwing. Sureties: Robert Laws, George Martin. Date: 2 March 1719/20.
- bond of Mary Cooper administratrix of Jonathon Cooper. Sureties: Edward Dicks, Robert Melvin. Date: 16 March 1719/20.
- bond of Robert Nairn, Jr. executor of David Rich. Surety: Robert Nairn, Sr. Date: 18 March 1719/20.

24:135
- bond of Bridgett Kirk executrix of John Kirk. Sureties: Donnock Dennis, John Dennis. Date: 17 March 1719/20.
- bond of John Kellam, Jr. executor of John Kellam, Sr. Sureties: John Murray, Christ. Glass. Date: 17 March 1719/20.
- will of Samuel Jones.
- will of Isaac Luke.
- will of David Rich.
- will of John Kirk.
- will of John Kellam.
- inventory of William Round.
- inventory of Esau Boston.
- inventory of Ephraim Polk.
- inventory of Manuell Johnson.
- inventory of William Wheatly.
- inventory of Ambross Archer.
- accounts of Joseph Jones administrator of John Jones.
- accounts of Mary Maddox administratrix of Alexander Maddox.
- accounts of William Hickman administrator of Signey Brown.

- accounts of Samuel Tarr & his wife administratrix of Henry Webb.
- accounts of William Richards administrator of Abraham Richards.
- accounts of John Cottman administrator of John Watters.

24:136 12 April. Exhibited from AA:
- additional inventory of John Stevens.

Mr. Phil. Feddeman (DO) exhibited:
- bond of Sarah Stanaway administratrix of Joseph Stanaway. Sureties: John Robson, Robert Paule. Date: 9 March 1719.
- bond of Richard Hart executor of Arthur Hart. Sureties: Richard Prichard, William Houlton. Date: 8 March 1719.
- bond of Mary Saldsbury executrix of Petegrew Saldsbury. Sureties: Benjamin Woodward, Edward Newton. Date: 10 March 1719.
- bond of Susannah Parrish administratrix of Richard Parrish. Date: 10 March 1719.

24:137
- bond of Sarah Conyers executrix of Henry Conyers. Sureties: William Perry, Stephen Flaharty. Date: 22 January 1719.
- will of Petegrew Saldsbury.
- will of Arthur Hart. Also widow's renunciation.
- will of Henry Conyers.
- inventory of Samuel Rawly.
- inventory of Godfrey Meottigg.
- inventory of William Sharpe.
- will of James Cullen.
- accounts of Kathe. Bruff executrix of Thomas Bruff.
- accounts of John Sharp administrator of William Sharp.

Samuel Hopkins (SO) exhibited:
- additional accounts of George Dashiell administrator of John Clark, passed before John Jones (g).

24:138 4 April. Philemon Lloyd, Esq. & James Loyd (g) vs. Madam Sarah Loyd executrix of Col. Loyd. Complaint against the

inventory. Appraisers: MM Thomas
Emmerson, Howell Powell. Mentions:
orphans.

- Mr. Thomas Emmerson deposed about:
  Negro Joan (over 40),

24:139 Negro Nan (crazed), Negro Frank
(over 60), Negro Tom (sorry of
Negro), Negro Bess (decrepit old
Negro woman).

- Mr. Howell Powell deposed that he
  believed that what Emmerson said is
  true.
- Mr. Robert Noble deposed about:
  Negro Joan (about 45 or 46, slow at
  work), Negro Nan (an old cross
  scolding Negro), Negro Frank (same
  as Mr. Emmerson), Negro Tom (age
  about 60), Negro Bess (past working
  in the ground).
- Howel Powel (Quaker) deposed.

24:140-142 ...

24:143 Mentions: children of Madam Lloyd,
Mr. Robert Ungle.

- Witnesses for the plaintiffs: Mr.
  Robert Noble, Mr. James Dawson,
  Capt. Smart, Andrew Wilkins, James
  Moody, John Sutton, Robert Ungle,
  Esq.,

24:144 Shadreck Kemp, Henry Jones, Thomas
Edmondson, Col. Mathew Tilghman
Ward, Thomas Crouch, William Arnold,
Mr. Robert Gouldesborough, John
Spriggnall.

- Witnesses for defendant: Vachel
  Denton, John Sutton, James Loyd,
  James Dawson.
- Philemon Loyd, Esq. deposed.

24:145 • Mr. James Loyd deposed.

24:146 • Foster Turbutt (TA) deposed.

- On 19 April 1720, Mr. Robert
  Gouldesborough to administer oath to
  MM

24:147 William Clayton & Daniel Sherwood as
appraisers in lieu of Thomas
Emmerson & Howell Powell.

- Ruling: said Philemon & James are
  brother of the dec'd.

24:148 Cites: amounts of the various
inventories.

24:149-150 ...

24:151 Said Sarah to render accounts as of
the 1st inventory.

24:152   Cited as witnesses in attendance:
         James Dawson, John Sprignal,
         Shadreck Kemp, John Sutton, Howell
         Powell,
24:153   Mr. Foster Turbutt.
       • Text of caveat. Date: 13 October
         1719.

24:154 Mr. Michael Howard for Mr. David
       Robinson (TA) vs. estate of Mrs.
       Elisabeth Low. Caveat exhibited.

       Mr. Foster Turbutt (TA) to grant LoA to
       James Dawson (TA) on estate of James
       Wright.

       13 April. Exhibited:
       • Elinor widow & executrix of Peter
         Bond had LoA on his estate on 16
         June 1718, & has since married Hill
         Savage. An inventory was returned,
         but no accounts. Therefore,
         distribution to
24:155   widow & 6 children. BA Court to
         take security.

       Exhibited from AA:
       • bond of John Powell administrator of
         Ann Thornberry. Sureties: Darby
         Conner, Benjamin Battee. Date: 26
         November 1719.

       Exhibited:
       • bond of Thomas Nevett administrator
         of Thomas Brettargh. Sureties:
         Walter Campbell, John Kirk. Date:
         13 April 1720. Appraisers: Gov.
         Loockerman, Charles Ungle. Henry
         Ennalls to administer oath.

       Thomas Nevett administrator of Thomas
       Brettargh vs. William Skinner (TA).
       Summons to answer complaint.

24:156 James Harris, Esq. (KE) exhibited:
       • bond of Edward Mitchell
         administrator of John Hancock, for
         use of Mr. Thomas Larkin.
         Sureties: Thomas Christian, Philip
         Holeadger.
       • bond of Pridddocks Blackiston
         administrator of John Blackiston,

    Jr. Sureties: Robert Dunn, Jr., William Dunn. Date: 12 March 1719/20.

- bond of William Ellis executor of John Ellis. Sureties: Philip Holeadger, William Burroughs. Date: 17 March 1719.
- will of Robert Foreman.
- will of John Ellis.
- deposition of John Worthington, regarding will of Dennis Sullivan.
- will of William Jones.
- will of Robert Jones.
- bond of Hannah Page administratrix of Jonathon Page. Sureties: Simon Wilmer, David Macbride. Date: 17 March 1719/20.

24:157
- bond of Hugh Mathews administrator of Dennis Sullivan. Sureties: John Hayden, James Breward. Date: 2 April 1720.
- inventory of William Lowcocks.
- additional accounts of Samuel Clark who married executrix of Dennis Clark.
- accounts of James Tibball administrator of William Harcom.
- additional inventory of William Harcom.
- accounts of Robert Meeks & his wife Susannah administratrix of William Darby.
- additional accounts of Abraham Redgrave, Jr. & Thomas Rayson executors of Philip Rason.
- accounts of Margaret Tumey administratrix of William Welch.

Petition of John Macclester (SO) that the bond on estate of John Bozman be assigned to him.

24:158 14 April. Mathias Vanderheyden (CE) exhibited:
- bond of Samuel Vans administrator of Edward Spencer. Sureties: Abell VanBurkeloo, Mathias Vanderheyden, Jr. Date: 26 March 1719.
- bond of Abigall Pullen administratrix of George Pullen. Sureties: James Alexander, Elias Alexander. Date: 1 December 1719.

- bond of Henry Ward administrator of Charles Fitzpatrick. Sureties: George Veazey, Richard Foster. Date: 13 January 1719/20.
- bond of Jacob VBebber administrator of John Beauman. Sureties: Ephraim Aug. Herman, John Hore. Date: 18 January 1719/20.
- bond of Bridget Robinson administratrix of James Robinson. Sureties: Francis Maudlin, William Dare. Date: 21 November 1719.
- bond of Abell VanBurkeloo administrator of Andrew Rosenquest. Surety: John Camble. Date: 3 February 1718.

24:159
- bond of Mary Bavington executrix of John Bavington. Sureties: John Ryland, Thomas Terry. Date: 7 December 1719.
- bond of Ann Elisabeth Vans executrix of Samuel Vans. Sureties: Running Bedford, John Pennington. Date: 20 February 1719.
- bond of Albert Cock executor of Guisbert Cock. Sureties: James Morgan, John Roberts. Date: 13 February 1719/20.
- bond of Mellice Hyland executrix of Nicholas Hyland. Sureties: John Pennington, Joseph Young. Date: 29 March 1720.
- will of Nicholas Hyland.
- will of John Bavington.
- will of Guisbird Cock.
- will of Samuel Vans.
- will of James Frisby.
- inventory of Edward Spencer.
- inventory of Michael Coulter.
- inventory of George Pullen.
- inventory of James Robinson.

24:160 Deputy Commissary (CH) to examine accounts of:
- Robert Hanson (g) who married Dorothy administratrix of John Parry (CH).

15 April. Deputy Commissary (SO) to examine accounts of:
- Mary Philips administratrix of Thomas Philips.

- Kath. West executrix of John West.

Patrick Hepburn (g, PG) exhibited:
- bond of John Pottenger & Sarah Pottenger executors of John Pottenger, Jr. Sureties: John Lamar, Samuel Pottenger. Date: 24 March 1719.
- will of
- inventory of Robert Hall.

24:161 Exhibited:
- accounts of John Harding executor of executrix of Morris Giddins.

16 April. Exhibited:
- additional accounts of George Dent executor of Col. William Herbert.

18 April. Deputy Commissary (CV) to examine accounts of:
- Benjamin Mackall & his wife Barbary administratrix of Thomas Holdsworth (CV).

19 April. Mr. John Baker (SM) to examine accounts of:
- Elisabeth Watts executrix of Peter Watts.

Mr. John Baker (SM) exhibited:
- bond of Mary Poore administratrix of James Poor. Sureties: William Harrison, William Loade. Date: 9 April 1720.
- bond of Anne Grasty administratrix of Samuell Grastey. Sureties: William Maria Farthing, Abraham Tennison. Date: 6 April 1720.
24:162 - bond of Mary Lee administratrix of Charles Lee. Sureties: William Lawrence, James Cox. Date: 4 April 1720.
- will of Thomas Reeves. Also depositions of John Ireland & John Hoskins.
- accounts of Elisabeth Oliver administratrix of Lewis Oliver.

Exhibited:
- bond of Winifred Holland administratrix of John Holland.

Sureties: Evan Jones, Richard Jones.
Date: 19 April 1720. Appraisers:
John Carter, John Stevens.
Valentine Carter to administer oath.

24:163 22 April. Deputy Commissary (SO) to
examine accounts of:
- Nicholas Dunn & his wife Elisabeth
  administratrix of John Walter (SO).

23 April. John Brewer was granted
continuance on estate of his father.

25 April. Mr. John Baker (SM)
exhibited:
- bond of Sarah Horne administratrix
  of Henry Horne. Sureties: John
  Horne, Thomas Aisquith. Date: 26
  APril 1720.
- bond of William Harrison
  administrator of James Doxey.
  Sureties: William Cutler, George
  Griggs. Date: 19 April 1720.
- bond of Elisabeth Cole executrix of
  Robert Cole. Sureties: John
  Greenwell, Robert Ford, Jr. Date:
  11 April 1720.
- bond of John Abbington administrator
  of John Woodward. Sureties: Richard
  Hopewell, John Seager. Date: 24
  February 1719.
24:164 - inventory of Thomas Reeves.
- will of William Kirby.
- will of Robert Cole.
- will of John Woodward.
- additional accounts of Thomas Sanner
  administrator of Vincent Langford.

Exhibited:
- accounts of William Yealdhall (AA)
  administrator of John Stevens.

Deputy Commissary (TA) to examine
accounts of:
- Edward Harden & Sarah Loveday
  administrators of Benjamin Giddens.

Francis Holland (g, BA) exhibited:
- bond of John Newsham administrator
  of Edward Harry. Sureties: Thomas
  Newsom, Peter Lester.
24:165 Date: 4 April 1720.

- bond of Joseph Johnson administrator of John Parker. Sureties: William Marshall, Richard King. Date: 30 March 1720.
- bond of Rowland Kimble executor of Samuel Jackson. Sureties: Thomas Cord, William Cook. Date: 5 April 1720.
- will of Samuel Jackson.
- inventory of Francis Street.
- accounts of Richard Gist administrator of Francis Street.
- accounts of Priscilla Freeborn administratrix of Richard Freeborn.
- accounts of John Cammeron & his wife administratrix of Daniel Maccentos.

29 April. Mr. Adderton Skinner (CV) exhibited:

24:166
- bond of Sarah Kidd administratrix of John Smith. Surety: Daniel Emmery. Date: 17 February 1719.
- bond of Mary Shepard executrix of John Shepherd. Surety: Thomas Marshall. Date: 5 March 1719.
- bond of Elisabeth Roden administratrix of John Roden. Sureties: Mathew Garner, William Edmunds. Date: 5 March 1719.
- will of John Shephard.
- inventory of Mary Boyle.
- inventory of Johanna Thompson.
- inventory of John Wilson.
- inventory of Richard Bond.
- inventory of William Pecock.
- inventory of Thomas Tongue.
- additional accounts of James Roberts son & heir of James Roberts executor of Robert Dixon.
- accounts of Roger Boyce administrator of Peter Madring.

24:167
- accounts of Susanna & David Hellen executors of David Hellen, Sr.

2 May. Exhibited from PG:
- additional inventory of Robert Brooks.

3 April. Exhibited:
- additional inventory of Col. Edward Lloyd. Also further additional inventory.

- renunciation of Mary Cole widow of
  John Cole (p, AA), recommending Col.
  William Holland (chief creditor).
  Date: 19 February 1719. Witnesses:
  Thomas Wells, Thomas Holland.

Court Session: 3 May 1720

24:168 Docket:
- E.J. for Thomas Gray vs. T.L. for
  John Gray. Libel & answer.
- R.T. for Jonathon Hopkins vs. W.C.
  for Harmanus Schee. Order for
  hearing.
- Michael Fletcher administrator of
  (N) Smithson vs. W.C. for J. Green &
  William Clayton. Agreed.

24:169 - W.C. for Mordecai Hammond & his wife
  vs. T.L. for Carpenter Lillingston,
  executor, etc. Sheriff (QA) to
  summon plaintiff for libel.
- M.H. for Benjamin Pemberton vs.
  Robert Grundy. Sheriff (TA) to
  summon defendant to pay
  distribution.
- W.C. for Thomas Nevett administrator
  of Thomas Brettargh vs. James Earle
  for William Skinner. Sheriff (TA)
  to summon plaintiff for libel.

24:170 - Edward Hall (sheriff, BA) to summon
  John Taylor executor of Abraham
  Taylor to give security. Order of
  contempt.
- Edward Hall (sheriff, BA) to summon
  Francis Dollahide administrator of
  Jonathon Hopkins to give security.
  Order of contempt.
- T.L. for Thomas Brannock vs.
  Nehemiah Beckwith. Summons for
  libel.

Court Session: 1720

24:171 3 May. Mr. Francis Holland (BA)
exhibited:
- will of Anthony Bale.
- will of James Philips.

4 May. Philip Feddeman (g) to examine
accounts of:
- Mary Bradley & his wife (!)
  administratrix of Thomas Woodward.

- Henry Oneall & his wife executrix of Thomas Vincent.

Foster Turbutt (g, TA) to examine accounts of:
- Ralph Person who married Elinor executrix of Thomas Booker.

Deputy Commissary (SM) to examine accounts of:
- Mary Clark executrix of Thomas Clark.

Exhibited:
- accounts of Ubgat Reeves executor of Thomas Reeves, Sr. (SM).

24:172 5 May. Dr. William Loch to prove will of:
- Nehemiah Birckhead (AA), constituting Mary Birckhead executrix.

Exhibited:
- accounts of John Craycroft administrator of Ignatius Craycroft (PG).
- additional accounts of Hugh Merrikin & his wife executrix of George Westall.

Mr. Alexander Contee (CH) exhibited:
- bond of Elisabeth Crabb executrix of Thomas Crabb. Sureties: Ralph Crabb, Henry Wright. Date: 22 March 1719.

24:173
- will of Thomas Crabb.
- inventory of Henry Franklin.

6 May. Petition of George Drew eldest son & heir of Anthony Drew (BA) for Deputy Commissary (BA) to prove said will.

Exhibited:
- accounts of John Bruce & his wife Judith executrix of John Warren (CH).

24:174 7 May. Exhibited:
- inventory of Norton Knatchbull (QA).

9 May. Mr. Patrick Hepburn (PG)
exhibited:
- bond of Magdalen Jarvis executrix of
William Jarvis. Sureties: Thomas
Willcoxen, Jeremiah Perdieu. Date:
30 April 1720.
- will of William Jarvis.

Exhibited:
- additional accounts of Thomas &
Joseph Wellman executors of Michael
Wellman.

10 May. Mr. Thomas Cockey
administrator of John Ingram was granted
continuance.

24:175 12 May. Katharine Craig (AA) widow of
John Craigh was granted continuance on
his estate. She is lame & not able to
travel.

15 May. Mr. Alexander Contee (CH)
exhibited:
- bond of Mary Miles executrix of
Henry Miles. Sureties: Thomas
Hagan, John Higdon, Sr. Date: 2 May
1720.
- will of Henry Miles.

16 May. Exhibited:
- bond of Mary Pumphry (late Mary
Cockey) administratrix of William
Cockey (BA). Sureties: Nathan
Pumphary, Walter Pumphary, Richard
Young. Date: 16 May 1720.
Appraisers: Benjamin Howard, Thomas
Randall.
24:176 Lancellot Todd to administer oath.

17 May. Exhibited:
- accounts of Richard Harrison
executor of Samuel Harrison.

18 May. Exhibited:
- accounts of Thomas Dillon
administrator of Mary Ganyott.

John Harcom (p, KE) vs. James Tippett
(KE). Summons to defendant to show
cause why LoA on estate of William
Harcom should not be repealed. Simon

Wilmer (sheriff) administered oath to said Tippett before Thomas Hynson & Thomas Rash. Date: 12 May 1720.

24:177 On 18 May, said John (brother of said William) & said James appeared. LoA to said James repealed. Said John was granted LoA.

19 May. James Harris, Esq. (KE) to examine accounts of:
* Richard Tulston & his wife Sarah administratrix of William Scott (KE).

Exhibited:
* accounts of Thomas Lingan executor of Edward Boteler (CV).

24:178 25 May. Mr. Patrick Hepburn (PG) exhibited:
* inventory of William Downe.
* additional inventory of James Shaw.
* accounts of Mary Shaw executrix of James Shaw.

26 May. Frances Dorsey administratrix of Nicholas Dorsey (BA) was granted continuance.

Deputy Commissary (CV) to examine accounts on estate of:
* David Bowen.
* John Shepard.

28 May. Dr. William Loch exhibited probate of will of Nehemiah Birckhead (AA).

24:179 John Dorsey (g) exhibited:
* additional accounts of William Marshall & his wife administratrix of George Wells (BA).

Mr. Francis Holland (BA) exhibited:
* bond of John Taylor executor of Abraham Taylor. Sureties: Francis Dollahide, Mathew Hale. Date: 11 August 1719.
* bond of Francis Dollahide administrator of John Hopkins. Sureties: Mathew Hale, Joseph Presbury. Date: 10 August 1719.

30 May. Mr. Foster Turbutt (TA) exhibited:

- bond of James Dawson administrator of James Wright. Sureties: Peter Harwood, Philip Horney. Date: 19 April 1720.

24:180
- bond of Benjamin Parrott one of executors of John Parrott. Sureties: Edward Clark, John Rathell. Date: 26 April 1720.
- bond of Rachel Mackway administratrix of Patrick Mackway. Sureties: John Morgan, John Bradshaw. Date: 26 April 1720.
- bond of Elinor Rigby administratrix of Arthur Rigby. Sureties: James Sandford, Morrice Orum. Date: 9 May 1720.
- bond of Tamer Berry (late Thamer Willson) executrix of Elisabeth Scott. Sureties: Thomas Dudly, John Willson. Date: 10 May 1720.
- bond of Tamer Berry administratrix of John Berry. Sureties: Thomas Dudley, John Wilson. Date: 10 May 1720.
- bond of John Bush administrator of Richard Brogden. Sureties: Michaell Fletcher, Thomas Sanders. Date: 24 May 1720.

24:181
- will of Anthony Voss.
- will of Elisabeth Scott.
- will of John Parrott.
- inventory of Joseph More.
- accounts of Elisabeth Hopkins administratrix of Turlo Huggins.
- accounts of Samuel Dickenson executor of Mathew Pickett.
- final accounts of John Henrix administrator of John Ludingham.

Deputy Commissary (TA) to grant LoA to:
- guardian of the children of Mary Eaton during their minority, or one of them if at age, on estate of Peter Anderton (TA).

24:182 Petition of John & James Pemberton (g, TA) executors of Thomas Beswick that the relations of the dec'd approve the inventory or show cause why they refuse.

Francis Holland (g, BA) exhibited:
- bond of Thomas Moulder administrator of Peter Bony. Sureties: John Hall, Esq., Thomas Cord. Date: 17 May 1720.
- bond of Henry Millan executor of William Norris. Sureties: Peter Lester, Thomas Newsome. Date: 21 May 1720.
- will of William Norris.
- will of Thomas Bucknall.

24:183 · will of Anthony Drew, with several depositions.

James Harris, Esq. (KE) exhibited:
- bond of John Inch administrator of William Jones. Sureties: Peter Debruler, Benjamin Blackleah. Date: 12 May 1720.
- bond of Andrew Nowell administrator of Philip Husitt. Sureties: Robert Randall, Joseph Right. Date: 20 April 1720.
- bond of Mary Davis administratrix of Edward Davis. Sureties: Thomas Recards, William Roberts. Date: 5 May 1720.
- bond of William Corse executor of James Corse. Sureties: Thomas Chandler, Thomas Midford. Date: 22 April 1720.

24:184 · bond of John Twigg & Anne Gyant executors of John Gyant. Sureties: John Reed, John Ashley. Date: 17 May 1720.
- will of James Corse.
- will of John Gyant.
- inventory of William Pope.
- additional accounts of William Woodland administrator of Thomas Parker.

2 June. Francis Holland (g, BA) exhibited:
- will of David Thomas, constituting Richard Ruff executor. Said Ruff was granted administration. Sureties: Peter Lester, Antle Deavor. Date: 28 May 1720.

3 June. Exhibited:
- additional accounts of Charles

Court Session: 1720

Nutter executor of William Piper.

24:185 9 June. Exhibited:
- accounts of Susannah Mather administratrix of George Mather (QA).

Philip Feddeman (DO) exhibited:
- will of Stephen Ross, constituting Katharine Ross executrix. Said Katharine was granted administration. Sureties: Anthony Rawlings, William Phillips. Date: 30 May 1720.
- bond of William Harper administrator of Richard Foster. Sureties: William Herron, Sr., William Cheattell. Date: 13 May 1720.
- bond of Elisabeth Jones administratrix of Isaac Jones. Sureties: Thomas Howell, David Peterkin. Date: 16 May 1720.
- inventory of Henry Conyer.
- additional accounts of Nehemiah Beckwith executor of Henry Beckwith.
- accounts of Henry Jones & his wife Rachel executrix of William Abbott.

24:186 10 June. Exhibited:
- accounts of Thomas Warren & his wife Mary executrix of Jonathon Jones (AA).
- inventory of Jonathon Jones.
- accounts of Otho Holland who married executrix of Charles Howard (AA).

Exhibited:
- accounts of Kathe. Creed administratrix of John Cread (AA).

14 June. Exhibited:
- accounts of Sarah Lloyd executrix of Edward Lloyd.

Foster Turbutt (TA) exhibited:
- bond of Thomas Turner administrator of John Turner. Sureties: Edward Turner, William Brown. Date: 31 May 1720.
24:187
- will of Maj. Thomas Emmerson.
- inventory of Robert Bishop.
- inventory of Samuel Martindale.

- accounts of Francis Neal administrator of Jonathon Neal.
- accounts of John Harrahan surviving administrator of Samuel Martindale.

Mr. John Baker (SM) exhibited:
- bond of Richard Fenwick, Cuthbert Fenwick, John Fenwick, Enoch Fenwick, & Ignatius Fenwick executors of John Fenwick. Sureties: William Thompson, Robert Clarke. Date: 19 May 1720.
- will of John Fenwick.
- inventory of Charles Lee.
- inventory of James Tubbs.
- accounts of John Guyther & his wife administratrix of Thomas Doxey.
- accounts of Hugh Hopewell executor of John King.
- accounts of Charles Brady & his wife executrix of Thomas Lawton.

24:188
- accounts of George Craft & his wife Elisabeth executrix of Richard Read.
- accounts of William Bradburne & his wife Elisabeth executrix of Francis Spinks.
- accounts of John Medly administrator of James Tubbs.
- accounts of Anne Read administratrix of James Meekins.
- accounts of William Jamstone & his wife administratrix of Thomas Barber.
- accounts of Robert Hutchins administrator of Francis Hutchins.

15 June. Exhibited from BA:
- inventory of John Rattenbury.

16 June. Exhibited from BA:
- will of Robert Gorsuch. Also bond of Robert Gorsuch administrator. Sureties: Thomas Gorsuch, Charles Gorsuch.

24:189
Date: 16 June 1720. Appraisers: Thomas Randall, Thomas Hughs (p). Capt. Richard Colegate to administer oath.

Exhibited:
- accounts of Jane Ridgley administratrix of William Ridgley,

Jr. (AA).

Dr. Patrick Hepburn (PG) to examine accounts of:
- William Smith executor of Dr. William Fisher.

Exhibited from BA:
- inventory of Peter Bonny.

Exhibited from QA:
- additional accounts of James Hutchins executor of John Hockens.

24:190 23 June. John Beale (g, AA) exhibited:
- will of Robert Ward, constituting Rebecca Ward executrix. Said Rebecca was granted administration. Sureties: William Brewer, Henry Leek. Date: 24 May 1720.
- will of John Carroll, constituting Mary Carroll executrix. Said Mary was granted administration. Sureties: Richard Snowden, Richard Evans. Date: 30 May 1720.
- bond of Elisabeth Hillyard & Daniel Hillyard, Jr. executors of Henry Hillyard. Sureties: Daniel Hillyard, Thomas Dawson. Date: 8 June 1720. Also will of said Henry.
- nuncupative will of James Williamson. Also bond of James Somervell administrator. Sureties: Patrick Sympson, William Black. Date: 3 May 1720.
- bond of Rachel Bordley administratrix of John Beard, Esq. Sureties: Thomas Bordley, Stephen Warman. Date: 29 December 1719.

24:191
- bond of William Holland, Esq. administrator of John Cole. Surety: John Beale. Date: 27 February 1719. Also renunciation of Mary Cole.
- bond of Amos Garrett administrator of Robert Thomas. Surety: John Beale. Date: 2 April 1720.
- bond of Thomas Price administrator of Philemon Hemsley, Esq., during minority of William Hemsley (son of dec'd). Sureties: Robert Noble, Mary Hemsley. Date: 4 April 1720.
- bond of Sarah Bryan administratrix

of Edward Bryan. Sureties: Thomas Brannock, John Davis, Gary Powell. Date: 28 April 1720.
* bond of John Welsh administrator of William Roseman. Surety: Richard Snowden. Date: 30 May 1720.
* inventory of Elinor Cross.
* inventory of John Cole.
* inventory of John Beard, Esq.

24:192
* inventory of William Nicholson.
* inventory of John Leakie.
* inventory of John Arnoldy.

Exhibited from QA:
* inventory of John Holland.

Exhibited bond of John Beale (g, AA) as Deputy Commissary (AA). Sureties: Stephen Warman, Vachel Denton. Date: 28 December 1719.

24:193 24 June. Mr. Adderton Skinner (CV) exhibited:
* bond of John Gray executor of Margaret Gray. Sureties: John Godsgrace, John Stennet. Date: 9 June 1720.
* bond of Thomas Gilley administrator of William Gilley. Sureties: William Dawkins, Darby Henly. Date: 21 May 1720.
* bond of Ann Lynam administratrix of John Lynam. Sureties: John Dickinson, Thomas Simmons. Date: 18 May 1720.
* bond of Elisabeth Deavour executrix of Gilbert Deavor. Sureties: William Willmott, James Freeman. Date: 7 May 1720.
* bond of Mary Stuart administratrix of William Stuart. Sureties: John Wood, Robert Jarman. Date: 23 April 1720.
* bond of Thomas Bourne executor of Elisabeth Bourn. Surety: James Heigh. Date: 7 June 1720.
* bond of Susanna, Mary, & Anne Nicholls executrices of Mary Nicholls. Sureties: John Brome, William Young. Date: 7 June 1720.

24:194
* bond of Abell Royston administrator of Rebecca Royston. Sureties:

Court Session: 1720

Kensey Johns, William Harris. Date:
18 June 1720.
• will of Gilbert Deavour, Sr.
• will of Elisabeth Bourne.
• will of Margaret Gray.
• will of Mary Nicholls.
• inventory of Gilbert Deavour.
• inventory of John Rodin.
• inventory of John Shepard.
• inventory of James Willmott.
• inventory of John Smith.
• inventory of Samuel Cluley.
• accounts of Jonathon Hollyday & his
  wife administratrix of John Owens.
• accounts of John James executor of
  John James.
• accounts of Sarah Kidd
  administratrix of John Smith.
• additional accounts of Robert Lee
  administrator of Nathaniel Miles.
• accounts of William Willmot
  administrator of James Willmott.

24:195 Exhibited:
• accounts of Anne Smith executrix of
  William Smith (AA).

28 June. Mr. Alexander Contee (CH)
exhibited:
• bond of Mary Boarman executrix of
  William Boarman. Sureties: William
  Boarman, Thomas Hagan, Joseph
  Routhorne. Date: 23 May 1720.
• bond of Priscilla Harrison executrix
  of William Harrison. Sureties:
  Charles Somersett Smith, Thomas
  Jameson. Date: 15 june 1720.
• bond of John Joye administrator of
  Thomas Clark. Sureties: Benjamin
  Douglas, John Browne. Date: 15 June
  1720.
• will of William Boarman.
• will of William Harrison.
• inventory of Jacob Miller.
• inventory of Charles Roch.
• inventory of George Short.
• accounts of Charles Musgrave
  administrator of William Musgrave.
• accounts of Thomas King & John
  Cooper executors of William
  Moncaster.
24:196 • additional accounts of Elisabeth

Court Session: 1720

Martin executrix of James Martin.
- accounts of William Denego administrator of John Denego.
- accounts of Patrick Mackenny & his wife executrix of John Barron.

Patrick Hepburn (g, PG) exhibited:
- bond of Roger Boyce executor of John Smith. Sureties: Joseph Chew, Henry French. Date: 11 June 1720.
- bond of Ellinor White executrix of Bernard White. Sureties: Joseph Belt, Thomas Sprigg. Date: 25 June 1720.
- will of Bernard White.
- inventory of Benjamin Berry.

24:197 2 July. Exhibited:
- inventory of William Cockey (BA).

Court Session: 5 July 1720

24:198 Docket:
- E.J. for Thomas Gray vs. T.L. for John Gray. Agreed.
- R.T. for Jonathon Hopkins vs. W.C. for Harmanus Schee. Dismissed with costs to plaintiff.
- W.C. for Mordecai Howard & his wife vs. T.L. for Carpenter Lillingston, executor, etc. Order for answer.
24:199 • W.C. for Thomas Nevett administrator of Thomas Brettargh vs. J.E. for William Skinner. Order for answer.
- T.L. for Thomas Brannock vs. Nehemiah Beckwith.
- W.C. for Jeremiah Finch & his wife vs. Sarah Frasier. Struck off.

John Gibson & Robert Mackillwain sworn as assistants to Commissary General.

24:200 Petition of Jane Taylor widow of Abraham Taylor (BA, d. 26 July 1719). When said Abraham died, there were 2 orphans which had been brought up by the petitioner:
- Mark Swift (age 15).
- Alice Cutchin (age 13).
The petitioner's son-in-law John Taylor (having LoA on said estate) is attempting to defraud the petitioner of part of said estate.

Court Session: 5 July 1720

24:201 Said Jane is very old & poor. Witness: George Read.
Ruling: handed over to BA County Court.

Exhibited:
- will of Anthony Drew, to be recorded, with depositions.

24:202 Mr. Samuel Hopkins to examine witnesses, regarding will of Mathew Nutter.

John & James Pemberton administrators of THomas Beswick (TA) vs. William Beswick & John Blackwell. Said William Beswick & John Blackwell are nearest of kin to said dec'd. Petition for reasons why they did not sign the inventory.

24:203 Mentions: children of dec'd.

5 July. Exhibited:
- additional accounts of Robert Tiler (g) administrator of James Mullakin.
- additional accounts of said Tiler administrator of John Reeves.

8 July. Exhibited:
- inventory of Francis Young (CV).

9 July. Alexander Contee (g, CH) to examine accounts of:
- Raphael Neal executor of James Neale.

Mathias Vanderheyden (g, CE) to examine accounts of:
- Mellice Hyland executrix of Nicholas Hyland.
- Elisabeth Merrit administratrix of Thomas Meritt.

24:204 James Harris, Esq. (KE) to examine accounts of:
- John Johnson & his wife executrix of William Blay (KE).

Alexander Contee (g, CH) to examine accounts of:
- Pidgeon Boye executrix of Jane Boye (CH).

Court Session: 5 July 1720

Summons rendered to:
- William Dalton & his wife executrix of Thomas Bradford to prove his will.
- Mary Cole executrix of her mother Mary Wells to take LoA.
- said Mary Cole executrix of her husband John Cole to take LoA.

James Harris, Esq. (KE) to grant LoA to:
- Arthur Miller on estate of Francis Jones (KE). Robert Jones (QA) to prove said will, as witnesses are in QA.

24:205 John Baker (g) to examine accounts of:
- Henry Cundlift administrator of Samuel Corbeslye.
- Vitus Herbert executor of Gilbert Turbevile.
- Richard Shirley & his wife Kath. executrix of John Wiseman.

12 July. Deputy Commissary (SO) to examine accounts of:
- Perthenia Morris administratrix of Thomas Morris.
- James Trewett & his wife Elisabeth administratrix of Philip Trewett.
- Susanna Dixon administratrix of Thomas Dixon.

Samuel Hopkins (SO) exhibited:
- bond of Katharine Tull administratrix of Thomas Tull. Sureties: George Tull, John Tull. Date: 23 June 1720.
- bond of Sarah Perkins administratrix of John Perkins. Sureties: John White, Daniel Caudry. Date: 21 June 1720.
- bond of Roger Woolford administrator of Mary Woolford. Sureties: Charles Ballard, George Dashiell. Date: 5 June 1720.
24:206 - bond of Mary Upshutt executrix of John Upshutt. Sureties: Donnock Dennis, William Noble. Date: 23 June 1720.
- bond of Anne Nutter administratrix of Mathew Nutter. Sureties: Benjamin Wailes, John Jones. Date:

22 June 1720.

- bond of William Whittington, Southy Whittington, Esther Whittington, & Hannah Whittington executors of Col. William Whittington. Sureties: William Faucit, Adam Spence, Nathaniel Hopkins. Date: 11 April 1720.
- bond of Elisabeth Bowen administratrix of Edward Bowen. Sureties: William Bowin, Jr., Abraham Smith. Date: 29 April 1720.
- bond of Elisabeth Fowler administratrix of John Fowler. Sureties: Edmon Beaucham, William Catling. Date: 5 May 1720.
- bond of Sarah Tull administratrix of Thomas Tull. Sureties: Samuel Handy, Solomon Colbourne. Date: 5 May 1720.

24:207
- bond of Thomas Williams executor of Thomas Williams. Sureties: William Planner, Thomas Dixon. Date: 5 May 1720.
- bond of Susanna Dixon executrix of Thomas Dixon. Sureties: William Planner, Samuel Handy. Date: 5 May 1720.
- bond of John Hampton administrator of John Chouvo. Sureties: Robert Nairne, Moses Fenton. Date: 20 May 1720.
- bond of John Hampton administrator of Patrick Donnock. Sureties: Robert Nairne, Moses Fenton. Date: 5 May 1720. Also renunciation of Mary Donnock.
- bond of Elisabeth Evans executrix of John Evans. Sureties: John Fawset, Sr., Ebenezar Franklyn. Date: 27 May 1720.
- bond of Elisabeth Schoolfield administratrix of Benjamin Schoolfield. Sureties: Samuel Davis, Joseph Schoolfield. Date: 31 May 1720.
- bond of Hill Drummond executor of Drake Drummond. Sureties: John Scarbrough, Henry Ayres. Date: 11 June 1720.

24:208
- bond of Thomas Houston administrator of Robert Houston. Sureties: Thomas

Baker, Barnet Ramsey.   Date: 21 June
1720.
- will of Thomas Tull.
- will of John Upshott
- will of Col. William Whittington.
- will of Thomas Williams. Also
  inventory.
- will of Capt. Thomas Dixon. Also
  inventory.
- will of John Evans. Also inventory.
- will of Benjamin Schoolfield.
- will of Drake Drummond
- will of Robert Houston.
- inventory of Thomas Tull, Jr.
- inventory of David Rich.
- inventory of John Kirk.
- inventory of John Irving.
- inventory of Samuel Jones.
- inventory of William Newbald.
- inventory of John Kellam.
- inventory of John Fowler.
- accounts of William Eskridge & his
  wife Abigall administratrix of
  William Newbald.

24:209
- accounts of Elisabeth Jones
  administratrix of John Jones.
- accounts of William Simpson
  administrator of Joseph Wouldhave.
- accounts of William Simpson
  administrator of Benjamin Wouldhave.

19 July. Deputy Commissary (SM) to
examine accounts of:
- Anne Coode executrix of John Coode.
- Bridget Richardson executrix of
  Nicholas Richardson.

26 July. Mr. Adderton Skinner (CV)
exhibited:
- accounts of Benjamin Mackall & his
  wife Barbara administratrix of
  Thomas Holdsworth.
- additional accounts of Grace Brook
  executrix of Robert Brook.
- inventory of John Lynam.
- inventory of William Gilley.
- inventory of Richard Johns, Jr.

24:210 Deputy Commissary (CV) to examine
accounts of:
- Ann Lynam administratrix of John
  Lynam.

Court Session: 5 July 1720

Capt. John Baker (SM) exhibited:
- will of Col. Henry Peregrine Jowles, constituting Dryden Jowles executrix. Said Dryden was granted administration. Sureties: Thomas Truman Greenfield, Richard Hopewell. Date: 9 June 1720.
- bond of Elisabeth Reader & Simon Reader executors of Benjamin Reader. Sureties: William Hardy, Thomas Alstone. Date: 8 June 1720.
- bond of Mary Rablin administratrix of Thomas Rabblin. Sureties: William Thorne, Samuel Wood. Date: 9 June 1720.
- additional inventory of William Herbert.
- inventory of Robert Cole.

24:211
- additional accounts of William Braburne & Nathaniell Cooper, Jr. executors of Edward Spink.
- accounts of Daniell Duggins & his wife Mary administratrix of Edward Miller, Jr.
- accounts of James Dillicoat executor of Henry Taylor, Sr.
- accounts of Patrick Fisher & his wife administratrix of John Noble.

James Harris, Esq. (KE) to examine accounts of:
- John Johnson & his wife executrix of William Blay.
- Rachel Medford executrix of Thomas Medford.
- John Johnson & his wife Catherine executrix of John Maddin.
- Mathew Pope administrator of William Pope.
- William Corse executor of James Corse.
- Andrew Norvill administrator of Philip Hissett.

27 July. Dr. Patrick Hepburn (PG) to examine accounts of:
- James Haddock & Col. Thomas Addison administrators of Andrew Hambleton.
- John & Samuel Pottenger executors of John Pottenger, Jr.
- Weldone Jefferson executor of Robert Hall.

24:212 Mr. Philip Feddeman (DO) exhibited:
- bond of Rebecca Pearson administratrix of John Pearson. Sureties: Anthony Rawlings, Thomas Peirson. Date: 13 June 1720.
- bond of Joseph Alford administrator of Elisabeth Halpin. Sureties: John Dawson, Thomas Barnitt. Date: 5 June 1720.
- bond of Mary Coursey administratrix of David Coursey. Sureties: John Eccleston, Charles Standford. Date: 14 June 1720.
- bond of Anne Lewis executrix of Gload Lewis. Sureties: Josiah Mace, Thomas Lewis. Date: 13 June 1720.
- inventory of Isaac Jones.
- inventory of Joseph Stanaway.
- inventory of Arthur Hart.
- inventory of John Pearson.
- inventory of Thomas Brettargh.
- additional accounts of Jonathon Clifton & his wife Mary administratrix of Manus Morris.

24:213
- additional accounts of Richard Pearson administrator of William Merchant.
- additional accounts of Sumer Addams & his wife administratrix of James Staples.
- additional accounts of Henry Oneale & his wife administratrix of Thomas Vinson.
- accounts of John Charlescraft & his wife administratrix of John Pearson.

Exhibited:
- accounts of Leonard Brooks executor of Richard Brooks (SM).
- additional accounts of Joseph Harrison administrator of Richard Harrison (CH).

Dr. Patrick Hepburn (PG) exhibited:
- inventory of William Brauner.
- inventory of William Jarvis.
- inventory of John Pottenger, Jr.
- accounts of Daniel Delhoser & his wife administratrix of William Brauner.
- accounts of William Smith executor of Dr. William Fisher.

Court Session: 5 July 1720

24:214 28 July. Exhibited:
- inventory of Samuel Jackson (BA).

30 July. Exhibited:
- bond of Margaret Birckhead executrix of Nehemiah Birckhead (AA). Sureties: Richard Snowden, Samuel Harrison (g). Date: 19 July 1720.

4 August. Exhibited:
- additional inventory of Henry Waters (AA).

6 August. James Harris, Esq. (KE) exhibited:
- additional accounts of James Tibball administrator of William Harcum.
- accounts of Robert Meeks executor of William Darby.

8 August. Exhibited:
- accounts of Sarah Jackson executrix of James Jackson (BA).

24:215 9 August. Mr. Francis Holland (BA) exhibited:
- bond of Sarah Perregoy administratrix of Joseph Perregoy. Sureties: William Loyall, Henry Perregoy. Date: 10 May 1720.
- will of John Bond.
- inventory of John Hopkins.

John Baker (g, SM) exhibited:
- accounts of Anne Coode executrix of John Cood.
- accounts of Bridget Richardson executrix of Nicholas Richardson.
- accounts of Elisabeth Watts executrix of Peter Watts.
- accounts of Pheby Harrard administratrix of William Harrard.
- accounts of Richard Shirley executor of John Wiseman.
- accounts of Joyce Haines administratrix of John Haines.
- accounts of Thomas Holland administrator of William Holland.
- accounts of Thomas Truman Greenfield administrator of Thomas Norman.
- accounts of Jane Butterworth executrix of Michael Butterworth.

Page 83

24:216   • inventory of John Fenwick.
      • inventory of Benjamin Reader.
      • inventory of Evan Howell.

John Baker (g, SM) to examine accounts of:
  • Richard, Cuthbert, John, Enoch, & Ignatius Fenwick executors of John Fenwick.
  • Kath. Reed executrix of William Reed.

<u>10 August</u>. Exhibited:
  • inventory of Philemon Hemsley, Esq. of goods in AA & in CH.
  • inventory of William Harcum (KE).
24:217   • inventory of Nehemiah Birckhead (AA).

<u>11 August</u>. Exhibited:
  • 2nd additional accounts of William Jones administrator of Morgan Jones (AA).

<u>16 August</u>. James Harris, Esq. (KE) exhibited:
  • bond of John Harcum administrator of William Harcum. Sureties: William Worrill, William Worrill, Jr. Date: 6 June 1720.
  • bond of James Wilson, Jr. & Peter Jones executors of William Jones. Sureties: Edward Holman, Sutton Burgin. Date: 9 July 1720.
  • bond of Nathaniel Hynson, Jr. administrator of John Hynson. Sureties: Hans Hanson, George Hanson. Date: 6 June 1720.
  • bond of Abigall Ackman administratrix of Grills Ackman. Sureties: William Woodland, Samuel Berry. Date: 5 August 1720.
  • will of Timothy Mulcan.
24:218   • inventory of Noah Laurence.
      • inventory of John Blackstone, Jr.
      • inventory of Dennis Sullivan.
      • inventory of William Hunt.
      • inventory of Michael Gaughagan.
      • inventory of John Ellis.
      • inventory of James Corse.
      • inventory of Col. Thomas Smith.
      • accounts of Mathew Pinar

administrator of William Hunt.
- accounts of Michael Hackett executor of Mary Bowles.
- accounts of William Spearman administrator of Michael Gahogon.
- accounts of Francis Thomas & his wife executrix of Philip Pryer.
- accounts of Predrick Blackiston administratrix of John Blackiston.

Mathias Vanderheyden (g, CE) exhibited:
- bond of James Collens administrator of Susanna Ricketts. Sureties: Thomas Gástelaw,

24:219
- James Bowers. Date: 18 June 1720.
- bond of Mary Young administratrix of Jacob Young. Sureties: William Price, Sr., William Price, Jr. Date: 16 April 1720.
- bond of John Ward administrator of William Ward. Sureties: William Veazy, Henry Hendrickson. Date: 13 May 1720.
- bond of Henry Peirce executor of Francis Smith. Sureties: George Douglas, Samuel Alexander. Date: 12 April 1720.
- bond of Samuel Alexander administrator of Daniel & Jane Canida. Sureties: John Smith, John Holtam. Date: 13 June 1720.
- inventory of Nicholas Hyland.
- inventory of Guisebird Cocks.
- inventory of Francis Smith.
- inventory of John Beamont.
- inventory of John Bavington.
- inventory of James Frisby.
- inventory of Thomas Merritt.
- inventory of William Ward.
- accounts of Abigall Pollen administratrix of George Pollen.

24:220 Mr. David Robinson (TA) vs. Nicholas Lowe executor of Mrs. Elisabeth Lowe. New appraisers: MM Henry Baily, Peter Sharp. [Note: the implication is that she has no legal representatives.]

24:221 Petition of Mr. Robert Noble for Mrs. Sarah Lloyd executrix of Col. Edward Lloyd. Said Sarah is widow of said Edward. Appeal to set aside the sentence.

24:222 Exhibited from AA:
- additional accounts of David Richards & his wife Anne administratrix of Henry Waters.
- accounts of John Powell & his wife Elisabeth executrix of William Pearce.

Exhibited:
- 2nd additional accounts of Elisabeth Cole surviving executrix of Robert Cole (SM).
- bond of Elisabeth Fraser administratrix of Alexander Fraser (BA). Sureties: George Walker, Thomas Taylor. Date: 16 August 1720. Appraisers: Lancelot Todd, John Ashman. Capt. Colegate to administer oath.

24:223 17 August. Exhibited:
- accounts of John Winchester & his wife Susanna widow & administratrix of Thomas Rouse (QA).

John Baker (g, SM) exhibited:
- bond of Elinor Baxter administratrix of Richard Baxter. Sureties: Thomas Griffin, John Bisco. Date: 9 August 1720.
- inventory of Henry Horne.
- inventory of Samuel Grasly.
- inventory of James Poor.

19 August. Exhibited:
- bond of Lancelott Todd administrator of John Lockett. Sureties: Maurice Baker, Charles Rockhold. Date: 19 August 1720. Appraisers: Benjamin Howard, John Ashman. Mr. John Israell to administer oath.

24:224 20 August. John Baker (g, SM) to examine additional accounts of:
- William Thompson administrator of William Herbert (SM).

22 August. Bond of Mary Barber administratrix of Thomas Barber (SM) was assigned to Thomas Sanders & his wife

Court Session: 5 July 1720

Eleanor.

23 August. Mr. Mathias Vanderheyden (g, CE) to examine accounts of:
- Mary Parsons executrix of William Parsons.
- Mary Bavington executrix of John Bavington.
- John Ward, Jr. administrator of William Ward.

Deputy Commissary (CH) to examine accounts of:
- Sarah Brett executrix of Henry Brett.
- Joseph Joye administrator of Thomas Clarke.
- Anne Short executrix of George Short.

24:225 Alexander Contee (g, CH) exhibited:
- will of John Blee. Also bond of Cleborne Lomax administrator. Sureties: Courts Keech, John Chandler. Date: 15 July 1720.
- will of Margaret Blee. Also bond of Cleborne Lomax administrator. Sureties: Courts Keech, John Chandler. Date: 15 July 1720.
- renunciation of Mr. John Fendall executor of said John Blee & Margaret Blee.
- will of John Brayfield, constituting Hudson Wathen executor. Said Wathen was granted administration. Sureties: Marmaduke Semmes, Thomas Barlow. Date: 12 July 1720.
- inventory of William Harrison.
- inventory of Thomas Clark.
- inventory of Henry Miles.
- inventory of Thomas Crabb.
- inventory of Henry Blanshet.
- additional inventory of Henry Franklin.

24:226
- accounts of Laurence Anders administrator of Henry Franklin.
- accounts of Thomas Matthews who married Susanna Yopp executrix of Isabell Dryden.
- accounts of John Smoot administrator of Gerrard Ocane.
- accounts of Thomas Mathews who

married Susannah Yopp executrix of Charles Yopp.
- accounts of John Smoot administrator of Lydia Ocain.
- additional accounts of Eleanor & John Philpott executors of Edward Philpott.

Richard Trensam procurator for Jonathon Hopkins (KE) vs. William Cumming procurator for Harmanus Schee (KE). Text of libel.

24:227 Plaintiff is natural brother of Philip Hopkins (KE, dec'd). Defendant married Johanna executrix of said Philip. Text of will of said Philip.

24:228-9 ...

24:230 Mentions: Simon Wilmer (sheriff, KE). Text of answer.

24:231 ...

24:232 Signed: John Beard for defendants.

24:233 Text of replication.

24:234-5 ...

24:236 Ruling: dismissed, with costs to be paid by plaintiff.

Mr. Foster Turbutt (TA) exhibited:
- bond of Katharine Buckingham administratrix of Thomas Buckingham. Sureties: Stephen Durden, William Dobson. Date: 19 July 1720.
- bond of Thomas Eaton administrator of Peter Anderton. Sureties: Hugh Spedden, John Botfield. Date: 13 June 1720.

24:237 • bond of William Clayton & Katharine Emmerson executors of Thomas Emmerson (g). Sureties: Jacob Loockerman, James Dawson. Date: 6 July 1720.
- will of William Parrott.
- inventory of Patrick Mackway.
- inventory of Thomas Taylor.
- additional inventory of David Fairbanks.
- inventory of David Witcherly.
- inventory of John Parrott.
- inventory of Thomas Buckingham.
- inventory of Elisabeth Scott.
- inventory of Joseph Bullock.
- accounts of Rebecca Webb executrix of Richard Webb.

Court Session: 5 July 1720

- accounts of Rebecca Love administratrix of John Love.
- accounts of Henry Bailey & his wife Elisabeth administratrix of Lambert Clements.
- accounts of John Harbert & his wife Ann administratrix of Joseph Bullock.
- accounts of Richard Morley & his wife Sarah administratrix of Rowland White.

25 August. Exhibited:
- additional accounts of John Brewer administrator of Joseph Brewer (AA).

24:238 Deputy Commissary (TA) to examine accounts of:
- Sarah Register administratrix of Robert Register.
- Hannah Parrott administratrix of Isaiah Parrott.
- Stephen Rashoon & his wife Ann administratrix of Edmond Dodd.
- Solomon Robinson & his wife Jane administratrix of Thomas Martin, Jr.
- Rachel Mackway administratrix of Patrick Mackway.
- Katharine Buckingham administratrix of Thomas Buckingham.

1 September. Francis Holland (g, BA) exhibited:
- bond of Mary Bucknall executrix of Thomas Bucknall. Sureties: Francis Holland, John Cottrell. Date: 29 August 1720.
- inventory of William Norris.

24:239 Exhibited:
- inventory of Thomas Macnemara, Esq. in CV, in BA, & in BA (!).

5 September. Exhibited:
- accounts of raphael Neale executor of James Neale the younger (CH).

John Baker (g, SM) exhibited:
- bond of Lidia Sanders administratrix of William Sanders. Sureties: John Sinnott, George Beverly. Date: 15 August 1720.

Court Session: 5 July 1720

- bond of Mary Aiskins administratrix of William Aiskins. Sureties: Thomas Waughop, John Morgan. Date: 29 August 1720.
- inventory of Thomas Rabling.
- accounts of Mary Clark administratrix of Thomas Clark.
- accounts of Richard Keen administratrix of William Creatchett.
- accounts of Francis Howel administratrix of Evan Howell.
- accounts of Katherine Scurlock administratrix of Richard Scurlock.

24:240 <u>6 September</u>. Patrick Hepburn (g, PG) exhibited:
- inventory of David Macdaniel.
- inventory of Joseph Jeans.
- accounts of Elisabeth Jeans executrix of Joseph Jeans.
- accounts of William Harris executrix of William Ransom.
- accounts of Thomas Davis & his wife administratrix of Thomas Finch.
- Johanna Edgar administratrix of Richard Edgar.
- accounts of John Bradford administrator of David MacDaniel.

Exhibited:
- accounts of Elisabeth Wood administratrix of John Wood (QA).
- accounts of William Cage administrator of Hannah Wilson.
- accounts of Frances Wells administratrix of Thomas Wells.
- inventory of John Leakings.
- inventory of Charles King.
- accounts of Honour Arden administratrix of Samuel Arden.
- accounts of Elisabeth wife of Thomas Stone administratrix of Richard Sampson.

Court Session: 6 September 1720

24:241 Docket:
- W.C. for Mordecai Hammond & his wife vs. T.L. for Carpenter Lillingston. executor etc. Order for answer.
- W.C. for Thomas Nevet administrator

of Thomas Brettargh vs. J.E. for William Skinner. Order for replication.

- T.L. for Thomas Brannock vs. Nehemiah Beckwith. Order for attachment.
- Daniel Dulany procurator for Benjamin Douglass, presumptive heir of Douglass Gifford (CH), petitioned for summons. Said Benjamin is cousin & heir at law.

24:242

- Regarding will of Francis Smith (CE). Mentions: representation of Rev. Mr. Richard Sewell on behalf of St. Stephen's Parish in CE. Ruling: not within the jurisdiction of this court.
- Benjamin Pemberton vs. Robert Grundy. Deposition of Mr. John Oldham, that he examined a copy of a "decretall" order made for said Pemberton against said Grundy, dated 3 May 1720.

24:243 Ruling: attachment to said Grundy.

John Oldham administrator of Cornelius Collins exhibited that he has not received any goods or chattels on said estate.

John Taylor (BA) administrator of Abraham Taylor exhibited 2 inventories, both of which are imperfect. Continuance was granted.

Deputy Commissary (BA) to examine accounts of:
- Jane Boon administratrix of John Boone.

24:244 Thomas Worthington administrator of William Catton exhibited that he has already exhibited accounts on said estate.

Summons rendered to Elisabeth Pearce to give better security on estate of William Pearce.

Executor of Thomas Hood (AA) was granted continuance.

Court Session: 6 September 1720

Exhibited:
- accounts of William Cage administrator of Hannah Wilson (CH).
- accounts of Raphael Neal executor of James Neale the younger (CH).

Stephen Warman (sheriff, AA) to summon:
- Richard Gott administrator of Richard Got to render accounts. Lives in BA.
- John Navarr administrator of John Brackhon to render accounts.
- Elisabeth Chew administratrix of John Chew to render accounts.
- Samuell Chew executor of Samuel Chew to render accounts.
- Sarah Simmonds administratrix of Richard Simmons to render accounts.
- William Holland administrator of John Steel to render accounts.
- Sarah Sparrow executrix of Solomon Sparrow to render accounts.

24:245
- Daniel Mariarte administrator of Edward Mariarte to render accounts.
- Anne Waters administratrix of Henry Waters to render accounts.
- James Mouat administrator of Jeremiah Sampson to render accounts.
- Samuel Chew administrator of Richard Powell to render accounts.
- Elisabeth Hinton administratrix of John Hinton to render accounts. "Not met".
- Patrick Creagh administrator of Mary Creagh to render accounts.
- Frances Campbell administratrix of James Campbell to render inventory.
- Fardinando Battee executor of Thomas Hood to render accounts.
- Amos Garret administrator of William Clark to render inventory.
- Amos Garret administrator of Richard Rawlins to render inventory.
- William Loch administrator of Alexander Watts to render inventory.

Stephen Warman (sheriff, AA) to render attachments to:
- John Slatter administrator of James Sweetlove to render accounts.

Court Session: 6 September 1720

Edward Hall (sheriff, BA) to summon:
- Jane Boon administratrix of John Boone to render accounts.
- Honour Arden administratrix of Samuel Arden to render accounts.
- John Taylor administrator of Abraham Taylor to render inventory.
- William Todd executor of Thomas Todd to render inventory. In VA.
- Stephen Gill administrator of John Leekins to render inventory.
- Francis Dollahide administrator of John Hopkins to render inventory.

Edward Hall (sheriff, BA) to render attachment to:
- Sarah Thomas executrix of John Thomas to render accounts. NEI.

24:246 Thomas Clagett (sheriff, PG) to summon:
- Tabitha Mills administratrix of William Mills to render accounts. In BA.
- Mary Tuel administratrix of Charles Tuell to render accounts.
- Mary Finch administratrix of William Finch to render accounts.
- Anne Jones administratrix of Evan Jones to render accounts.
- Catharine Prather administratrix of John Prather to render accounts.
- Martha Brown administratrix of John Brown to render accounts.
- Frances Wells administratrix of Thomas Wells to render accounts.
- Thomas Stoddart administrator of Thomas Harvey to render accounts. Dead.
- James Stoddart administrator of Thomas Robins to render accounts.
- Johanna Edgar administratrix of Richard Edgar to render accounts.
- James Stoddart administrator of John Hamilton to render accounts.
- John Bradford administrator of David MacDaniel to render inventory.

Thomas Clagett (sheriff, PG) to render attachment to:
- Richard Lancaster administrator of Luke Ray to render inventory.

Court Session: 6 September 1720

Sab. Sollers (sheriff, CV) to summon:
- Benjamin Mackall executor of Mary Mackall to render accounts.
- Francis Wallis administrator of Samuel Wallis to render accounts.
- Priscilla Johns executrix of Richard Johns to render inventory.
- Thomas King administrator of Charles King to render inventory.
- Alexander Parran administrator of John Hennyman to render inventory.

24:247 Sab. Sollers (sheriff, CV) to render attachment to:
- Richard Turner administrator of William Turner to render accounts.

John Howard (sheriff, CH) to summon:
- Elisabeth Hardy executrix of William Hardy to render accounts. Married Joshua Holden.
- Isabell Dryden administratrix of George Dryden to render accounts. Mort.
- Isabel Dryden administratrix of Anne Coulson to render accounts. Mort.
- William Cage administrator of Hannah Wilson to render accounts.
- Susanna Yopp executrix of Charles Yopp to render accounts.
- John Sinnot administrator of Lidia Ocain to render inventory.
- John Butt & James Maddox administrators of Thomas Gooly to render inventory.
- Raphael Neal executor of James Neal to render accounts.

John Howard (sheriff, CH) to render attachment to:
- Joseph Harrison administrator of Robert Kerr to render accounts. Mort.
- Frances Loften administratrix of John Loften to render inventory.

T. T. Greenfield (sheriff, SM) to summon:
- Robert Scott administrator of William Guthrick to render accounts.
- James Dallicoat executor of Henry Taylor to render accounts.

Court Session: 6 September 1720

- Thomas Truman Greenfield administrator of Thomas Norman to render accounts.
- William Gouldesborough administrator of William Hasler to render accounts.
- Thomas Waughop administrator of Laurence Dillon to render accounts.
- John Stapleton administrator of Henry Stapleton to render inventory.
- William White administrator of Edward Diall to render inventory.
- Mary Miller administratrix of Edward Miller, Sr. to render inventory.
- Frances Howell administratrix of Evan Howell to render inventory.
- Sarah Barrett executrix of Edward Barrett to render inventory. Removed to PG.
- Agnus Penny administratrix of John Penny to render inventory. Removed to PG.

24:248 Summons to SO:
- Wyborough Evans administratrix of William Evans to render accounts.
- Edward Driskill executor of Edward Hammond to render inventory.
- William Kennet executor of John Kennet to render inventory.
- Sarah Dashiel executrix of Robert Dashiel to render accounts.
- Samuel Powel administrator of John Powell to render accounts.
- Adam Heath administrator of John Shore to render inventory.
- Arabella Collins administratrix of John Collins to render accounts.
- Elisabeth Stevens administratrix of Thomas Stephens to render accounts.
- Thomas Holdbrook executor of John Holdbrook to render accounts.
- Mary Larey executrix of Daniel Larey to render accounts.
- Mary & Richard Beathers executors of William Beather to render accounts.
- Alexander Wilson executor of Alexander Wilson to render accounts.
- William Whittington executor of Stephen White to render inventory.
- Edward Round executor of William Round to render accounts.

Court Session: 6 September 1720

- Elisabeth Bratten executrix of John Bratten to render accounts.
- Nathaniell Walley administrator of Edward Waley to render accounts.
- Charles Ballard administrator of Robert Coller to render inventory.
- William Faucit administrator of John Gray to render accounts.
- Elisabeth Jones executrix of John Jones to render accounts.
- Elisabeth Polk administratrix of Ephraim Polk to render accounts.
- Tabitha Kellam administratrix of William Kellam to render accounts.
- Warren Hadder executor of Warren Hadder to render accounts.
- William Simson administrator of Benjamin Wouldhave to render accounts.
- William Simson administrator of Joseph Wouldhave to render accounts.
- Mary Fall executrix of Abraham Fall to render inventory.
- Naomy Shiles administratrix of Thomas Shiles to render inventory.
- Henry Philips administrator of Charles Philips to render inventory.
- Abigall Newbold administratrix of William Newbold to render inventory.
- Robert Martin administrator of James Manuell to render inventory.
- Robert Penton & his wife executrix of Isaac Lukes to render inventory.
- James Perry administrator of Mary Larey to render inventory.

24:249

Attachments to SO:
- Susanna Jones administratrix of Daniel Jones to render inventory.
- Margaret Gray executrix of Miles Gray to render accounts.
- Arthur Warren administrator of Samuel Davis to render accounts.
- Hugh Porter & his wife Margaret executrix of Edward Bray to render inventory.
- Anne Renshaw administratrix of John Renshaw to render inventory.
- Samuel Tingle executor of Robert Cobb to render accounts.
- Mary Philips administratrix of Thomas Philips to render accounts.

Court Session: 6 September 1720

- Mary Redmond administratrix of Walter Redmond to render accounts.
- Katherine Porter executrix of Hugh Porter to render accounts.
- Elisabeth Johnson administratrix of John Johnson to render accounts.
- William Kibbe executor of John Higgins to render accounts.

Cha. Ungle (sheriff, DO) to summon:
- Anne Maudsley executrix of James Maudsley to render inventory. Dead.
- Elisabeth Ennalls executrix of Thomas Ennalls to render accounts.
- John Hodson & Henry Ennalls administrators of John Ennalls to render accounts.
- Rasanna Cannon administratrix of James Cannon to render accounts.
- John Dawson executor of Anne Dawson to render accounts.
- Phillis Marrott executrix of William Marrott to render accounts.
- Anne Woodward administratrix of Thomas Woodward to render accounts.
- Anne Hooper administratrix of Richard Hooper to render inventory.
- Sarah Stanaway administratrix of Joseph Stanaway to render inventory.
- Richard Hart executor of Arthur Hart to render inventory.
- Mary Saldsberry executrix of Petegrew Saldsberry to render inventory.
- Susannah Parish administratrix of Richard Parish to render inventory.
Date: 29 August 1720.

Thomas Bozman (sheriff, TA) to summon:
- Elinor Cottner (also Elinor Catnor) administratrix of Alexander Cottner to render accounts. NEI.
- John Spriggnall executor of Anthony Wise to render accounts.
- John Oldham administrator of Cornelius Collins to render accounts.
- Peter Cullen & his wife Mary administratrix of Pierce Welsh to render accounts.
- David Robinson & William Aires administrators of Sarah Collins to

24:250

render accounts.

- John & James Pemberton executors of Thomas Beswick to render accounts & perfect inventory. NEI.
- Elisabeth Field administratrix of Christo. Field to render accounts. NEI.
- Robert Grundy administrator of John Cooks to render inventory.
- George Shanahan administrator of Margaret Reglace to render accounts.
- Joseph Eason administrator of John Eason, Jr. to render accounts.
- Jacob Gibson administrator of Robert Bishop to render accounts.
- Jane Martin administratrix of Thomas Martin to render accounts.
- Rebecca Love administratrix of John Love to render accounts. NEI.
- John Green & William Clayton, Jr. administrators of Mary Smithson to render accounts.
- Elisabeth Martindale administratrix of Henry Martindale to render inventory.
- Robert Ungle administrator of Thomas Collter to render inventory.
- Michael Fletcher administrator of Thomas Smithson to render inventory.
- John Stevens & Sarah Webb executors of Sarah Stephens to render inventory.
- Sarah Webb executrix of Henry King to render inventory.
- Elisabeth Smith administratrix of Daniel Smith to render inventory.

24:251 T. Bozman (sheriff, TA) to render attachment to:
- John & Robert Fellows administrators of Robert Fellows to render accounts.
- Rebecca Pitts executrix of John Pitts to render accounts.
- Thomas Emmerson, Jr. executor of Anne Emmerson to render accounts. NEI.
- John Kemball administrator of Peter Hoskins to render inventory.
- Heneritta Crump administratrix of Walter Crump to render inventory.
- Anne Bullock administratrix of

- Joseph Bullock to render inventory.
- Elinor Cotner administratrix of Alexander Cotner to render inventory. NEI.

Cha. Ungle (sheriff, DO) to render attachment to:
- Mary Warner administratrix of Stephen Warner to render accounts. "Languidus".
- George Fee administrator of Mathew Oneal to render accounts. Not found in DO.

24:252 Edward Wright (sheriff, QA) to summon:
- Edward Wright administrator of James Hepburn to render accounts.
- William Shield administrator of Bryan Shield to render accounts.
- Catherine Santee administratrix of Philemon Santee to render inventory.
- John Tootall administrator of John Tootall to render accounts.
- Edward Shield administrator of William Harvey to render accounts.
- Elisabeth Coursey executrix of William Coursey to render accounts.
- Robert Jones & his wife Neriah administratrix of Nathaniel Wright to render accounts.
- Sarah Gold administratrix of Christ. Gold to render accounts.
- John Wright administrator of Thomas Willotson to render accounts.
- Arthur Emory executor of Julian King to render accounts.
- Anne Barbor administratrix of Newton Barbor to render accounts.
- George Empey (also George Impey) administrator of Patrick Craven to render inventory.
- Thomas Bannon administrator of John Bannon to render accounts.
- George Philips administrator of Elisabeth Philips to render inventory.
- Elisabeth Blangey executrix of Jacob Blangey to render inventory.
- Edward Jones executor of William Arland to render inventory.
- Judith Brown administratrix of John Brown to render inventory.

Court Session: 6 September 1720

- James Coudon administrator of Augustin Finn to render inventory.
- Frances & Joseph Jackson executors of Barbary Jackson to render inventory.
- Nicholas Marsey administrator of James Bennett to render inventory.

24:253 Edward Wright (sheriff, QA) to render attachment to:
- Anne Kerby executrix of William Kerby to render accounts.
- Earnall Hawkins executor of John Hawkins to render accounts.
- Johanna Impy administratrix of William Impy to render inventory.
- Samuel Hunter administrator of John Hayes to render inventory.
- Arnault Hawkins administrator of John Spry to render inventory.
- Peter Falcom executor of Peter Falcom to render accounts.
- Barbery Jackson administratrix of William Draper to render inventory.
- Sarah Dancy administratrix of Peter Dancy to render inventory.
- Elinor Pratt administratrix of William Pratt to render inventory.
- Sarah Tool administratrix of Timothy Tool to render inventory.
- Frances Nicholson executrix of John Nicholson to render inventory.
- Joseph West administrator of John Farrow to render inventory.
- Hannah Bryon administratrix of Cornelius Bryon to render inventory.
- John Wright administrator of Thomas Willson to render inventory.

Gid. Pearce (sheriff, KE) to summon:
- Thomas Eubanks administrator of Richard Eubanks to render inventory. In TA.
- Martha Fillingham executrix of Richard Fillingham to render accounts.
- Theodotia Roberts administratrix of John Peters to render inventory. In QA.
- William Dean administrator of Anthony Wilkinson to render accounts.

Court Session: 6 September 1720

- Martha Smith executrix of Thomas
  Smith to render inventory.
- William Spearman administrator of
  Michael Gaughagan to render
  inventory.

24:254 • William Glanvil & Col.
  Nathaniel Hynson administrators of William
  Glanvil to render inventory.
- Mathew Piner administrator of
  William Hunt to render inventory.
- Thomas Browning administrator of
  Noah Laurence to render inventory.
  In CE.

Gid. Pearce (sheriff, KE) to render
attachment to:
- Susanah Darby administratrix of
  William Darby to render accounts.
- Dennis Towney administrator of
  William Welsh to render accounts.
  Dead, leaving a widow named Sarah.
- Margaret Pryor administratrix of
  William Pryon to render accounts.

Summons to CE:
- Thomas Price administrator of John
  Shuttleberry to render accounts.
- Cornelius Tobie administrator of
  George Struten to render inventory.
  NE.
- Mary Thomas executrix of William
  Dare to render accounts. NE.
- Henry Ward administrator of Charles
  FitzPatrick to render inventory.
24:255 • Jacob VanBebber administrator
  of John Beaumans to render
  inventory.
- Abell Vanburkelo administrator of
  Andrew Rosenquest to render
  accounts.
- Mary Bavington executrix of John
  Bavington to render inventory. NE.

James VBebber (sheriff, CE) to render
attachment to:
- Elisabeth Hethrington administratrix
  of Thomas Hithrington to render
  inventory. Married Henry
  Hendrickson.
- Johana Damper administratrix of
  Daniel Damper to render accounts.
  NE.

Court Session: 6 September 1720

- Johana Gray administratrix of Thomas Corne to render inventory. Not known.

Court Session: 1720

7 September. Deputy Commissary (SM) to examine accounts of:
- Jonathon Cay & George Gillaspie executors of George Irvan.
- (additional) Thomas Underwood administrator of Timothy Sullivant.

Bond of Edward Jones executor of William Arland (son & heir of Ralph Arland (QA)) is assigned to said Jones.

24:256 Deputy Commissary (QA) to examine accounts of:
- Arthur Emory executor of Julian King.
- Sarah Tucker administratrix of Nathaniel Tucker.

Deputy Commissary (CH) to grant LoA to:
- Rosaman widow of Douglas Gifford on his estate.

Deputy Commissary (PG) to examine accounts of:
- Aron Webb & his wife Martha administratrix of John Browne (PG).

John Israel (g) to prove will of Samuel Hinton (BA), constituting Elisabeth Hinton (alias Elisabeth Stone) executrix.

12 September. Mary Reeves widow of Thomas Reeves (SM) vs. Ubgate Reeves executor of said Reeves. Caveat against passing additional accounts.

24:257 Exhibited from PG:
- inventory of Luke Ray.
- accounts of Richard Lancaster administrator of Luke Ray.

Exhibited from AA:
- inventory of James Campbell.

Exhibited from CE:
- accounts of Charles Ramsey executor of Charles Ramsey.

Exhibited from KE:
- final accounts of Benjamin Pearce who married Mary executrix of John Hynson.

Exhibited from BA:
- inventory of Robert Gorsuch.

13 September. Exhibited from AA:
- inventory of Alexander Watts.
- accounts of Samuel Chew administrator of Richard Powell.
- accounts of Elisabeth Chew administratrix of John Chew.

Exhibited from CE:
- inventory of Charles FitzPatrick.

24:258 14 September. Exhibited from BA:
- accounts of Hill Savidge & his wife administratrix of Peter Bond.

Foster Turbutt (TA) exhibited:
- bond of Peter Russam administrator of Thomas Greenwood. Sureties: Samuel Neale, William Sheild. Date: 16 August 1720.
- bond of Sarah Maccotter administratrix of Alexander Maccotter. Sureties: William Watts, William Bexley. Date: 12 September 1720.
- additional inventory of Edm. Dodd.
- inventory of Thomas Grundy.
- inventory of John Berry.
- inventory of Sarah Stevens.
- inventory of Ambross Ford.
- inventory of James Wright.
- accounts of Issabell Grundy administratrix of Thomas Grundy.
- accounts of Edward Hardin & Sarah Loveday administrators of Benjamin Githins.

24:259
- accounts of Philip Casey & Peter Sanders executors of David Fairbanks.
- accounts of Stephen Rashoon & his wife Anne administratrix of Edm.

Dodd.

Samuel Hopkins (g, SO) exhibited:

- bond of Mary Griffin administratrix of John Griffin. Sureties: Daniel Caudry, John Webb. Date: 19 August 1720.
- bond of Thomas Bannister executor of William Bannister. Sureties: Robert King, William Mitchell. Date: 17 August 1720.
- bond of Thomas Gilliss executor of John Gillis. Sureties: Robert King, Ezekel Gillis. Date: 15 August 1720.
- bond of Sarah Bounds administratrix of James Bounds. Sureties: John Gunby, William Kibble. Date: 17 August 1720.
- bond of Thomas Fowler administrator of Edward Sermon. Sureties: Thomas Renshaw, Benjamin Esam. Date: 17 August 1720.
- bond of Abigall Parsons administratrix of John Parsons. Sureties: William Kibble, Richard Stevens. Date: 18 August 1720.
- bond of Elisabeth Waters one of executors of Richard Waters. Also renunciation of William Waters. Sureties: Robert King, William Planner. Date: 15 August 1720.
- bond of Margaret Tilman executrix of Gideon Tilman. Sureties: Alexander Hall, William Wheeler. Date: 19 August 1720.
- bond of John Murray administrator of John Murray. Sureties: John Scarbrough, Robert Hall. Date: 2 July 1720.
- bond of Quandan Bratten executor of James Bratten. Sureties: Samuel Bratten, James Bratten. Date: 1 July 1720.
- bond of Esther Denwood administratrix of Arthur Denwood. Sureties: Levin Denwood, Thomas Gillis. Date: 12 July 1720.
- bond of John Tunstal administrator of Joseph Crundwell. Surety: Ephraim Wilson. Date: 12 July 1720.

24:260

- will of William Bannister.
- will of Gideon Tilman.
- will of John Gillis.
- will of Richard Waters.
- will of James Bratten.
- inventory of Drake Drummond.
- inventory of Thomas Tull, Sr.

24:261
- inventory of Joseph Crandwell.
- inventory of John Perkins.
- inventory of Mary Lary.
- accounts of Sarah Dashield administratrix of Robert Dashield.
- accounts of Mary Powel administratrix of Thomas Powell.
- accounts of Sarah Roach administratrix of John Roach.
- accounts of Lewis Rigby & his wife Elisabeth administratrix of Peter Elzey.
- accounts of Nicholas Dunn & his wife administratrix of John Waller.
- inventory of Edward Bowin.

17 September. Deputy Commissary (PG) to administer oath to Mr. Benjamin Hall one of executors of Charles Carroll, Esq. (Annapolis).

Deputy Commissary (CE) to examine accounts of:
- Mary Bavington widow & executrix of John Bavington (CE).

Deputy Commissary (CH) to examine accounts of:
- Mary Boarman executrix of William Boarman (CH).

24:262 Exhibited from AA:
- accounts of Fardinando Battee executor of Thomas Woods.
- inventory of Capt. George Browne.

Exhibited from BA:
- accounts of Richard Gist administrator of Francis Street.

18 September. John Beale (g, AA) exhibited:
- bond of James Carroll administrator of George Browne. Sureties: Samuel Peele, Thomas Gassaway. Date: 13

September 1720.
- bond of Elisabeth Simmons executrix of George Simmons. Sureties: Roger Crudgenton, Samuel Guichard. Date: 15 August 1720.
- bond of Mary Jones administratrix of Joshua Jones. Sureties: John Merrikin, Nathaniel Stinchcomb. Date: 8 August 1720.

24:263
- bond of Thomas Crutchley administrator of George Man. Sureties: Thomas Harris, Mordecai Price. Date 1 August 1720.
- inventory of Daniel Hilliard.
- inventory of Robert Ward.
- inventory of James Williamson.
- LoD of John Brice.
- accounts of Samuel Peele administrator of John Ward.
- accounts of William Nichols & his wife administratrix of Richard Symons.
- accounts of John Powel administrator of Anne Thornberry.
- accounts of Patrick Creagh administrator of Mary Creagh.

<u>19 September</u>. James Harris, Esq. (KE) exhibited:
- bond of Agnes MacDonnell administratrix of John MacDonnell. Sureties: Fredrick Hanson, John Darick. Date: 25 August 1720.
- bond of Christopher Hale administrator of Stephen Denning. Sureties: John Smothers, William Smothers. Date: 17 August 1720.
- inventory of Philip Hissitt.
- inventory of William Jones.

24:264
- accounts of Samuel Parsons administrator of Agnes Parsons.
- accounts of John Johnson & his wife administratrix of John Maddin.

Exhibited:
- additional accounts of John Woodall administrator of Edward Plestoe.
- additional accounts of Sarah Lloyd executrix of Col. Edward Lloyd.

Adderton Skinner (g, CV) exhibited:
- bond of John Cox administrator of

Court Session: 1720

Col. Henry Cox. Surety: John
Brooke. Date: 3 August 1720.
- bond of Margaret Ashcom
administratrix of Nathaniel Ashcom.
Surety: John Rousby, Esq. Date: 10
September 1720.
- will of Col. Henry Cox.
- will of Amy Batson.
- inventory of Elisabeth Bourn.
- inventory of William Stuart.

24:265
- accounts of Mary Shepard executrix
of John Shepard.
- accounts of James Brown
administrator of Joanna Thompson.
- accounts of James Murrain & his wife
executrix of Elisha Sedgwick.
- account of Samuel Griffith of
legacies paid in obedience to his
mother's assignment.
- accounts of James Deavour & his wife
executrix of David Bowen.

Mathias Vanderheyden (g, CE) exhibited:
- bond of Ariana Frisby executrix of
James Frisby. Sureties: James
Harris, Stephen Knight. Date: 22
March 1720.
- bond of Anne Lewis executrix of
Richard Lewis. Sureties: Johannes
Numbers, John Boyer. Date: 4 August
1720.
- inventory of Daniel & Jane Canaday.
- accounts of Elisabeth Merrit
administratrix of Thomas Merritt.

24:266 20 September. John Baker (g, SM)
exhibited:
- bond of John Wheatly administrator
of James Wheetly. Sureties: John
Ford, Stephen Nottingham. Date: 1
September 1720.
- inventory of Edmond Doyall.
- accounts of William White
administrator of Edmond Doyall.
- accounts of Elisabeth Aisquith
executrix of Col. William Aisquith.
- additional accounts of Hugh Hopewell
executor of John King.

21 September. Exhibited:
- additional accounts of John Gibb
executor of Ralph Arland.

Court Session: 1720

<u>23 September</u>. Deputy Commissary (SM) to
examine accounts of:
* Frances Merrit executrix of John
  Merrit (SM).

Daniel Mariartee (g) administrator of
Edward Mariartee (PG) was granted
continuance.

24:267   Robert Jones (g, QA) exhibited:
* bond of Margaret Martin & Charles
  Neale administrators of William
  Martin. Sureties: Patrick Sexton,
  Ferdinando Callaghace. Date: 1 July
  1720.
* bond of Roger Murphey administrator
  of Thomas Jones. Sureties: Thomas
  Murphey, Francis Jackson. Date: 22
  March 1719.
* bond of Joanna Wyat executrix of
  James Wyat. Sureties: William Wyat,
  Charles Meloyd. Date: 4 June 1720.
* bond of John Clemons administrator
  of John Clemons. Sureties: Edmond
  Prior, Roger Murphey. Date: 1 July
  1720.
* bond of Thomas Godman administrator
  of Robert Porter. Sureties: Solomon
  Clayton, James Miller. Date: 29
  June 1720.
* bond of John Maconnakin
  administrator of John Dobs.
  Sureties: Robert Walters, John Legg.
  Date: 15 April 1720.
* bond of John Hacket administrator of
  Maj. William Hackett. Sureties:
  John Collins, Robert Hollins. Date:
  20 July 1720.
* bond of Sarah Tucker administratrix
  of Nathaniel Tucker. Sureties: John
  Wright, Solomon Wright. Date: 25
  March 1720.
24:268 * bond of Edward Brown administrator
  of Robert Walker. Sureties: John
  Chaires, William Austin. Date: 21
  May 1720.
* bond of William Clayton
  administrator of William Turloe.
  Sureties: Edward Wright, James
  Earle. Date: 2 July 1720.
* bond of William Hemsley & Robert
  Noble executors on the Eastern Shore

of Philemon Hemsley. Sureties: James Pemberton, Solomon Clayton. Date: 31 March 1720.
- bond of Mary Benton executrix of Francis Benton. Sureties: Michael Moore, John Roberts. Date: 15 April 1720.
- bond of Katharine Williams executrix of James Williams. Sureties: Peter Wild, Henry Wright. Date: 5 May 1720.
- bond of Katharina Wright & Robert Norris Wright executors of Charles Wright. Sureties: John Wright, John Chaires. Date: 4 July 1720.
- bond of Mary Hinds executrix of Thomas Hinds. Sureties: Thomas Hinds, Thomas Ford. Date: 30 July 1720.

24:269
- bond of Hester Hacket executrix of Maj. William Hackett. Sureties: John Collins, William Hollins. Date: 21 March 1719.
- will of Maj. William Hackett.
- will of James Williams.
- will of Thomas Hind, Sr.
- will of James Wyat.
- will of Francis Benton.
- will of William Sweatnam.
- will of Charles Wright.
- inventory of James Williams.
- inventory of Jacob Blangy.
- inventory of Robert Walker.
- inventory of Patrick Craven.
- inventory of John Clemond.
- inventory of Francis Benton.
- inventory (of goods on the Eastern Shore) of Philemon Hemsley, Esq.
- inventory of Augustine Finn.
- inventory of Edward Pain.
- inventory of Elisabeth Cavener.
- inventory of James Bennett.
- inventory of Nathaniel Tucker.
- accounts of Edmond Shield administrator of William Harvey.
- accounts of James Condon administrator of Augustine Finn.

24:270 24 September. Philip Feddeman (DO) exhibited:
- bond of Mary Hooper executrix of Henry Hooper. Sureties: Roger

Woolford, Mathew Travis. Date: 30 August 1720.
- bond of Mary Harper executrix of William Harper. Sureties: John Griffin, Francis Griffin. Date: 10 August 1720.
- bond of Cornely Mackall executrix of David Mackall. Sureties: Edward Ross, Peter Ross. Date: 8 August 1720.
- bond of Elisabeth Bartington administratrix of Enock Bartington. Sureties: Edward Poole, John Minnish. Date: 6 September 1720.
- will of Henry Hooper.
- will of William Harper.
- will of David Mackall.
- inventory of Petigrew Saldsberry.
- inventory of Richard Foster.
- inventory of Stephen Warner.
- inventory of Richard Hooper.
- inventory of David Cousey.

24:271
- inventory of Stephen Ross.
- accounts of Mary Warner administratrix of Stephen Warner.
- accounts of Henry Tripp administrator of Austin Parker.
- accounts of John Harwood executor of James Noell.
- accounts of Thomas Stimson executor of Elisabeth Sear.
- accounts of Mary Coursey administratrix of David Coursey.
- accounts of Henry Bradley & his wife administratrix of Thomas Woodward.

27 September. Deputy Commissary (DO) to examine accounts of:
- Richard Hart executor of Arthur Hart.
- Mary Saldsbury executrix of Petegrew Saldsbury.
- John Hudson Secundus & Henry Ennalls administrators of John Ennalls.

Exhibited:
- accounts of James Stoddart administrator of Thomas Harvie (PG).

24:272 28 September. Alexander Contee (g, CH) exhibited:
- bond of John Butts & Stephen Mankin

administrators of Elisabeth Haley.
Sureties: George Goodrick, Josias
Mankin. Date: 18 August 1720.
- renunciation of William Hunter of
  administration on estate of
  Elisabeth Haley.
- inventory of Thomas Gooley.
- inventory of William Boarman.
- accounts of Joseph Joye
  administrator of Thomas Clarke.
- accounts of John Butts & James
  Maddox administrators of Thomas
  Gooly.

Exhibited from CE:
- accounts of Benjamin Pearce & his
  wife executrix of Edward Cooper.

29 September. Exhibited from SM:
- inventory of Col. Henry Jowles.

24:273 30 September. Francis Holland (g, BA)
exhibited:
- bond of George Drew executor of
  Anthony Drew. Sureties: Francis
  Dollahide, William Lenox. Date: 13
  September 1720.
- bond of Arrabello Loney
  administratrix of William Loney.
  Sureties: Francis Holland, William
  Cook, Benjamin Osburn. Date: 8
  September 1720.
- will of Thomas Bucknall.
- inventory of William Loney.
- inventory of Abraham Taylor.

1 October. John Baker (g, SM)
exhibited:
- accounts of Vitus Herbert executor
  of Gilbert Turbevile.
- additional accounts of William
  Thompson & his wife administratrix
  of William Herbert.
- inventory of John Woodward.

3 October. Exhibited from BA:
- inventory of Alexander Fraser.
- inventory of John Lockett.

24:274 6 October. Exhibited:
- accounts of Elisabeth Ensor
  administratrix of Abraham Ensor.

9 October. Mathias VanBibber (g) to examine accounts of:
- Mathias Vanderheyden administrator of James Barbot (CE). Mr. John Ward is to be present.

12 October. MM Thomas Cockey, Thomas Worthington, & Patrick Sympson are to appraise the estate of Charles Carroll, Esq.

Exhibited from BA:
- bond of Mary Bond executrix of John Bond. Sureties: William Bond, Robert Smith. Date: 3 August 1720.

Exhibited from TA:
- inventory of Maj. William Turloe.
- inventory of Maj. Thomas Emmerson.

24:275 Adderton Skinner (g, CV) exhibited:
- bond of Abraham Bowen executor of Charles Bowen, Sr. Sureties: Charles Bowen, Isaac Bowen. Date: 27 September 1720.
- will of Charles Bowen, Sr. Also inventory.
- inventory of Margaret Gray.
- inventory of Rebecca Royston.

13 October. Mathias Vanderheyden (g, CE) exhibited:
- bond of Sarah Smith executrix of John Smith. Sureties: Robert Wood, Lawrence Guilshiott. Date: 29 September 1720.
- will of John Smith.
- inventory of Susannah Reckcott.
- accounts of James Collens administrator of Susannah Rickcott.
- additional accounts of James Numberon who married widow of John Husband.
- accounts of Henry Ward administrator of Charles FitzPatrick.
- accounts of Johanna Dampier administratrix of Daniel Dampier.
- accounts of John Ward administrator of William Ward.

24:276 15 October. Gilbert Falconar (g, KE) vs. Hannah Bryan widow of John Bryan

(KE). Sheriff (KE) to summon defendant
to prove said will.

18 October. Exhibited:
- will of Nicholas Rogers (BA),
  constituting Elinor Rogers
  executrix. Said Elinor was granted
  administration. Sureties: William
  Hamilton, John Gorsuch. Date: 18
  October 1720. Appraisers: Lancelot
  Todd, Hu. Hughs (p). John Israel to
  administer oath.
- accounts of James Mouat
  administrator of Capt. Jeremiah
  Sampson.

24:277 19 October. James Harris, Esq. (KE)
exhibited:
- bond of Arthur Miller executor of
  Francis Jones. Sureties: Simon
  Wilmer, James Moore. Date: 6
  October 1720.
- bond of John Fanning administrator
  of Daniel Dunahow. Sureties: Daniel
  Ferrill, Daniel Delahunt. Date: 12
  October 1720.
- inventory of John Giant.
- accounts of John Twig & Ann Giant
  executors of John Giant.

Exhibited:
- accounts of Samuel Magruder
  administrator of James Gardner (PG).

Exhibited from BA:
- bond of Hannah Orrick administratrix
  of William Orrick. Sureties: John
  Orrick, John Howard. Date: 19
  October 1720. Appraisers: Col.
  Thomas Hammond, John Gardner. John
  Israel to administer oath.

Deputy Commissary (CV) to examine
accounts on estate of:
- Sampson Warren.
- Samuel Wallis.

24:278 20 October. Exhibited:
- additional inventory of Henry Lowe,
  Esq.
- additional accounts of Henry &
  Bennet Lowe executors of said Low.

21 October. Exhibited:
* accounts of Richard Bennet, Esq.
  administrator of Norton Knatchbull.

23 October. Exhibited:
* accounts of Thomas Truman Greenfield
  & James Greenfield executors of Col.
  Thomas Greenfield.
* accounts of Thomas Truman Greenfield
  & James Greenfield executors of Col.
  Thomas Greenfield on estate of Col.
  Thomas Holliday.

24 October. Foster Turbut (g, TA)
exhibited:
* accounts of Hannah Parrot
  administratrix of Isaiah Parrot.
* additional inventory of Prudence
  Woolman.
* inventory of Arthur Rigby.
* inventory of Peter Anderton.

Mr. David Robinson one of executors of
Mrs. Elisabeth Lowe (TA) vs. Mrs.
Margaret Lowe wife of Mr. Nicholas Lowe
one of executors of said Elisabeth.
24:279 Deposition of Margaret Lowe that she
never meddled in said estate.

25 October. Exhibited:
* LoD of Madam Elisabeth Lowe (TA).

26 October. Exhibited:
* additional inventory of Elisabeth
  Low.

27 October. Richard Cole & his wife
executors of Renatus Smith were granted
continuance.

Deputy Commissary (SO) to examine
accounts of:
* Francis Ervin administratrix of John
  Ervin.
* Katherine MacNeale executrix of Hugh
  MacNeale.

Exhibited:
* accounts of Samuel Maxwell
  administrator of Henry King.

24:280 2 November. Exhibited:
- accounts of William Ennalls one of executors of Col. Thomas Ennalls.

9 November. John Baker (g, SM) exhibited:
- inventory of William Harrison.
- additional accounts of John Heard administrator of John Doagins.
- additional accounts of Joseph Hardyn administrator of John Welch.
- accounts of Anne Read executrix of William Read.
- additional accounts of Mary Jessop executrix of Joseph Jessop.
- accounts of Thomas Turner administrator of Joshua Turner.

Court Session: 12 November 1720

24:281 Docket:
- W.C. for Mordecai Hammond & his wife vs. Thomas Larkin for Carpenter Lillingston executor, etc. Libel, answer, & replication. MM William Turbutt & Robert Jones to examine witnesses.
- W.C. for Thomas Nevet administrator of Thomas Brettargh vs. J.E. for William Skinner. Libel, answer, & replication.
- T.L. for Thomas Brannock vs. Daniel Dulany procurator for Nehemiah Beckwith. Charles Ungle (sheriff, DO) rendered attachment to defendant.

24:282
- T.L. for Vestry of St. Michael's Parish vs. Daniel Dulany procurator for Michael Fletcher. Libel. T. Bozman (sheriff, TA) to summon defendant.
- Summons rendered to Hannah Bryan widow of John Brian (KE) to prove his will.
- Lord Proprietor vs. Robert Grundy. At petition of Daniel Dulany procurator for Benjamin Pemberton, T. Bozman (sheriff, TA) rendered attachment to defendant.

24:283 Said defendant is "mortuus est".
- will of Douglass Gifford (CH) is to be recorded.

Court Session: 12 November 1720

23 November. John Beale, Esq. (AA)
exhibited:
- will of Charles Carroll, Esq.,
  constituting Henry Darnall (g),
  James Carroll (g), & Daniel Carroll
  (g) executors. Said executors were
  granted administration, during
  absence or inability of Charles &
  Daniel Carroll executors in chief).
  Sureties: Benjamin Tasker, Jacob
  Henderson, Charles Digges, John
  Digges. Date: 23 August 1720.
- will of Dr. Mordecai Moore,
  constituting Deborah Moore & Richard
  Moore executors. Said Deborah &
  Richard were granted administration.
  Sureties: Samuel Chew, Samuel
  Harrison. Date: 4 November 1720.

24:284
- bond of Hannah Cross administratrix
  of Robert Cross. Sureties: James
  Smith, Peter Goslin. Date: 21
  October 1720.
- inventory of Joshua Jones.
- accounts of Albertus Greening
  administrator of John Arnoldy.
- accounts of William Whitehead & his
  wife executrix of Elinor Cross.

24 November. Exhibited:
- bond of Sidney Peirpoint, wife of
  Charles Peirpoint, sister,
  next-of-kin & administratrix of
  William Chew (BA). Sureties:
  Charles Peirpoint, William
  Hambleton, Peter Shipley. Date: 15
  November 1720. Appraisers: Benjamin
  & John Howard. John Israel to
  administer oath.

26 November. Appointment of Mr. John
Israel as Deputy Commissary (BA).

24:285 28 November. John Baker (g, SM)
exhibited:
- will of John Tany, constituting
  Katharine Taney executrix. Said
  Katharine was granted
  administration. Sureties: Richard
  Hopewell, Robert Hutchins. Date: 1
  November 1720.
- will of William Morgan, constituting
  Elisabeth Browne executrix. Said

Browne was granted administration.
Sureties: William Maria Farthing,
John Abell. Date: 5 November 1720.
• accounts of Richard, Cuthbert, John,
Enoch, & Ignatius Fenwick executors
of John Fenwick.

Deputy Commissary (SM) to examine
accounts of:
• Sarah Horne administratrix of Henry
Horne.
• Jonathon Cay & George Gillaspie
executors of George Ervin.
• Robert Ford administrator of Peter
Smith.

Deputy Commissary (DO) to examine
accounts of:
• Elisabeth Bartington administratrix
of John Bartington.

24:286 29 November. Philip Feddeman (g, DO)
exhibited:
• bond of Mary Mallahane
administratrix of Patrick Mallahane.
Sureties: Anthony Chillcutt, Govert
Loockerman. Date: 17 October 1720.
• will of Benjamin Woodward,
constituting Mary Woodward
executrix. Said Mary was granted
administration. Sureties: Thomas
Brannock, Isaac Nicholls. Date: 14
November 1720.
• inventory of Enoch Bartington.
• inventory of William Harper.
• inventory of Glood Lewis.
• accounts of Dennis Mackcarty & his
wife Phillis executrix of William
Marrett.
• additional accounts of John Samuell
& his wife administratrix of Mathew
Oneale.

24:287 30 November. Exhibited:
• additional accounts of Carp.
Lillingston executor of Joseph
Lambert.

4 December. Alexander Contee (CH)
exhibited:
• will of Edward Sanders, constituting
Thomas Sanders & Charles Sanders

executors. Said Thomas & Charles
were granted administration.
Sureties: John Causeen, Isaac
Gilpin. Date: 4 October 1720.
- bond of William Hoskins executor of
Philip Hoskins. Surety: Robert
Hanson. Date: 14 November 1720.
- inventory of Elisabeth Haley.
- inventory of John Brayfield.
- inventory of John Blee.
- inventory of Margaret Blee.
- accounts of Anne Short executrix of
George Short.
- additional accounts of Edward
Milstead who married Mary executrix
of John Shekertie.
- accounts of Pidgeon Boye executrix
of Jane Boye.
- accounts of John Suttle
administrator of Thomas Waterman.
- accounts of Sarah Brett executrix of
Henry Brett.
- accounts of Walter Storey who
married Anne administratrix of
Thomas Dixon.

24:288 8 December. Samuel Galloway (CV) vs.
estate of his father Samuel Galloway.
Caveat against the will of said estate.

Deputy Commissary (CV) to examine
accounts on estate of:
- Thomas Tongue.
- Richard Harris.
- Rebecca Royston.

Exhibited:
- bond of Mary Barnet administratrix
of William Barnet (BA). Sureties:
John Merriken, William Cumming, John
Smith, Nathaniel Stinchicomb. Date:
8 December 1720. Also the
deposition of Mary Dun, regarding
the nuncupative will of the dec'd.

24:289 13 December. James Harris, Esq. (KE)
exhibited:
- bond of Elinor Jones administratrix
of Robert Jones. Sureties: George
Murfee, William Arland. Date: 25
December 1720.
- bond of Daniel Pearce administratrix

of John Bryan. Sureties: John
Johnson, St. Leidger Codd. Date: 18
November 1720.
- will of John Bryant.
- will of William Howard, constituting
  Elisabeth Howard executrix. Said
  Elisabeth was granted
  administration. Sureties: James
  Thomas, John Magner. Date: 28
  November 1720.
- will of Isaac England, constituting
  Elisabeth England executrix. Said
  Elisabeth was granted
  administration. Sureties: Samuel
  Smith, Francis Thomas. Date: 16
  November 1720.
- inventory of Grill Ackman.
- accounts of Anne Browning executrix
  of Thomas Browning administrator of
  Noah Laurence.

24:290 Exhibited:
- inventory of Edward Bryan (AA), for
  goods in AA & DO.

15 December. Dr. Patrick Hepburn (PG)
exhibited:
- will of John Burch, constituting
  Elisabeth the wife of James Read
  executrix. Said Elisabeth was
  granted administration. Sureties:
  Charles Beavan, John Dowhite. Date:
  21 November 1720.
- bond of Samuel Perrie administrator
  of Thomas Polson. Sureties: James
  Haddock, John Docwra. Date: 21
  October 1720.
- bond of Jean Prather administratrix
  of Jonathon Prather, Jr. Sureties:
  William Ray, Sr., Anthony Drane.
  Date: 26 November 1720.
24:291 - additional inventory of John
  Prather.
- inventory of John Smith.
- accounts of John Docwra & his wife
  Salome administrators of James
  Robinson.
- accounts of Thomas Addison, Esq.
  administrator of Andrew Hamilton.
- accounts of Terence Bryan & his wife
  administrators of Charles Tuell.
- accounts of John & Sarah Pottenger

executors of John Pottenger, Jr.
- accounts of Katharine Prather administratrix of John Prather.

16 December. Exhibited:
- additional accounts of Ubgate Reeves executor of Thomas Reeves.

20 December. Exhibited:
- LoD on estate of William Nicholson (AA).

29 December. Bazel Warring (g, PG) vs. estate of Ignatius Craycroft. Caveat exhibited.

24:292   Col. James Haddock attorney for executors of Capt. Thomas Wharton vs. estate of Gabriel Burnham. Caveat exhibited.

31 December. Exhibited:
- inventory of William Orrick (BA).

2 January. Exhibited:
- renunciation of Samuel Galloway on estate of his father.

10 January. Deputy Commissary (PG) to examine accounts of:
- Mary Barry executrix of Benjamin Barry (PG).

Court Session: 10 January 1720

24:293   Docket:
- W.C. for Mordecai Hammond & his wife vs. T.L. for Carpenter Lillingston executor, etc. Libel, answer, & replication.
- W.C. for Thomas Nevett administrator of Thomas Brettargh vs. J.E. for William Skinner. Libel, answer, replication.
- T.L. for Thomas Brannock vs. D.D. for Nehemiah Beckwith. Libel; attachment for answer.
- T.L. for Vestry of St. Michael's Parish vs. D.D. for Michael Fletcher. Libel.

24:294   • deposition of Charles Hutton that he was a witness for George Forbes at

Court Session: 10 January 1720

> suit of Mary Cheseldyne executrix of Kenelm Cheseldyne.
> - David Robinson vs. estate of Elisabeth Lowe (TA). Caveat exhibited. Nicholas Low is administrator.

Court Session: 1720

24:295 11 January. Exhibited bond of John Israel as Deputy Commissary (BA). Sureties: Benjamin Howard, John Howard. Date: 26 November 1720.

John Israel (g, BA) exhibited:
- bond of Charles Merryman, Jr. administrator of John Henderson. Sureties: Thomas Rutter, Thomas Gorsuch. Date: 5 December 1720.

12 January. Foster Turbutt (g, TA) exhibited:
- will of Mr. Robert Grundy. Also bond of James Lloyd & his wife Anne & John Pemberton & his wife Deborah executors. Sureties: John Sherwood. Howell Powell. Date: 29 November 1720.
- will of Frances Sherwood (female), constituting Daniel Powell executor. Said Powell was granted administration. Sureties: Howell Powell, John Bullen. Date: 29 November 1720.
- bond of Elisabeth Helsby administratrix of James Helsby. Sureties: David Robinson, John Pattison. Date: 30 November 1720.

24:296
- bond of Rebecca Tibbolls administratrix of Abraham Tibbolls. Sureties: David Robinson, Dennis Rock. Date: 30 November 1720.
- inventory of Thomas Greenwood.
- inventory of Timothy MacDaniel.
- inventory of Richard White.
- additional inventory of Peter Webb.
- inventory of Laughlin MacDaniell.
- inventory of Henry King.
- accounts of John Oldfield & his wife administratrix of Joseph Moore.
- accounts of Edward Turner executor of Thomas Tyler.

- accounts of Anne Cockayne administratrix of Thomas Cockayne.
- accounts of John Bartlet & his wife administratrix of Edgar Webb.
- accounts of Rebecca Pitt executrix of John Pitts.
- election of Mrs. Anne Dàwson widow & executrix of John Dawson (TA). Date: 1 October 1720.

24:297

14 January. Thomas Gassaway (g) to grant LoA to Anne Galloway executrix of Samuel Galloway.

18 January. Exhibited:
- accounts of James Stoddart administrator of John Hambleton.
- accounts of James Stoddart administrator of Thomas Robins.
- additional inventory of Thomas Robins.

20 January. At the request of Thomas Reeves son of Thomas Reeves (SM, dec'd), John Baker (SM) to examine witnesses to will of said Thomas (dec'd) that they have not already done so.

24:298 20 January. Philip Feddeman (g, DO) exhibited:
- accounts of Richard Hart executor of Arthur Hart.

23 January. Exhibited:
- accounts of Nicholas Lowe & David Robinson executors of Elisabeth Lowe.

25 January. Deputy Commissary (CH) to examine accounts of:
- Daniel Jenifer & his wife administrators of John Rogers (CH).

26 January. Gerard Slye (g, SM) vs. estate of Garret Vansweringen (SM). Caveat against administration dbn.

24:299 27 January. Adderton Skinner (g, CV) exhibited:
- bond of Jane Meeds executrix of William Meads. Sureties: Thomas Hardisty, William Harrison. Date:

Court Session: 1720

17 December 1720.
- will of Elisabeth Mauldin.
- inventory of Col. Henry Cox.
- inventory of Mary Nicholls.
- additional inventory of Samuel Wallis.
- accounts of John Pearson & his wife Anne on estate of John Lynam.
- accounts of Frances Wallis administratrix of Samuel Wallis.
- accounts of Richard Turner administrator of William Turner.
- accounts of William Kemp & his wife administratrix of Sampson Warring.

30 January. John Baker (g, SM) exhibited:
- will of Daniel Smith, constituting Elisabeth Smith executrix. Said Elisabeth was granted administration. Sureties: James Waughop, John Medley. Date: 21 April 1720.

24:300 - bond of Mary Coombes administratrix of Thomas Coombes. Sureties: Luke Lee, John Edwards. Date: 21 January 1720.
- bond of Mary Dean administratrix of John Dean. Sureties: Robert Hawkins, John Welsh. Date: 14 January 1720.
- bond of Thomas Waughop administrator of Thomas Dyer Smith. Sureties: Daniel of St. Thomas Jenifer, Charles Hoskins. Date: 11 December 1720.
- bond of Mary Vansweringen administratrix of Joseph Vansweringen. Sureties: Thomas Waughop, Vitus Herbert. Date: 23 January 1720.
- inventory of James Wheatly.
- inventory of Mary Aiskin.
- inventory of Richard Baxter.
- accounts of Henry Cunclift administrator of Samuel Corbes.
- accounts of Sarah Horne administratrix of Henry Horne.
- accounts of Thomas Waughop administrator of Laurence Dillon.

24:301 31 January. Josias White (North Carolina) vs. Anne widow of Gabriel Burnham (PG). Summons to take LoA.

Exhibited:
* accounts of Elisabeth Bond executrix of Richard Bond (CV).

1 February. Exhibited:
* additional accounts of John Smith & his wife Dorothy administrators of Thomas Williamson (BA).

2 February. At the petition of Charles Yates & his wife Jane daughter & representative of William Ludwell (dec'd), the bond of Thomas Emms administrator was assigned to them.

24:302 4 February. At petition of Amos Garret, Esq., sheriff (SM) to summon Cuthbert Sawell & sheriff (CH) to summon Mary Green to cause the will of their brother John Sawell to be proved.

10 February. Exhibited:
* accounts of Amos Garret administrator of Edward Hancock.
* accounts of Amos Garret administrator of Michael Sinclear.

11 February. Exhibited:
* inventory of William Chew.

13 February. Exhibited:
* bond of John Watkins & John Talbot administrators of Benjamin Laurence. Surety: Stephen Warman. Appraisers: Joshua & John Dorsey. John Israel (g) to administer oath.

16 February. Exhibited:
* additional inventory of Thomas Macnemara, Esq.
24:303 * accounts of John Swann & his wife administratrix of John Foster (PG).
* inventory of Richard Rawlings (AA).
* additional inventory of Richard Rawlings (AA).

17 February. Exhibited:
* accounts of Amos Garret, Esq.

Court Session: 1720

administrator of Rev. Edward
Butler.

21 February. Exhibited:
* additional accounts of Richard
  Fulstone administrator of William
  Scott.

Deputy Commissary (KE) to examine
accounts of:
* John Inch administrator of William
  Jones.

Benjamin Pearce (g) to examine accounts
of:
* Mathias Vanderheyden administrator
  of James Barbot.

23 February. Deputy Commissary (TA) to
examine accounts of:
* Sarah Register administratrix of
  Robert Register.
* Solomon Robinson & his wife Jane
  administrators of Thomas Martin, Jr.
* Rachel Mackway administratrix of
  Patrick Mackway.
24:304 * Katharine Buckingham administratrix
  of Thomas Buckingham.

William Cumming & his wife Elisabeth vs.
William Turbutt (QA) surviving
administrator of James Coursey. Summons
to answer libel.

John Israel (g, BA) exhibited:
* bond of William Osburne executor of
  William Cottam. Sureties: Aquila
  Hall, Benjamin Hanson. Date: 8
  December 1720.
* bond of William Hollis administrator
  of Clark Hollis. Sureties: John
  Stokes, Francis Ogg. Date: 14
  November 1720.
* bond of John Hall, Esq. & Thomas
  Randall administrators of Richard
  King. Sureties: Roger Mathews,
  Christ. Randall. Date: 4 August
  1720.
24:305 * will of William Cottam.
* inventory of John Parker.

At the request of Arthur Connar &
Absolom Thrift, exhibited distribution
of estate of Pierce Welsh (TA):
- Peter Cullen & his wife Mary
  (widow's thirds).
- remaining 2/3rds to 3 children.

24 February. John Israel (g, BA)
exhibited:
- bond of Aquila Hall who married
  Johanna executrix of Col. James
  Phillips. Sureties: John Hall,
  Esq., Roger Mathews, Edward Hall,
  John Clark. Date: 30 December 1720.

24:306 • bond of Hezekiah Balch administrator
of William Jenkins. Sureties:
Thomas Johnson, John Duely. Date:
27 December 1720.
- bond of Edgar Tippar administrator
  of Edward Carney. Sureties: John
  Stoaks, John Clark. Date: 10
  October 1720.
- bond of Margaret Standifer
  administratrix of John Standifer.
  Sureties: John Fuller, James Hicks,
  Nehemiah Hicks. Date: 4 November
  1720.
- inventory of Thomas Bucknall.
- inventory of Thomas Cannon.
- inventory of William Cottam.

Exhibited:
24:307 • inventory of Anthony Drew (BA).
- inventory of George Simmons (AA).
- accounts of George Drew executor of
  Anthony Drew.
- inventory of Nicholas Rogers. Also
  LoD.

28 February. Deputy Commissary (CH) to
examine accounts on estate of:
- John Blee.
- Margaret Blee.
- Edward Sanders.

Samuel Hanson (g, CH) exhibited:
- bond of Thomas Holland administrator
  of Douglas Gifford. Sureties: John
  Courts, Charles Courts. Date: 14
  January 1720.
- bond of Mary Ching administratrix of
  John Ching. Sureties: Robert St.

Court Session: 1720

Clare, William Throne. Date: 14
February 1720.

24:308 Deputy Commissary (CE) to examine
accounts of:
• Josiah Crouch administratrix of
Anthony Knowlman (KE).

Benjamin Pemberton vs. James Lloyd &
John Pemberton executors of Robert
Grundy. Caveat exhibited.

Exhibited:
• accounts of Timothy Macnemara who
married Jane widow & executrix of
Robert Leeks (DO).
• accounts of Amos Garret
administratrix of Edward Cheeny.
• accounts of Robert Cole
administrator of Renatus Smith.

Summons rendered to John Talbot (p, AA)
to show cause why administration on
estate of Benjamin Laurence should not
be revoked &
24:309 granted to Rachel the widow.

3 March. Capt. St. Ledger Codd (KE)
attorney for John Potts (ENG) vs.
Gideon Pearce (KE) executor of Maj.
William Potts (KE). Summons to
defendant.

Exhibited:
• accounts of Charles Hammond & his
wife Rachel executrix of Col.
Charles Greenberry.
• inventory of Henry Hooper (DO).
• accounts of Mathew Travis
administrator of William Chaplin.
• accounts of Thomas Marshall executor
of Samuel Chuvly.
• accounts of David Young
administrator of Edward Payne (QA).

24:310 8 March. MM George Dent & Daniel
Jenifer to examine accounts of:
• Robert Hanson & his wife Dorothy
administrators of John Parry (CH).

13 March. Patrick Hepburn (g, PG)
exhibited:

- will of Philip Gittings, constituting Anne Gittings executrix. Said Anne was granted administration. Sureties: Enoch Combes, Thomas Lucas. Date: 25 February 1720.
- bond of Stephen Jermain administrator of Samuel Westly. Sureties: William Elliot, Thomas Kinderick. Date: 1 March 1720.
- inventory of Jonathon Prather, Jr.
- accounts of Mary Berry executrix of Benjamin Berry.

24:311 John Baker (g, SM) exhibited:
- will of Thomas Orion, constituting William Gibson executor. Said Gibson was granted administration. Sureties: Thomas Boult, William Sanders. Date: 10 March 1721.
- bond of Mary Briscoe administratrix of George Briscoe. Sureties: James Swann, Philip Briscoe. Date: 7 March 1720/1.
- bond of Res. Dillion administratrix of Thomas Dillion. Sureties: Robert Ford, Sr., James Wildman. Date: 9 March 1720/1.
- bond of Mary Howard administratrix of Nathaniel Howard. Sureties: John Bta. Carbery, James Wildman. Date: 1 March 1720.
- bond of Mary Boomer administratrix of John Boomer. Sureties: Anthony Simms, Joseph Hebb. Date: 13 February 1721.
- bond of Owen Smithson administrator of George Beveridge. Sureties: Jacob Williams, William Cole. Date: 10 February 1720.

24:312
- inventory of William Sanders.
- additional inventory of William Thompson.
- inventory of John Taney.
- accounts of Robert Ford, Sr. administrator of Peter Smith.
- accounts of Agnus Penny administratrix of John Penny Smith.

Court Session: 14 March 1720

24:313 Docket:

- W.C. for Mordecai Hammond & his wife vs. T.L. for Carpender Lillingston executor, etc. Libel, answer, replication. Daniel Dulany, Esq. procurator for defendant moved that Mr. James Heath who married executrix of Dr. Edward Chatham & his wife be parties in the suit.

24:314
- W.C. for Thomas Nevett administrator of Thomas Brettargh vs. J.E. for William Skinner. Libel, answer, replication

- T.L. for Thomas Brannock vs. D.D. for Nehemiah Beckwith. Libel. Attachment to defendant.

- T.L. for Vestry of St. Michaell's Parish vs. D.D. for Michael Fletcher. Libel. Attachment to defendant.

- Mrs. Mary Vansweringen widow of Joseph Vansweringen (SM) appeared, as per petition of Mr. Gerard Sly.

24:315
- D.D. & T.L. for Acquila Paca & his wife vs. R.T. for Acquila Hall & his wife executrix of James Philips. Libel.

- W.C. for Harmanus Schee vs. Jonathon Hopkins & his wife. Execution for costs.

- Summons to Cuthbert Sawell (SM) & Mary Green (CH) to prove will of their brother John Sawell. Attachment to said Green.

- W.C. for William Cumming & his wife Elisabeth vs. William Turbutt surviving administrator of James Coursey. Struck off.

24:316
- D.D. for Benjamin Pemberton vs. Richard Trensam for James Lloyd & John Pemberton executors of Robert Grundy. Defendants "imparle" until the next court.

- Daniel Dulany procurator for widow Benjamin Laurence (BA) vs. Thomas Larkin procurator for John Talbott. Rachel Laurence (the widow) exhibited that the dec'd died at the house of her brother Daniel Mariartee on 19 December last. Said Rachel has been unable to administer said estate. Said Talbott was granted LoA.

24:317   Mentions: exchange of land between said Benjamin & said Talbot; Mr. Francis Wasson.

24:318   Stephen Warman (sheriff, AA) exhibited summons.
Ruling: LoA granted to said Talbot & John Watkins repealed, & LoA granted to said Rachel.

24:319   • St. Leidger Codd vs. Benjamin Pearce executor of William Pott. Coroner (KE) to summon defendant.

       • At request of Henry Costin, Edward Wright (sheriff, QA) summoned Roger Murphey (QA) administrator of Thomas Jones to render inventory. Said Murphey exhibited an inventory.

24:320   • James Macnemara (g) vs. Rev. Jacob Henderson (g). Sheriff (AA) to summon MM James Carroll, Edward Griffith, & Robert Moulen to testify for the plaintiff. Thomas Clagett (sheriff, PG) summoned defendant. Said Henderson deposed that he does not know of any will of Thomas Macnemara, Esq. (Annapolis).

       • Stephen Warman (sheriff, AA) summoned Sarah & Thomas Harris to show cause why they, as relations, refused to sign the inventory of William Pearce (AA).

Court Session: 1720

24:321 10 March. Samuel Hopkins (g, SO) exhibited:
       • accounts of John Handy & his wife executrix of John Winder.
       • accounts of Warren Hadder administrator of Warren Hadder.
       • accounts of Mary Stevens administratrix of John Stevens.
       • inventory of Edward Shores.

17 March. Richard Colegate (g) to administer oath to John Israel, Lancelott Todd, & John Eager as appraisers of estate of Thomas Todd.

20 March. Daniel of St. Thomas Jenifer & his wife Elisabeth one of daughters of Nathaniel Ashcom (brother of Samuel Ashcom) vs. Martha Dansey executrix of

Charles Ashcom one of brothers &
administrator of said Samuel.
24:322 Summons to said Dansey

22 March. Appointment of Mr. Samuel
Turbott as Deputy Commissary (TA).

Exhibited:
- accounts of Margaret Rattenbury
  administratrix of Dr. John
  Rattenbury (BA).
- accounts of Mary Rock (CH) widow &
  administratrix of Charles Rock.

John Israell (g, BA) exhibited:
- bond of Thomas Sheredine
  administrator of Thomas Long.
  Sureties: Richard Gist, Thomas
  Biddeson. Date: 7 March 1720.
24:323
- bond of Diana Hale administratrix of
  Mathew Hale. Sureties: John Stokes,
  Thomas Talley. Date: 8 March 1720.
- bond of Elisabeth Hinton (alias
  Elisabeth Stone) executrix of Samuel
  Stone. Sureties: Jonathon Tipton,
  Edward Maham. Date: 25 February
  1720.
- bond of Mary Phipps administratrix
  of John Willis. Sureties: Jonathon
  Plowman, Thomas Taylor. Date: 22
  February 1720.
- bond of Susannah Coale executrix of
  Joseph Coale. Sureties: John Coale,
  George Hitchcock. Date: 13 March
  1720.
- bond of Hannah Teale executrix of
  Edward Teale. Sureties: William
  Baker, William Hamilton. Date: 14
  January 1720.
- James Holliday administrator of Jane
  Treadway. Sureties: William
  Perkins, Elisha Perkins. Date: 7
  March 1720.
- will of Ann Felk.
- will of Samuel Hinton.
- will of Joshua Cockey.
- will of Joseph Coale.
- will of Edward Teale.
- inventory of Humphry Lewis.
- inventory of John Standifer.
- inventory of John Henderson.
- inventory of Edward Teale.

- inventory of David Thomas.
24:324 • accounts of Philip Sindall executor of Jacob & Jane Peacock.

23 March. Exhibited:
- accounts of Amos Garret, Esq. administrator of William Clark (AA).
- inventory of said William Clark.
- inventory of William Barnet (AA).

Court Session: 1721

31 March. Sheriff (TA) to summon Frances Bowes (TA) widow of George Bowes to prove his will.

4 April. Adderton Skinner (g, CV) exhibited:
- will of Thomas Howe, constituting Sarah Howe executrix. Said Sarah was granted administration. Sureties: John Mackall, Charles Clagett. Date: 16 March 1720.
24:325 • will of Thomas Gilley, constituting William Dawkins, Sr. executor. Said Dawkins was granted administration. Sureties: William Dawkins, Jr., David Hellen. Date: 24 January 1720.
- bond of William Malden & James Malden executors of Elisabeth Malden. Sureties: James Somervell, John Kent, John Young. Date: 16 March 1720.
- will of William Strabry, constituting Anne Strabry executrix. Said Anne was granted administration. Sureties: Thomas Buttenshire, Thomas Freeman. Date: 23 March 1720.
- bond of John Wilkinson administrator of Elisabeth Mears. Surety: Thomas Edmonds. Date: 23 March 1720.
- bond of Margaret Willymott administratrix of William Willymott. Sureties: John Jarman, William Edmonds. Date: 23 March 1720.
- inventory of William Meads.

24:326 Samuel Hopkins (g, SO) exhibited:
- bond of Rachel Powell executrix of Samuel Powell. Sureties: Edward

Clarke, John Tull. Date: 9 March 1720.

- bond of Elisabeth Walton administratrix of Elisha Walton. Sureties: William Walton, John Holland. Date: 9 March 1720.
- bond of Elisabeth Powell administratrix of William Powell. Sureties: Charles Ratcliff, Robert Gant. Date: 10 March 1720.
- bond of Joyce Johnson & Peter Johnson executors of Leonard Johnson. Sureties: John Rickards, Thomas Mumford. Date: 10 March 1720.
- bond of Elisabeth Roach executrix of Nathaniel Roach. Sureties: John Roach, Michael Roach. Date: 24 February 1720.
- bond of Nathaniel Ratcliff administrator of William Ratcliff. Sureties: Henry Smock, Elias Pointer. Date: 28 February 1720.
- bond of Ellis Hudson & Dennis Hudson executors of Henry Hudson. Sureties: John Devorecks, John Dennis. Date: 7 March 1720.

24:327 • Robert Gantt executor of Margaret Towers. Sureties: John Tull, Richard Logwood. Date: 9 March 1720.
- bond of Richard Webb administrator of Mark Webb. Sureties: Thomas Mumford, Robert Gantt. Date: 9 March 1720.
- bond of Thomas Collins one of executors of Thomas Collins. Sureties: Andrew Collins, Lodowick Fleming. Date: 8 March 1720.
- bond of Elisabeth Johnson executrix of Robert Johnson. Sureties: Robert Gantt, Richard Webb. Date: 9 March 1720.
- bond of Katherine Wood executrix of Robert Wood. Sureties: Adam Spence, William Stevenson. Date: 9 March 1720.
- bond of Esther Skirven executrix of William Skirven. Sureties: William Whittington, Southy Whittington. Date: 21 February 1720.
- bond of Lazarus Maddox executor of

Mary Stevens. Sureties: Bruff Bratten, John Bratten. Date: 24 March 1720.

- bond of Elisabeth Bratten & Bruff Bratten executors of John Bratten. Sureties: Lazarus Maddux, William Holland. Date: 24 March 1720.

24:328
- bond of Charles Rackliffe administrator of Nathaniel Rackliffe. Sureties: John Purnell, William Fausit. Date: 23 March 1720.
- bond of Charles Rakliffe executor of Nathaniel Rackliffe. Sureties: John Purnell, William Fausit. Date: 23 March 1720.
- bond of Elisabeth Owen administratrix of Moses Owen. Sureties: Philip Conner, John Conner. Date: 20 March 1720.
- bond of Arthur Warwick executor of William Warwick. Sureties: George Tull, Gideon Tilman. Date: 20 March 1720.
- bond of Boiz Walstone executor of James Curtis. Sureties: John Tull, Charles Revell. Date: 20 March 1720.
- bond of Mary Cornely administratrix of Darby Cornely. Sureties: John Gibbins, Cornelius Ward. Date: 20 March 1720.
- bond of Alce Pusey administratrix of William Pusey. Sureties: William Bolithoe, Joseph Lankford. Date: 20 March 1720.

24:329
- will of Samuel Powell.
- will of William Powell.
- will of Leonard Johnson.
- will of Nathaniel Roach.
- will of Henry Hudson.
- will of Margaret Towers.
- will of Thomas Collings.
- will of Robert Johnson.
- will of Robert Wood.
- will of William Skirven.
- will of Mary Stevens.
- will of John Bratten.
- will of Nathaniel Ratcliff.
- will of Nathaniel Ratcliff, Sr.
- will of William Warwick.
- will of James Curtis.

- inventory of Thomas Shiles.
- inventory of William Bannister.
- inventory of John Watts.
- inventory of John Gilley.
- accounts of Francis Erwing administratrix of John Erwing.

Exhibited:
- additional inventory of Phileon Hemsley (AA), of goods in CH.
- additional accounts of Daniel Jenifer & his wife executrix of John Rogers (CH).

5 April. Samuel Hopkins (g, SO) to examine accounts of:
- Levin Denwood administrator of Samuel Groome.

24:330 John Pitts (g, DO) to examine accounts of:
- William Cullen & his wife Sarah administratrix of Edward Bryon (AA).

Mathias Vanderheyden (g, CE) exhibited:
- bond of Anne Browning executrix of Thomas Browning. Sureties: William Veazey, Richard Foster. Date: 31 October 1720.
- bond of Hugh Mathews administratrix of Owen Mackreigh. Sureties: Ephraim Aug. Herman, John Camble. Date: 27 December 1720.
- bond of Gunning Bedford administrator of Samuell & Anne Elisabeth Vaus. Sureties: Abell VanBurkeloo, Robert Eyre. Date: 29 October 1720.
- bond of Henry Gilder administrator of Daniel Caniday. Sureties: Daniel Hewen, Jacob Caulk. Date: 16 March 1720.
- inventory of John Smith.
- inventory of Jacob Young.
- inventory of Richard Lewis.
24:331 - accounts of Bridget Robinson administratrix of James Robinson.
- additional accounts of Mary Thompson administratrix of John Thompson.
- accounts of Mary Thompson executrix of William Dare, Sr.
- accounts of Mary Parsons executrix

of William Parsons.
- accounts of Thomas Price administrator of John Suttleberry.
- accounts of John Court administrator of Edward Webb.
- accounts of Albert Cox executor of Guysbert Cox.

Robert Jones (g, QA) exhibited:
- bond of Margaret Bordon executrix of John Bordon. Sureties: John Kinnimont, Ambross Kinimont. Date: 1 March 1720.
- bond of Marmaduke Goodhand executor of Hannah Goodhand. Sureties: Carpender Lillingston, Mord. Hammond. Date: 24 November 1720.
- bond of Rachell Meloyd administratrix of Charles Meloyd. Sureties: Richard Jagg, Robert Hollingsworth. Date: 21 January 1720.
- bond of Mary Parsons administratrix of Samuel Parsons. Sureties: Thomas Godwin, George Holliday. Date: 26 November 1720.

24:332 • bond of Richard Tilghman, Esq. administrator of Richard Bishop. Sureties: Augustine Thompson, Thomas Godman. Date: 28 November 1720.
- will of John Borden.
- will of Hannah Goodhand.
- will of John Dob.
- inventory of Thomas Jones.
- inventory of Charles Wright.
- inventory of William Martain.
- inventory of Thomas Hinds.
- inventory of John Brown.
- inventory of James Wyat.
- additional inventory of Philemon Hemsley, Esq., of goods on the Eastern Shore.

Exhibited:
- will of Foster Turbut (TA), constituting Samuel Turbutt & Henry Turbutt executors. Said Samuel & Henry were granted administration. Sureties: Nicholas Lowe, Thomas Bozman. Appraisers: Richard Coward, Jonathon Taylor. Robert Ungle, Esq. to administer oath.

24:333 6 April. Exhibited:
* inventory of William Glanwill (KE).

7 April. James Harris, Esq. (KE) exhibited:
* bond of Samuel Wickes administrator of Michael Wilson. Sureties: Edward Rogers, Sr., William Simcocks. Date: 28 November 1720.
* bond of Elinor Reading administratrix of William Reading. Sureties: Nicholas Waterman, Walter Meeks. Date: 22 March 1720.
* bond of Anne Hayden executrix of John Haydon. Sureties: James Brewer, George Gleives. Date: 22 March 1720.
* bond of John Cookson administrator of Jos. Hartley. Sureties: Benjamin Griffith, William Mackey. Date: 13 March 1720.
* bond of Daniel Pearce administrator of Mary Browne. Sureties: Arthur Miller, Laughlin Flinn. Date: 22 March 1720.

24:334 * will of William Pearce.
* will of John Hardyn.
* inventory of William Howard.
* inventory of John Mackdoniell.
* inventory of Stephen Denning.
* inventory of Edward Davis.
* inventory of Francis Jones.
* inventory of William Jones.
* accounts of Arthur Miller executor of Francis Jones.
* accounts of William Course executor of James Course.
* accounts of Rachel Midford executrix of Thomas Midford.
* accounts of John Jack & his wife executrix of William Jones.

8 April. Exhibited:
* accounts of Robert Hanson & his wife Dorothy administratrix of John Parry (CH).

10 April. Exhibited:
* accounts of Jane Boon administratrix of John Boon (BA).

24:335 <u>11 April</u>. Samuel Hopkins (g, SO) exhibited:

- bond of John Murray executor of Hugh Porter. Sureties: Charles Nicholson, William Oshannas. Date: 15 February 1720.
- bond of Thomas Peel & Sarah Wate executors of Elias Wate. Sureties: Woney Mackclamy, Samuel Dirckson. Date: 10 February 1720.
- bond of Tobias Pepper executor of Tobias Pepper. Sureties: Henry Brownbitt, William Pepper. Date: 7 February 1720.
- bond of John Woodcraft administrator of Thomas Wildgoes. Sureties: Thomas Mumford, James Hogg. Date: 2 February 1720.
- bond of John Bratten executor of David Linsey. Sureties: John Taylor, Gideon Tilmon. Date: 28 January 1720.
- bond of Robert Martin administrator of Edward Martin. Sureties: William Whittington, William Robeson. Date: 31 December 1720.
- bond of Anne Watts administratrix of John Watts. Sureties: Joseph Venables, John Venables. Date: 2 November 1720.
- bond of Elisabeth Ramxy administratrix of Barnett Ramsey. Sureties: Isaac Pypor, Samuel Gillitt. Date: 10 October 1720.
- bond of Jennett Mills executrix of William Smith. Sureties: Robert Mills, Isaac Pyper. Date: 10 October 1720.

24:336
- will of Hugh Porter.
- will of Elias Wate.
- will of Tobias Pepper.
- will of David Linsey.
- will of Barnett Ramsey.
- will of William Smith.
- inventory of John Griffith.
- inventory of John Upshott.
- inventory of Mathew Nutter.
- inventory of James Bounds.
- inventory of Barnett Ramsey.
- inventory of John Parsons.
- inventory of Robert Howston.
- inventory of Gideon Tilmon.

Court Session: 1721

- inventory of Jonathon Cooper.
- inventory of Isaac Luke.
- accounts of Mary Phillips administratrix of Thomas Phillips.
- accounts of Henry Jarmen & his wife Elisabeth administratrix of Philip Trewit.

13 April. Deputy Commissary (CV) to examine accounts of:
- Mary Tongue administratrix of Thomas Tongue.

Court Session: 13 April 1721

24:337 Docket:
- Capt. St. Leidger Codd (g, KE) for John Potts (minor, GB) vs. Gideon Pearce executor of Maj. William Potts. William Ringgold (coroner, KE) summoned defendant. Text of libel: said Codd exhibited will of said Potts, bequeathing to his son Joseph Potts & if he dies then to said John Potts. Said Joseph died soon after,
24:338   before he came of age.
24:339   Text of answer.
24:340-1 ...
24:342   Text of replication.
24:343   Ruling: Marmaduke Tilden & John March to examine witnesses.

Court Session: 1721

14 April. Exhibited:
- accounts of Mary Stuard administratrix of William Stuard (CV).
- accounts of William Richardson administrator of Anne Burton.

Deputy Commissary (CV) to examine accounts of:
- Anne Meed executrix of William Meed.
- Abraham Bowen executor of Charles Bowen.

Patrick Hepburn (g, PG) exhibited:
- will of Benjamin Hall, constituting Mary Hall executrix. Said Mary was granted administration. Sureties:

Clement Hill, William Digges. Date: 29 March 1721.

24:344
- bond of James Young administrator of David Palton. Sureties: Edward Marloe, Timothy Mahann. Date: 4 April 1721.
- bond of John Modesley administrator of Richard Lambeth. Sureties: Francis Piles, Sr., Francis Piles, Jr. Date: 29 March 1721.
- inventory of Philip Gittings, Sr.
- inventory of John Burch.

15 April. Samuel Hanson (g, CH) exhibited:
- bond of Ralph Bagly administrator of John Wilson. Sureties: Thomas Swann, William Thorne. Date: 3 April 1721.
- bond of Thomas Osburn administrator of George Gader. Surety: Thomas Stone, Jr. Date: 28 March 1721.
- bond of Thomas Annis administrator of Thomas Anniss. Sureties: William Benson, Thomas Hatcher. Date: 17 March 1720.

24:345
- additional inventory of John Blee.
- inventory of Edward Sanders.
- accounts of Thomas Mathews & his wife executrix of Isabel Dryden.
- accounts of Jos. Joy administrator of Thomas Clark.
- accounts of John & Richard Ashman & Richard Ancoram administrators of Anne Foster.
- accounts of Cleborn Lomax administrator of Margaret Blee.
- accounts of Cleborn Lomax administrator of John Blee.
- additional accounts of Thomas Mathews & his wife executrix of Charles Yopp.
- additional accounts of Thomas Mathews administrator of Edward Chapman.

16 April. Henry Ennalls (g, DO) vs. Thomas Taylor (g, DO). Summons to defendant to show cause why he detains certain goods of the estate of John Ennalls (DO).

21 April. Exhibited:
- inventory of John Hynson (KE).
- inventory of Richard King (BA).

24:346 22 April. John Pitts (g, DO) exhibited:
- bond of Robert Johnson, Jr. executor of Robert Johnson, Sr. Sureties: John Robson, Michael Todd. Date: 17 March 1720.
- bond of Roger Woolford administrator of John Sharply. Sureties: Theod. Madkin, Anthony Tall. Date: 20 February 1720.
- bond of Mary Ellis administratrix of William Ellis. Sureties: Edward Newton, Isaac Nicholls. Date: 16 March 1720.
- bond of Mary Lecompte, Philip, Samuel, & Joseph Lecompte executors of Moses Lecompte. Sureties: John Brannock, Nehemiah Beckwith. Date: 20 March 1720.
- bond of Lewis Griffen administrator of James Foxen. Sureties: Timothy Macnemara, William Robinson. Date: 16 March 1720.
- bond of Walter Quinton administrator of David Clark. Sureties: James Hayes, Govert Loockerman. Date: 14 February 1720.
- will of Robert Johnson.
- will of Thomas Smith.
- will of Moses Lecompt.

24:347
- accounts of Katharine Ross executrix of Stephen Ross.
- accounts of Elisabeth Jones administratrix of Isaac Jones.
- accounts of Oliver Fairbrother & his wife administratrix of Mathew Barnes.
- inventory of Elisabeth Halpin.
- inventory of Stephen Ross.

24 April. Exhibited:
- additional inventory of James Coursey (QA).

25 April. Daniel Dulany, Esq. vs. Charles Egan & his wife Elinor. Sheriff (PG) to summon defendants & other kindred of Jonathon White (clerk, dec'd), estate unadministered by Bernard

White (dec'd).

Deputy Commissary (CE) to examine accounts of:
- Abell VanBurkeloo administrator of Andrew Rosenquest.

Deputy Commissary (DO) to examine accounts of:
- Mary Saldsbury executrix of Alexander Fisher.

24:348 Exhibited:
- inventory of Richard Galloway (AA).

27 April. Exhibited:
- will of Mary Hammond (AA), constituting John Beale executor. Said Beale was granted administration. Sureties: Stephen Warman, Vachel Denton. Date: 25 April 1721. Appraisers (g): Caleb Dorsey, John Worthington.

2 May. Deputy Commissary (CV) to examine accounts of:
- William Young administrator of George Young, Jr.
- William Young administrator of Francis Young.

3 May. Exhibited:
- additional accounts of Susanna Mather administratrix of George Mather (QA).
- accounts of Martha Smith executrix of Col. Thomas Smith (KE).
24:349 - bond of Anne Burrell administratrix of Samuel Burrell. Sureties: Edward Smith, John Treadhoun. Date: 3 May 1721.

Col. William Holland administrator of John Steele (g) was granted continuance.

Samuel Chew executor of Samuel Chew was granted continuance.

4 May. Deputy Commissary (DO) to examine accounts of:
- Mary Button executrix of John Button (DO).

Court Session: 1721

6 May. Deputy Commissary (TA) to examine accounts of:
- John Fellows & Robert Fellows administrators of Robert Fellows.

9 May. Deputy Commissary (TA) to examine accounts of:
- Judith Lord executrix of James Lord.
- **24:350** Thomas Eton executor of Peter Anderton
- Rachel Mackway administratrix of Peter Mackway.
- Solomon Robinson & his wife administratrix of Thomas Martin.
- John Spriggnal executor of Anthony Wise.
- Isabella Taylor executrix of James Taylor.
- Sarah Register administratrix of Robert Register.
- Mathew Jenkins administrator of Thomas Jenkins.
- Robert Ungle administrator of Thomas Collier.

Court Session: 9 May 1721

24:351 Docket:
- W.C. for Mordecai Hammond & his wife vs. T.L. for Carp. Lillingston executor, etc. & James Heath & his wife executrix of Edward Chetham. Libel, answer, replication, duplication. Attachment rendered to defendants.
- W.C. for Thomas Nevett administrator of Thomas Brettargh vs. P.K. & J.E. for William Skinner. Libel, answer, replication.
- **24:352** T.L. for Thomas Brannock vs. William Cumming & Daniel Dulany, Esq. for Nehemiah Beckwith. Libel.
- T.L. for Vestry of St. Michael's Parish vs. D.D. for Michael Fletcher. Libel. Sheriff (TA) to summon defendant to render answer.
- **24:353** D.D. & T.L. for Acquila Paca & his wife vs. R.T. for Acquila Hall & his wife executrix of James Phillips. Libel. Attachment to render answer.
- estate of James Sawell vs. Mary Green & Cuthbert Sawell. Defendants

are siblings of dec'd. Attachment rendered to defendants.

- D.D. for Benjamin Pemberton vs. R.T. for James Lloyd & John Pemberton executors of Robert Grundy. Order for answer.
- St. Leidger Codd for John Potts vs. Gideon Pearce executor of William Potts.

24:354 • R.T. for Henry Costin vs. W.C. for Roger Murphey administrator of Thomas Jones. Libel. Order for answer.

- W.C. for Daniel of St. Thomas Jenifer vs. Philip Key (g) procurator for Martha Dansey executrix of Charles Ashcom. T. T. Greenfield (sheriff, SM) to summon defendant to render answer.
- Richard Trensam (g) procurator for David Robinson vs. Philip Key & William Cumming procurators for Nicholas Lowe executor of Elisabeth Lowe. T. Bozman (sheriff, TA) to summon defendant to render answer.

24:355 • Thomas Bozman (sheriff, TA) to summon Frances Bowes widow of George Bowes to prove his will or renounce administration.

- Henry Ennalls vs. Thomas Taylor. Charles Ungle (sheriff, DO) to summon defendant.
- Robert Gouldesborough, William Wood, & Ambrose Wood to prove will of Col. Thomas Smithson. Summoned by sheriff (TA).

24:356
24:357-8 ...
24:359 They deposed.

Mr. Michael Fletcher to pay witnesses for their attendance.

- Rachel Laurence widow of Benjamin Lawrence vs. John Talbot & John Watkins administrators of said Benjamin. Said Rachel was sick when LoA were granted to said Talbot & Watkins. Said Rachel was granted LoA & to pay defendants.
- administrator of Thomas Brettargh vs. William Skinner. Defendant says that he did not receive more than was mentioned in the inventory.

24:360

Court Session: May 1721

<u>9 May</u>. Mr. Michael Fletcher deposed regarding the estate of Col. Thomas Smithson (TA).

Amos Garrott, Esq. administrator of Richard Rawlings was granted continuance.

Mary Carroll executrix of John Carroll was granted continuance, as the inventory was not signed by creditors & next-of-kin.

Exhibited:
- accounts of Richard Galloway & his wife executrix of Solomon Sparrow.

24:361 MM Philip Key & Alexander Frazier were admitted as procurators before the Court.

David Robinson one of administrators of Sarah Collins was granted continuance.

Exhibited:
- inventory of William Guthrie. Administrator: Robert Scott.
24:362 - inventory of Peter Huskins. Administrator: James Campbell.

Sheriff (PG) to summon Charles Egan & his wife Elinor & other relations of Jonathon White (clerk, dec'd), unadministered by Bernard White (dec'd) to show cause why LoA should not be granted to Daniel Dulany, Esq. & executor of Thomas Macnemara, Esq.

Stephen Warman (sheriff, AA) to summon:
- John Talbott & his wife executrix of Richard Bickerdike to render accounts.
- Margaret Macnemara administratrix of Thomas Macnemara to render accounts.
- Mary Carroll (late Mary Forrister) executrix of Peter Forrister to render accounts.
- Thomas Larkin administrator of John Leckie to render accounts.
- Elisabeth Hinton administratrix of John Hinton to render accounts.
- Rachel Bordley administratrix of

John Beard, Esq. to render accounts.
In CH; not determined.

- Mary Carroll executrix of John
  Carroll to render inventory.

24:363
- Amos Garrett administrator of Robert
  Thomas to render inventory.
- Henry Darnall, James & Daniel
  Carroll executors of Charles Carroll
  to render inventory.

Sheriff (AA) to render attachment to:
- Samuel Chew administrator of Samuel
  Chew to render accounts.
- William Holland, Esq. administrator
  of John Steele to render accounts.
- Richard Galloway & his wife
  executrix of Solomon Sparrow to
  render accounts.
- Francis Campbell administratrix of
  James Campbell to render accounts.
- Amos Garrett administrator of
  Richard Rawlings to render accounts.
- Daniel Mariartee administrator of
  Edward Mariartee to render accounts.

Edward Hall (sheriff, BA) to summon:
- John Lowe administrator of William
  Lowe to render accounts.
- John Wilmott executor of John
  Wilmott to render accounts.
- Stephen Gill administrator of John
  Leekins to render accounts.
- Tabitha Mills administratrix of
  William Mills to render accounts.
- John Newsham administrator of Edward
  Harry to render inventory.
- Joseph Johnson administrator of John
  Parker to render inventory.
- Francis Dollahide administrator of
  John Hopkins to render accounts.
- Sarah Perregoy administratrix of
  Joseph Perregoy to render inventory.
- Mary Bond executrix of John Bond to
  render inventory.
- John Hall, Esq. & Thomas Randall
  administrators of Richard King to
  render inventory.
- Richard Gott administrator of
  Richard Gott to render accounts.

24:364
Edward Hall (sheriff, BA) to render
attachment to:

Court Session: May 1721

- Jane Boone administratrix of John Boone to render accounts.

Thomas Claggett (sheriff, PG) to summon:
- Elisabeth Brook administratrix of Roger Brook to render accounts.
- William Trunker & his wife Elisabeth administratrix of Thomas Clark to render accounts.
- William Clark & his wife Anne administratrix of William Nicholls to render accounts.
- James Haddock & Weldone Jefferson executors of Robert Hall to render accounts.
- Sarah Barrett executrix of Edward Barrett to render inventory.
- Dr. Hagan & his wife executrix of Bernard White to render inventory.

Thomas Claggett (sheriff, PG) to render attachment to:
- Anne Jones administratrix of Evan Jones to render accounts. Not found.
- Martha Browne administratrix of John Brown to render accounts. Not found.

Sab. Sollers (sheriff, CV) to summon:
- Mary Tongue administratrix of Thomas Tongue to render accounts.
- William Young administrator of Francis Young to render accounts.
- Priscilla Johns executrix of Richard Johns to render accounts.
- Margaret Ashcom administratrix of Nathaniel Ashcom to render inventory.

Sab. Sollers (sheriff) to render attachment to:
- Alexander Parran administrator of John Kennyman to render inventory.

24:365 Sheriff (CH) to summon:
- Philip Lee administrator of Francis Ibettson to render accounts.
- John Courts administrator of Jacob Miller to render accounts.
- John Brown & Edward Anderson administrators of to render

accounts.
- Margaret Yopp administratrix of Roger Yopp to render accounts.
- Joseph Harrison administrator of Richard Harrison to render accounts.
- Thomas Jameson executor of Winifred Lee to render accounts.
- Elinor Sanders executrix of Mathew Sanders to render inventory.

Attachments to CH:
- Elisabeth Hardy executrix of William Hardy to render accounts.

T. T. Greenfield (sheriff, SM) to summon:
- Thomas Lowe administrator of Thomas Hargis to render accounts.
- John Jane executor of Thomas Kendelo to render accounts.
- Mary Miller administratrix of Edward Miller, Sr. to render accounts.
- Mary Cheseldyne executrix of Kenlem Cheseldyne to render accounts.
- Elinor Heardman administratrix of James Heardman to render accounts.

T. T. Greenfield (sheriff, SM) to render attachment to:
- Robert Scott administrator of William Guthrie to render accounts.
- William Gouldesborough administrator of William Hasler to render accounts.
- John Stapleton administrator of Henry Stapleton to render inventory.
- Mary Miller administratrix of Edward Miller, Sr. to render inventory.

24:366 Summons to SO:
- Weighborough Evans administratrix of William Evans to render accounts. Dead, no effects.
- Dennis Driskill executor of Edward Hammond to render inventory.
- William Kennett executor of John Kennet to render inventory.
- Samuel Powell administrator of John Powell to render accounts. Dead; Rachel his widow is administratrix.
- Adam Hitch administrator of John Shore to render inventory.

- Arabella Collins administratrix of John Collins to render accounts.
- Elisabeth Stephens administratrix of Thomas Stephens to render accounts.
- Thomas Holdbrook executor of Thomas Holebrook to render accounts.
- Mary Larey executrix of Daniel Larey to render accounts.
- William & Richard Beathers executors of William Beather to render accounts.
- Alexander Wilson executor of Alexander Wilson to render accounts. Runaway.
- William Whittington executor of Stephen White to render inventory.
- Edward Round executor of William Round to render accounts.
- Elisabeth Bratten executrix of John Bratten to render accounts.
- Nathaniel Waley administrator of Edward Waley to render accounts.
- Charles Ballard administrator of Robert Cotter to render inventory.
- William Faucit administrator of John Gray to render accounts.
- Elisabeth Polk administratrix of Ephraim Polk to render accounts.
- Tabitha Kellam administratrix of William Kellam to render accounts. Married Joseph Holston.
- Warren Hadder executor of Warren Hadder to render accounts.
- Pierce Read executor of Walter Read to render accounts. Dead; his widow is administratrix.
- Mary Fall executrix of Abraham Fall to render inventory.
- Mary Fountain executrix of John Browne to render accounts.
- Naomy Shiles administratrix of Thomas Shiles to render accounts. Pauper.
- Sarah Wheatly administratrix of William Wheatly to render accounts.
- Henry Philips administrator of Charles Philips to render inventory. Nothing found; he himself a "Sen.".
- Richard Holland administrator of Charles Shewell to render accounts.
- Esau Boston administrator of Esau Boston to render accounts.

24:367
- Robert Martin & John Devoricks administrators of James Manuell to render inventory.
- Lewis Jones executor of Samuel Jones to render inventory.
- Robert Ponton who married executrix of Isaac Lukes to render accounts.
- James Perry administrator of Mary Larey to render accounts.
- Esther Denwood administratrix of Arthur Denwood to render inventory.
- Quantan Bratten executor of James Bratten to render inventory.
- Elisabeth Waters executrix of Richard Waters to render inventory.
- John Murray administrator of John Murray to render inventory.
- Thomas Fowler administrator of Edward Sermon to render inventory.
- Elisabeth Schoolfield executrix of Benjamin Schoolfield to render inventory. Married Adam Spence.
- William, Southy, Esther, & Hannah Whittington executors of Col. William Whittington to render inventory.
- John Hampton administrator of John Chonvo to render inventory.
- John Hampton administrator of Patrick Donnock to render inventory.

Attachments to SO:
- Susannah Jones administratrix of Daniel Jones to render inventory.
- Margaret Gray executrix of Miles Gray to render accounts. Dead; William Turpin is her administrator.
- Arthur Warren administrator of Samuel Davis to render accounts.
- Hugh Porter & his wife Mary executrix of Edward Bray to render inventory. Both dead; John Murray is executor to said Hugh.
- Anne Renshaw administratrix of John Renshaw to render inventory.
- Samuel Tingle executor of Robert Cobb to render accounts. Dead; no effects.
- Mary Redmond administratrix of Walter Redmond to render accounts. Married John Goslin & said John is dead.

Court Session: May 1721

- Katherine Porter executrix of Hugh Porter to render accounts.
- Elisabeth Johnson administratrix of John Johnson to render accounts.
- William Kebble executor of John Hoggins to render accounts.

Charles Ungle (sheriff, DO) to render attachment to:
- John Hudson Secundus & Henry Ennalls administrators of John Ennalls to render accounts.
- Rosanna Cannon administratrix of James Cannon to render accounts.
- Susannah Parish administratrix of Richard Parish to render inventory.

24:368 Charles Ungle (sheriff, DO) to summon:
- John Dawson executor of Anne Dawson to render accounts.
- Mary Barnes administratrix of Mathew Barnes to render accounts.
- Anne Hooper executrix of Richard Hooper to render accounts.
- Mary Rawley administratrix of Samuel Rawley to render accounts.
- Joseph Alford administrator of Elisabeth Halpin to render inventory.
- Cornely Mackall executrix of David Mackall to render inventory.

T. Bozman (sheriff, TA) to summon:
- Elinor Cotner administratrix of Alexander Cotner to render accounts.
- Elisabeth Field administratrix of Christ. Field to render accounts.
- Mathew Jenkins executor of Thomas Jenkins to render accounts.
- Isabella Taylor executrix of James Taylor to render accounts.
- Sarah Register administratrix of Robert Register to render accounts.
- Elisabeth Martindale administratrix of Henry Martindale to render accounts.
- Risdon Bozman & his wife executrix of Philip Sherwood to render accounts.
- Anne Turner administratrix of Edward Turner, Sr. to render accounts.
- Robert Ungle, Esq. administrator of

Thomas Collier to render accounts.
- Michael Fletcher administrator of Thomas Smithson to render accounts.
- John Stephens & Sarah Webb executors of Sarah Stephens to render accounts.
- Elisabeth Rippeth administratrix of James Rippeth to render accounts.
- Christ. Arrington administrator of Prudence Woolman to render accounts.
- Sarah Webb executrix of Henry King to render accounts.
- Edward Harding executor of Mary Githens to render accounts.
- Sarah Harrison administratrix of John Harrison to render inventory.
- William Harrison executor of William Harrison to render inventory.
- Anne Dawson executrix of John Dawson to render inventory.

24:369
- John Bush administrator of Richard Brogden to render inventory.
- Thomas Turner administrator of John Turner to render inventory.
- Sarah Maccotter administratrix of Alexander Maccotter to render inventory.
- Thomas Eubanks administrator of Richard Eubanks to render inventory.

T. Bozman (sheriff, TA) to render attachment to:
- Elinor Cotner administratrix of Alexander Cotner to render inventory.
- John & Robert Fellows administrators of Robert Fellows to render accounts.
- Thomas Emmerson, Jr. executor of Anne Emmerson to render accounts.
- John Kemball administrator of Peter Hoskins to render inventory.
- Heneritta Crump administratrix of Walter Crump to render inventory.
- John Spriggnall executor of Anthony Wise to render accounts.
- David Robinson & William Airs administrators of Sarah Collins to render accounts.
- John & James Pemberton executors of Thomas Beswick to render accounts.
- George Shanhan administrator of

- Margaret Reglace to render accounts.
- Joseph Eason administrator of John Eason, Jr. to render accounts.
- Jane Martin administratrix of Thomas Martin to render accounts.
- John Green & William Clayton, Jr. administrators of Mary Smithson to render accounts.
- Elisabeth Martindale administratrix of Henry Martindale to render inventory.
- Robert Ungle, Esq. administrator of Thomas Collier to render inventory.
- Michael Fletcher administrator of Thomas Smithson to render inventory.
- Elisabeth Smith administratrix of Daniel Smith to render inventory.

24:370 Summons to QA:
- William Shield administrator of Bryant Shield to render accounts.
- Katharine Santee administratrix of Philemon Santee to render inventory.
- John Tootall administrator of John Tootall to render accounts.
- Elisabeth Coursey executrix of William Coursey to render accounts.
- Sarah Gold administratrix of Christ. Gold to render accounts.
- Anne Barber administratrix of Newton Barber to render accounts.
- Daniel Harris administrator of Morte Bryant to render accounts.
- Robert Basnet administrator of John Barnes to render inventory.
- Thomas Bannan administrator of John Bannan to render accounts.
- Robert Jones administrator of William Sweatnam to render accounts.
- Elisheba Erreckson executrix of Charles Erreckson to render accounts.
- George Phillips administrator of Elisabeth Cavenah to render accounts.
- Elisabeth Blangy executrix of Jacob Blangy to render accounts.
- Edward Jones executor of William Arland to render inventory.
- Judith Brown administratrix of John Brown to render inventory.
- Nicholas Marsey administrator of

- James Bennet to render accounts.
- John Hackett administrator of William Hackett to render inventory.
- Mary Hinds executrix of Thomas Hinds to render inventory.
- Joanna Wyat executrix of James Wyat to render inventory.
- Katherine & Robert Wright executors of Charles Wright to render inventory.
- Thomas Godman administrator of Robert Porter to render inventory.
- John Macconakin administrator of John Dobs to render inventory.
- Margaret Martin & Charles Neal administrators of William Martin to render inventory.

24:371 Attachments to QA:
- Anne Kerby executrix of William Kerby to render accounts.
- Ernault Hawkins executor of John Hawkins to render accounts.
- Johanna Impey administratrix of William Impey to render inventory.
- Samuel Hunter administrator of John Hays to render inventory.
- Ernault Hawkins administrator of John Spry to render inventory.
- Peter Falcom executor of Peter Falcom to render accounts.
- Barbara Jackson administratrix of William Draper to render inventory.
- Sarah Deny administratrix of Peter Deney to render inventory.
- Elinor Pratt administratrix of William Pratt to render inventory.
- Sarah Tool administratrix of Timothy Toole to render inventory.
- Frances Nicholson executrix of John Nicholson to render inventory.
- Joseph West administrator of Robert Farrow to render inventory.
- Hannah Bryan administratrix of Cornelius Bryan to render inventory.
- John Wright administrator of Thomas Willotson to render inventory.
- Arthur Emory executor of Julian King to render accounts.
- Francis & Joseph Jackson executors of Barbary Jackson to render inventory.

Court Session: May 1721

G. Pearce (sheriff, KE) to summon:
- Martha Smith executrix of Thomas Smith to render accounts.
- William Glanvil & Nathaniel Hynson administrators of William Glanvil to render accounts.
- Rachel Medford executrix of Thomas Medford to render accounts.
- John Atwick administrator of William Lowcock to render accounts.
- Mathew Pope administrator of William Pope to render accounts.
- Hannah Page administratrix of Jonathon Page to render inventory.
- Mary Davis administratrix of Edward Davis to render inventory.
- Agnes MacDonnell administratrix of John MacDonell to render inventory.
- Christ. Hall administrator of Stephen Denning to render inventory.
- James Wilson & Peter Jones administrators of William Jones to render inventory.
- Nathaniel Hynson, Jr. administrator of John Hynson to render inventory. In CE.

24:372

G. Pearce (sheriff, KE) to render attachment to:
- Margaret Pryer administratrix of William Pryer to render accounts.
- Martha Fillingham executrix of Richard Fillingham to render accounts.
- William Dean administrator of Anthony Wilkinson to render accounts. NE.

Summons to CE:
- Joseph Young administrator of Thomas Corne to render accounts.
- Cornelius Tobie administrator of George Strutton to render inventory.
- Mary Thompson executrix of William Dare to render accounts.
- Adam Browne administrator of Michael Coulter to render accounts.
- Sarah Smart administratrix of John Smart to render inventory.
- Bridget Robinson administratrix of James Robinson to render accounts.
- Mary Bavington executrix of John

Bavington to render accounts.
- Mary Young administratrix of Jacob Young to render inventory.
- Sarah Smith executrix of John Smith to render inventory.
- Anne Lewis executrix of Richard Lewis to render inventory.

24:373 Attachments to CE:
- Henry Hendrickson & his wife Elisabeth administratrix of Thomas Hitherington to render inventory.
- Joseph Young administrator of Thomas Corne to render inventory.
- Thomas Price administrator of John Shuttleberry to render accounts.
- Abel VanBurkeloo administrator of Andrew Rosenquest to render accounts.

Deputy Commissary (TA) to examine accounts of:
- Judith Lord executrix of James Lord.
- Thomas Eaton executor of Peter Anderton.
- Rachel Mackway administratrix of Peter Mackway.
- Solomon Robinson & his wife administratrix of Thomas Martin.
- John Spriggnall executor of Anthony Wise.
- Isabella Taylor administratrix of James Taylor.
- Sarah Register administratrix of Robert Register.
- Mathew Jenkins executor of Thomas Jenkins.
- Robert Ungle, Esq. administrator of Thomas Collier.

Samuel Turbutt (g, TA) exhibited:
- bond of William Oston & Jacob Faulkner administrators of Jacob Gregory. Sureties: James Benney, Robert Stonestreet. Date: 18 April 1721.
- bond of Ambros Kinnimont administrator of Alexander Kinnimont. Sureties: Richard Barrow, Charles Stevens. Date: 25 April 1721.

24:374 - bond of Caleb Clarke administrator

of Elisabeth Mears. Sureties: John Baggs, Richard Swift. Date: 25 April 1721.

- bond of Frances Bowes executrix of George Bowes. Sureties: Enion Williams, Edward Turner. Date: 25 April 1721.
- will of George Bowes.
- inventory of Daniel Smith.
- inventory of Elisabeth Mears.
- additional inventory of John Start.
- inventory of Richard Brogden.
- inventory of John Turner.
- inventory of William Harrison.
- inventory of Thomas Collier.
- inventory of Walter Crump.
- accounts of John Bush administrator of Richard Brogden.
- accounts of Charles Springall & his wife Heneritta administratrix of Walter Crump.

Exhibited:
- inventory of Robert Grundy (TA).
- additional inventory of Thomas Beswick.
- inventory of Peter Huskins.

24:375 Exhibited from AA:
- accounts of Margaret Macnemara administratrix of Thomas Macnemara, Esq.
- accounts of Richard Galloway & his wife executrix of Solomon Sparrow.

Exhibited from SM:
- inventory of William Guthrie. Administrator: Robert Scot.

10 May. James Harris, Esq. (KE) exhibited:
- bond of William Yearly administrator of Thomas Hilliard. Sureties: John Huff, Thomas Stippard. Date: 12 April 1721.
- bond of Charles Smith & William Dicas executors of Sarah Jewres. Sureties: Abrahanm Ambros, James Tibbatt. Date: 26 April 1721.
- bond of Margaret Ray administratrix of James Ray. Sureties: Abraham Redgrave, William Simpson. Date: 18

April 1721.
* bond of Isabella Pearce executrix of William Pearce. Sureties: John Denning, John Rogers. Date: 27 April 1721.
* bond of James Tibball administrator of Thomas Maslin. Sureties: Robert Green, Charles Smyth. Date: 26 April 1721.

24:376
* will of Sarah Jewies.
* inventory of Robert Jones.
* inventory of Jonathon Page.
* additional accounts of Mathias Vanderheyden (g) administrator of James Barbott, examined by Benjamin Pearce (g).
* accounts of Josias Crouch administrator of Anthony Knowlman.

Exhibited:
* accounts of John & James Pemberton executors of Thomas Beswick.

11 May. Vitus Harbert vs. William Thompson (g, SM) administrator of William Harbert. Summons to answer libel.

12 May. Deputy Commissary (KE) to examine accounts of:
* Hannah Page administratrix of Jonathon Page.
* Mary Davis administratrix of Edward Davis.
* Agnes MacDaniel administratrix of John MacDaniel.
* James Wilson, Jr. & Peter Jones executors of William Jones.

24:377 12 May. Deputy Commissary (CE) to examine accounts of:
* Henry Pierce executor of Francis Smith (CE).

John Baker (g, SM) exhibited:
* will of James Thompson, constituting James Thompson executor. Said executor was granted administration. Sureties: William Harrison, William Cutler. Date: 21 April 1721.
* will of Charles Dafft, constituting Elisabeth Dafft executrix. Said

Elisabeth was granted
administration. Sureties: Nicholas
Mills, Sr., Francis Nevet. Date: 22
April 1721.
- will of Elisabeth Burrell,
constituting James Thompson
executor. Said Thompson was granted
administration. Sureties: George
Thompson, Thomas Vanrisweek. Date:
22 April 1721.
- will of Henry ONeal, constituting
Eliner Oneale executrix. Said
Eliner was granted administration.
Sureties: William Harrison, Daniel
Norris. Date: 15 April 1721.
- bond of Rachel Wright administratrix
of William Wright. Sureties: John
Glover, William Johnson. Date: 29
April 1721.
- bond of Mary Readish administratrix
of Daniel Readish. Sureties:
William Loard, Daniel Norris. Date:
15 April 1721.

24:378
- inventory of Joseph Vansweringen.
- accounts of Anne Bryarly executrix
of Timothy Sullivant.
- accounts of Mary Lee administratrix
of Charles Lee.
- accounts of John Henning
administrator of James Powers.

13 May. Deputy Commissary (SO) to
examine accounts of:
- Sarah Wheatly administratrix of
William Wheatly.
- Mary Fountain executrix of John
Browne.

16 May. Exhibited:
- accounts of Winifret Holland
administratrix of John Holland (QA).

Patrick Hepburn (PG) exhibited:
- inventory of Bernard White.
- accounts of Samuel Magruder
administrator of James Gardiner.
- renunciation of Henry Witham (PG)
who married widow of Mr. Benjamin
Hall (PG).

24:379
Date: 12 May 1721. Attested by
Patrick Hepburn on 14 May 1721.

17 May. Deputy Commissary (PG) to
examine accounts of:
- Robert Gorden & his wife Mary
  administratrix of William Downes.
- Magd. Jarvis executrix of William
  Jarvis.

23 May. Samuel Hanson (g, CH)
exhibited:
- additional inventory of John Parry.
- inventory of William Boarman.
- additional accounts of Laurence
  Anders administrator of Henry
  Franklin.
- accounts of Mary Boarman executrix
  of William Boarman.

25 May. Acquila Paca & his wife vs.
Acquila Hall & his wife executrix of
James Phillips.

24:380 John Dorsey (g) & Roger Mathews (g) to
take oath of the defendants regarding
their answer.

Mordecai Hammond & his wife vs. James
Heath & his wife Mary. Lambert Wilmer
(g, KE) to take oath of defendants
regarding their answer.

John Israell (g, BA) exhibited:
- bond of Judith Welsh administratrix
  of William Welsh. Sureties: Thomas
  Carr, Thomas Ford. Date: 1 April
  1721.
- bond of Rachel Laurence
  administratrix of Benjamin Laurence.
  Sureties: John Dorsey (son of
  Edward), John Howard. Date: 27
  March 1721.
- bond of Margaret Wills
  administratrix of John Wills.
  Sureties: Robert Parker, Thomas
  Taylor. Date: 10 May 1721.
- bond of Francis Dollahide
  administrator of Francis Dollahide.
  Sureties: James Maxwell, John
  Roberts. Date: 2 May 1721.
- bond of Elisabeth Petit
  administratrix of John Petit.
  Sureties: James Durham, Joseph
  Ellidge. Date: 2 May 1721.
- bond of John Mackenzy administrator

of John FitzRedmond. Sureties: John
Maccarty, Henry Carrington. Date:
29 April 1721.

24:381 • bond of Laurana Shields
administratrix of Henry Shields.
Sureties: Hugh Johns, Henry Jones.
Date: 24 April 1721.

• bond of Elinor Rogers executrix of
Jabez Peirpoint. Sureties: Jonathon
Hanson, Moses Edwards. Date: 24
April 1721.

• bond of Mary Webster executrix of
John Webster, Jr. Sureties:
Benjamin Wheeler, William Hunter.
Date: 11 April 1721.

• will of Walter Pumphary,
constituting Mercy Pumphary
executrix. Said Mercy was granted
administration. Sureties: Ebenezar
Pumphary, Anthony Johnson. Date: 25
March 1721.

• will of William Jenkins, Jr.,
constituting Sarah Jenkins
executrix. Said Sarah was granted
administration. Sureties: Jeremy
Downes, Cadwalader Jones. Date: 2
May 1721.

• inventory of William Jenkins, Sr.
• inventory of Jane Treadway.
• inventory of Bray Platt.
• inventory of John Bond.
• additional inventory of John Bond.
• accounts of John Taylor executor of
Abraham Taylor.
• accounts of Sabra Durant
administratrix of Anthony Durant.

Exhibited:
• accounts of Col. William Holland
administrator of John Steele.

24:382 26 May. Exhibited:
• accounts of Amos Garrett, Esq.
administrator of Richard Rawlings.

27 May. Exhibited:
• accounts of William Trunker & his
wife administratrix of Thomas Clark
(PG).

30 May. John Baker (g, SM) exhibited:
• will of Robert Thomas, constituting

Court Session: May 1721

Mary Thomas executrix. Said Mary
was granted administration.
Sureties: John Fodery, Robert
Terrin. Date: 20 May 1721.
- bond of Elisabeth Dillicoat
administratrix of James Dillicoat.
Sureties: James Campbell, John
Taylor, Jr. Date: 20 May 1721.
- bond of Agnus Green administratrix
of James Green. Sureties: John
Squires, Robert Terrin. Date: 20
May 1721.
- inventory of William Wright.
- inventory of John Daines.
- additional accounts of Richard,
Cuthbert, John, Enoch, & Ignatius
Fenwick executors of John Fenwick.
- additional accounts of George
Gillespie & Jonathon Cay executors
of George Ervin.

24:383   Exhibited bond of Samuel Turbutt as
Deputy Commissary (TA). Sureties:
Robert Ungle, Esq., Nicholas Lowe (g).

John Pitts (g, DO) exhibited:
- bond of Margaret Poole executrix of
Edward Poole. Sureties: William
Guy, William Eruin. Date: 14 April
1721.
- will of Edward Poole.
- accounts of Rosanna Cannon
administratrix of James Cannon.

31 May. Deputy Commissary (SO) to
examine accounts of:
- Francis Martin & his wife Katherine
administratrix of Thomas Tull, Sr.
- Robert Weers & his wife
administratrix of John Kirk.
- Sarah Davis administratrix of Thomas
Davis.
- John Medcalf administrator of John
Cullen.
- John White & his wife Sarah
administratrix of Thomas Beaucham.
- Price Collins & his wife Mary
administratrix of John Cropper.

Deputy Commissary (BA) to examine
accounts of:
- Henry Millan administrator of

Page 162

Court Session: May 1721

William Norris.

24:384 Thomas Buckannan & his wife Mary
(daughter of Anne Dorset (widow, PG,
dec'd)) vs. Thomas Dorset (PG).
Sheriff (PG) to summon said Dorset to
exhibit will of said Anne.

Deputy Commissary (QA) to examine
accounts of:
- David Young administrator of Edward
  Pain.
- Sarah Tucker administratrix of
  Nathaniel Tucker.
- Mary Hinds administratrix of Thomas
  Hinds.
- Katharine & John Chairs executors of
  John Chaires.
- Arthur Emory executor of Julian
  King.

Sheriff (BA) to summon Susannah Long
widow of Thomas Long (BA).

Summons to Charles Carroll executor of
Charles Carroll to render accounts on
estates of Thomas Docwra & of John Dodd.

24:385 John Beale, Esq. (AA) exhibited:
- will of Samuel Galloway,
  constituting Anne Galloway
  executrix. Said Anne was granted
  administration. Sureties: Richard
  Galloway, John Galloway, Peter
  Galloway. Date: 23 January 1720.
- bond of Darcus Wayman administratrix
  of Leonard Wayman. Sureties:
  Richard Snowden, Edmund Wayman.
  Date: 6 April 1721.
- bond of William Loch, Esq.
  administrator of Thomas Veazean.
  Sureties: John Beale, Vachel Denton.
- bond of Elisabeth Rablin
  administratrix of David Rablin.
  Sureties: John Merrikin, Robert
  Boone. Date: 4 February 1720.
- bond of Charles Carroll one of
  executors of Charles Carroll, Esq.
  Sureties: James Carroll, Henry
  Darnall, William Digges. Date: 21
  January 1720.
- bond of Thomas Pratt administrator

of Jane Pratt. Sureties: John Norris, John Cheshire. Date: 13 March 1720.
- bond of Cornelius Brooksby administrator of Thomas Brett. Sureties: Richard Trensam, Thomas Holmas. Date: 15 March 1720.

24:386
- inventory of Robert Cross.
- inventory of George Man.
- inventory of Alexander Scott.
- inventory of William Roseman.
- accounts of John Slatter administrator of James Sweetlove.
- accounts of Albertus Greening administrator of John Arnoldy.
- accounts of William Loch, Esq. administrator of Alexander Watts.

Exhibited:
- accounts of Elisabeth wife of Thomas Stone executrix of Richard Sampson (BA).
- inventory of Samuel Hinton.

1 June. Deputy Commissary (PG) to examine accounts of:
- Elisabeth Brooks administratrix of Roger Brooks (PG).

Deputy Commissary (CV) to examine accounts of:
- Priscilla Johns executrix of Richard Johns (CV).

24:387 5 June. Deputy Commissary (SM) to examine accounts of:
- Elisabeth Cole executrix of Robert Cole.
- Elinor Baxter administratrix of Edward Baxter.

7 June. Exhibited:
- inventory of John Renshaw (SO).

Francis Bright administratrix of Thomas Bright (KI) vs. Michael Moore. Summons to defendant.

Deputy Commissary (SO) to examine accounts of:
- Anne Renshaw administratrix of Francis Roberts.

- said Anne administratrix of John Renshaw.

Deputy Commissary (SM) to examine accounts of:
- William Watts & his wife executrix of John Taney.
- Simon & Elisabeth Reader executors of Benjamin Reader.
- Dryden Jowles executrix of Col. Henry Peregrine Jowles.

11 June. Exhibited:
- additional inventory of William Chew (BA).

24:388 Mathias Vanderheyden (g, CE) exhibited:
- will of Hendrick DHoff, constituting Slyntie DHoff executrix. Said Slyntie was granted administration. Sureties: Charles Mollen, Laurence Gailshiott. Date: 17 May 1721.
- will of Thomas Smith, constituting Mary Smith executrix. Said Mary was granted administration. Sureties: John Ward, Thomas Pearce. Date: 31 May 1721.
- will of William Price, constituting Mary Price executrix. Said Mary was granted administration. Sureties: George Veazey, William Price, Jr. Date: 24 April 1721.
- bond of Thomas Simmons administrator of Robert Simmons. Sureties: Francis Mauldin, Richard Whitton. Date: 22 April 1720.
- inventory of Owen Megraw.
- inventory of Thomas Browning.
- inventory of Robert Simmons.
- accounts of Thomas Simmons administrator of Robert Simmons.

12 June. Deputy Commissary (TA) to examine accounts of:
- Perry Benson & his wife executrix of Michael Russell.

24:389 Deputy Commissary (SO) to examine accounts of:
- William Richardson administrator of Robert Johnson.
- Elisabeth Bishop administratrix of

Court Session: May 1721

John Bratten.

Samuel Hopkins (g, SO) exhibited:
- bond of Comfort Oxford & Anne Mary Oxford administratrices of Thomas Oxford. Sureties: Samuel Turner, William Turner. Date: 26 May 1721.
- bond of Mary Pope one of executors of John Pope. Sureties: John Purnell, John Pope. Date: 26 May 1721.
- bond of Elisabeth Holland executrix of Nehemiah Holland. Sureties: Fisher Walton, William Aydelot. Date: 11 May 1721.
- bond of John Hopkins administrator of Thomas Kendall. Sureties: Adam Heath, David Johnson. Date: 16 May 1721.
- bond of Richard Hudson administrator of Jonathon Hudson. Sureties: Thomas Collins, John Patrick. Date: 11 April 1721.
- bond of Joseph Henderson executor of William Henderson. Sureties: John Henderson, Samuell Dorman. Date: 29 April 1721.
- bond of Robert Hudson administrator of Henry Hudson. Sureties: Richard Pennewell, Isaiah Bredell. Date: 25 April 1721.
24:390 - bond of Francis Erwing administratrix of Robert Anderson. Sureties: John Jones, Levin Gale. Date: 18 April 1721.
- bond of Betty Gale executrix of Samuel Morris. Sureties: Thomas Gillis, Thomas Lawes. Date: 18 April 1721.
- bond of Underwood Renshaw executor of Jane Alsey. Sureties: William Wheeler, Thomas Renshaw. Date: 21 April 1721.
- bond of Sarah Woolford administratrix of Levin Woolford. Sureties: William Jones, William Turpin. Date: 21 April 1721.
- bond of Elisabeth Reed administratrix of Pierce Reed. Sureties: John Sturgis, Sr., John Sturgis, Jr. Date: 13 April 1721.
- bond of William Richardson

administrator of James Mills.
Sureties: Mathew Scarborough, John
Scarborough. Date: 6 April 1721.

- bond of Mary Heap executrix of
Charles Wharton. Sureties: John
Henderson, Bruff Bratton. Date: 29
April 1721.
- bond of George Tull executor of
Jonathon Noble. Sureties: Daniel
Caudry, Samuel Dorman. Date: 29
April 1721.

24:391
- will of Thomas Oxford.
- will of John Pope.
- will of Nehemiah Holland.
- will of William Henderson.
- will of Samuel Morris.
- will of Jane Alsey.
- will of Charles Wharton.
- will of Jonathon Noble.
- inventory of Patrick Donnock.
- inventory of Edward Surman.
- inventory of William Warwick.
- inventory of John Chove.
- inventory of James Manuell.
- inventory of Thomas Wildgoose.
- inventory of Benjamin Schoolfield.
- accounts of Elisabeth Stevens
administratrix of Thomas Stevens.
- accounts of William Faucit
administrator of John Gray.
- accounts of Thomas Fowler
administrator of Edward Serman.
- accounts of Elisabeth Johnson
administratrix of John Johnson.
- accounts of Elisabeth Reed
administratrix of Pierce Reed.
- accounts of Esau Boston
administrator of Esau Boston.
- accounts of Arthur Warwick
administrator of Samuel Davis.
- accounts of Anne Disheroon
administratrix of Michael Disheroon.
- accounts of William Kibble
administrator of John Hoggin.
- accounts of Katharine Mackneel
administratrix of Hugh Mackneel.
- Susanna Dixon administratrix of
Thomas Dixon.
- accounts of Naomy Shiles
administratrix of Thomas Shiles.

14 June. Deputy Commissary (SM) to
examine accounts of:
- William Langly & his wife
  administratrix of Richard Baxter
  (SM).

24:392 • William Jameson & his wife
  administratrix of Thomas Barber.

15 June. Exhibited:
- further accounts of Woolman Gibson &
  his wife on estate of Lambert
  Clements, proved before Robert
  Ungle, Esq.

17 June. Exhibited:
- inventory of David Mackall (DO).

19 June. Exhibited:
- pretended will of Mary Willson (CH),
  with depositions taken before Samuel
  Hanson (g, CH). Also, renunciation
  of William Cood on said estate.
  "Probate is short & doubt full."

Exhibited from AA:
- inventory of John Carroll.
- inventory of Jane Pratt.
- accounts of Rebecca Ward executrix
  of Robert Ward.

24:393 20 June. Samuel Hanson (g, CH)
exhibited:
- bond of John Smoot administrator of
  Lidia Beanes. Sureties: William
  Heard, William Decrego. Date: 14
  May 1721.
- bond of Francis Brown & his wife
  administrators of Giles Thompkins.
  Sureties: John Brown, Percival
  Fearson. Date: 22 May 1721.
- will of Thomas Orrell.

John Baker (g, SM) exhibited:
- bond of Sarah Birch administratrix
  of Benjamin Birch. Sureties: George
  Forbes, Thomas McWilliams. Date: 7
  June 1721.
- inventory of Mary Boomer.
- inventory of George Briscoe.
- inventory of John Penney.
- accounts of Elisabeth Reader & Simon
  Reader executors of Benjamin Reader.

- accounts of Elisabeth Cole executrix of Robert Cole.

26 June. Deputy Commissary (KE) to examine accounts of:
- Christopher Hall & his wife administratrix of Stephen Denning.
- Martha Pope administratrix of William Pope.
- Andrew Norwell administrator of Philip Hissitt.
- Elisabeth England administratrix of Isaac England.

24:394 Deputy Commissary (BA) to examine accounts of:
- Hill Savadge & his wife administratrix of Peter Bond.

Adderton Skinner (g, CV) exhibited:
- bond of Robert Heigh, Jr. executor of Robert Heigh, Sr. Sureties: James Heigh, Abraham Downes. Date: 10 May 1721.
- bond of John Binyon administrator of Richard Garnum. Sureties: John Loutherland, Jacob Roberts. Date: 2 May 1721.
- bond of Samuel Griffith administrator of Henry Johnson. Surety: Ephraim Gover. Date: 26 May 1721.
- bond of Sarah Day executrix of Robert Day. Sureties: John Greves, Thomas Littell. Date: 2 May 1721.
- bond of Elisabeth Williams administratrix of Hugh Williams. Sureties: Samuel Peacock, Joseph Owen. Date: 15 April 1721.
24:395 - bond of Jannett Tucker administratrix of John Tucker. Sureties: William Smith, John Dorrumple. Date: 21 June 1721.
- will of Robert Day.
- will of William Meade.
- will of Robert Heighe.
- will of William Williams.
- inventory of William Willymott.
- inventory of Elisabeth Meares.
- additional inventory of Thomas Tongue.
- inventory of John Kenman.

- inventory of William Strabry.
- inventory of Nathaniel Ashcom.
- accounts of Abraham Bowen executor of Charles Bowen.
- accounts of William Davis & his wife administratrix of William Peacock.
- accounts of Abel Royston administrator of Rebecca Royston.
- accounts of Mary Tongue administratrix of Thomas Tongue.

Exhibited:
- accounts of Elishabe Erreckson executrix of Charles Erreckson (QA).

27 June. St. Ledger Codd (g, KE) for John Potts (GB) vs. Gideon Pearce (KE) executor of Maj. William Potts (KE). Summons to render answer.

24:396 Exhibited:
- additional accounts of Samuell Howell who married executrix of Richard Freeborne (BA).

28 June. Deputy Commissary (CE) to examine accounts of:
- Mary Price executrix of William Price (CE).

1 July. Exhibited:
- inventory of David Rablin (AA).

6 July. Exhibited:
- accounts of Margarett Birchead executrix of Nehemiah Birchead (AA).

7 July. Exhibited:
- accounts of George Harris executor of William Harris (CV).

Deputy Commissary (CH) to examine accounts of:
- John Brown & Edward Anderson administrators of Richard Morris.
- Sarah Day executrix of Robert Day.

24:397 10 July. John Baker (g, SM) exhibited:
- bond of Rose Dillion administratrix of Thomas Dillion. Sureties: Robert Forde, Sr., James Wildman. Date: 9 March 1720/1.

- will of Elisabeth Brady, constituting Owen Brady executor. Said Owen was granted administration. Sureties: John Hoskins, John Jane. Date: 7 June 1721.
- inventory of Charles Dafft.
- inventory of Thomas Orion.
- inventory of Capt. Nathaniel Howard.
- inventory of Daniel Smith.
- inventory of Thomas Dillion.
- inventory of Jame Dilliotte.

Dr. Patrick Hepburn (PG) exhibited:
- bond of Thomas Dorsett executor of Anne Dorsett. Sureties: Aaron Lomax, William Harris. Date: 5 June 1721.

24:398
- bond of Francis King administrator of David Jones. Sureties: William & Joseph West. Date: 17 June 1721.
- bond of Daniel Dulany administrator of Jonathon White. Sureties: Jacob Henderson, Alexander Contee. Date: 30 June 1721.
- will of Anne Dorsett.
- inventory of Thomas Polson.
- inventory of David Patten.
- additional accounts of Charles Egan & his wife executors of Bernard White.
- accounts of Magdalen Jervis executrix of William Jervis.

Court Session: 11 July 1721

24:399 Docket:
- William Cumming procurator for Mordecai Hammond (g, AA) & his wife Frances vs. Thomas Larkin procurator for Carpender Lillingston (g, QA) executor, etc. & James Heath & his wife executrix of Edward Chetham.
Text of libel: Said Frances is a daughter of Mr. John Lillingston (QA, dec'd) & one of the legatees of Richard Macklin (St. Paul's Parish, TA). Said Carpender is executor of Joseph Lambert (QA) with said Lambert.

24:400   Said Joseph Lambert was executor of Mr. John Lillingston (QA). Said Lillingston & Chetham were executors of said Macklin. Said Macklin died on 31 May 1704. Will of said Macklin bequeathed to the 4 younger children of Mr. John Lillingston.

24:401   After the inventory was filed, said Chetham renounced executorship.

24:402   Said John Lillingston bequeathed to his son & 3 daughters, from estate of said Macklin: Carpender, Jane, Mary, Frances. Said Mary died a minor.

24:403   Mathew Tilghman Ward & Edward Chetham renounced executorship of said Lillingston's estate. The other executor was Joseph Lambert. John Wells renounced executorship on estate of said Joseph Lambert.

24:404   Said Carpender refuses to pay the plaintiff her share.

24:405   Summons to said Carpender
24:406   by Edward Wright (sheriff, QA).
24:407   Text of answer.
24:408-9 ...
24:410   Text of replication.
24:411 ...

24:412   William Turbutt & Robert Jones commissioned to examine witnesses. Daniel Dulany procurator for defendants moved that Mr. James Heath who married executrix of Dr. Edward Chetham be parties to the suit.

24:413   Richard Tilghman, Esq., age 47, deposed.

24:414   Mentions: Said Macklin practiced as an attorney in several counties, books of Mr. Michael Earle, said Lillingston's children by his 2nd wife (Carpender, Jane, Mary,
24:415   Frances.

Christ. Denny, age 67, deposed.
24:416   Charles Warner, age 30, deposed. Mentions: servant woman of said Macklin named Scotch Mogzy. Deponent was a hired servant of said Macklin at the time of his death. Margaret Jones, age 38, deposed. She was a servant of Macklin at the time of his death.

Court Session: 11 July 1721

24:417   Interrogations (list of questions).
24:418   Answers by Carpender Lillingston (g,
          QA). Mentions: John Bullen
          (chyrurgeon, TA).
24:419 ...
24:420   Received from: MM Dunkin Munroe,
          George Philips, John Bennet, John
          Newman, John Hammilton, John
          Coursey, Charles Wright. Mentions:
          legacy to Richard Tilghman.
          Payments to: Mr. Richard Tilghman,
          Mr. Dulany, Mr. Thomas Hammond,
24:421   Mr. John Wells, Mord. Hammond.
24:422   Mentions unrecovered debts from:
          Renatus Smith, Nicholas Clouds,
          Edward Wright.
          List of inventory items in question.
24:423 ...
24:424   Richard Trensam procurator for James
          Heath & his wife Mary.
24:425   Text of answer of said Heath.
24:426-8 ...
24:429   Ruling: plaintiff.
24:430 • William Cumming procurator for
          Thomas Nevett administrator of
          Thomas Brettargh vs. P.K. & James
          Earle procurator for William Skinner
          (g, TA).
          Text of libel. Said Nevett
          (merchant, DO) is attorney for John
          Baily (linen draper, Warrington,
          Lancaster) administrator of Thomas
          Brettargh (TA).
24:431   LAC on the estate of said Brettargh
          were granted to said Skinner.
24:432   Said LAC were revoked.
24:433 ...
24:434   Thomas Bozman (sheriff, TA).
24:435   Text of answer.
24:436-441 ...
24:442   Text of replication.
24:443-4 ...
24:445   Ruling: payment is not allowed to
          John Brannock
24:446   & defendant, save for payment of
          disallowed items.
        • T.L. for Thomas Brannock vs. W.C. &
          D.D. for Nehemiah Beckwith. Libel &
          answer.
24:447 • T.L. for the Vestry of St. Michael's
          Parish vs. D.D. for Michael
          Fletcher. Libel.

Court Session: 11 July 1721

- D.D. & T.L. for Acquila Paca & his wife vs. R.T. for Acquila Hall & his wife executrix of James Phillips. Libel.
- Attachment rendered to Cuthbert Sawel (SM) & to Mary Green (CH) to prove will of their brother John Sawell or to show cause.
- D.D. for Benjamin Pemberton vs. R.T. for James Lloyd & John Pemberton executors of Robert Grundy. Struck off.
- R.T. for Henry Costin vs. W.C. for Roger Murphey administrator of Thomas Jones. Libel.

24:448
- W.C. for Daniel of St. Thomas Jenifer vs. P.K. for Martha Dansey executrix of Charles Ashcom. Libel.
- R.T. for David Robinson vs. P.K. & W.C. for Nicholas Lowe executor of Elisabeth Lowe. Attachment to render answer.
- W.C. for Vitus Herbert vs. Daniel Dulany procurator for William Thompson administrator of William Herbert. Libel. T. T. Greenfield (sheriff, SM) to summon defendant.
- W.C. for the same vs. D.D. for the same. Libel.
- W.C. for Thomas Buckannan & his wife Mary daughter of Anne Dorset vs. Thomas Dorset.

24:449   Sheriff (PG) to summon defendant.

Court Session: 1721

Sheriff (BA) summoned Susannah Long widow of Thomas Long. Said Susannah deposed. Mentions: Thomas Sheredine to whom dec'd sold "Dixon's Neck" & "Long's Addition". Said Long died before the sale was complete.

24:450   Stephen Warman (sheriff, AA) to summon Charles Carroll (g) executor of Charles Carroll, Esq. to render accounts on the estates of Thomas Docwra & of John Dodd.

Francis Bright administratrix of Thomas Bright (KI) vs. William Cumming procurator for Michael Moore. Edward Wright (sheriff, QA) summoned

Page 174

Court Session: 1721

24:451 defendant. Said Moore deposed.

24:452 Mr. Samuel Hanson (CH) exhibited:
- pretended will of Mary Willison.

William Cumming & his wife vs. William Turbutt surviving administrator of James Coursey. Sheriff (QA) to summon defendant.

Joshua George was admitted as procurator before the Court.

Court Session: July 1721

25:1 St. Ledger Codd for John Potts (residuary legatee of William Pott) vs. Gideon Pearce executor of William Potts. William Ringold (coroner, KE) summoned defendant.
Text of petition.
25:2 Text of questions.
25:3 Text of plea & answer.
25:4 Signed: Joshua George.
Text of answers to questions.
25:5 ...
25:6 John Beck, Sr. (KE) deposed on 5 May 1721.
25:7 Thomas Browning deposed. Signed: John March.
Ruling: mentions accounts of John Bruffett.
25:8 Case dismissed.

Court Session: 1721

25:9 14 July. Exhibited:
- accounts of Elisabeth Frazer administratrix of Abraham Frazer (BA).

15 July. John Pitts (g, DO) exhibited:
- bond of Elisabeth Quinnally administratrix of Patrick Quinnally. Sureties: Stephen Owins, David Herrin. Date: 13 June 1721.
- bond of John Richardson administrator of Simon Richardson. Sureties: Richard Michell, Dennis Mackarty. Date: 14 June 1721.
- will of Thomas Bradshaw, constituting Mary Bradshaw

Page 175

executrix. Said Mary was granted
administration. Sureties: Richard
Lawson, Henry Tucker. Date: 8 June
1721.
- inventory of James Foxen.
- inventory of William Elles.
- inventory of Edward Poole.
- inventory of Robert Johnson, Sr.
- inventory of Richard Parish.
- accounts of William Harper
administrator of Richard Foster.
- accounts of Mary Button executrix of
John Button.
- accounts of Mary Coursey
administratrix of David Coursey.
- accounts of Lewis Griffin
administrator of James Foxen.
- accounts of Mary Rawley
administratrix of Samuel Rawley.
- accounts of Joseph Alford
administrator of Elisabeth Halpen.
- accounts of William Cullen & his
wife administrators of Edward Bryan.

25:10 17 July. Exhibited:
- 4th additional accounts of John Scot
& his wife Jane executrix of Peter
Dent.
- additional accounts of Cornelius
Howard one of executors of Cornelius
Howard.

18 July. Exhibited from SM:
- inventory of James Green.
- inventory of Daniel Reddish.
- inventory of Henry Oneal.

Exhibited from CH:
- bond of Mary Williams administratrix
of Edward Williams. Sureties:
Stephen Mankin, Richard Price.
Date: 13 June 1721.
- inventory of Mathew Sanders.
- inventory of John Wilson.
- additional accounts of Cleabourn
Lomax administrator of Margaret
Blee.
- additional accounts of Walter Storey
& his wife administratrix of Thomas
Dixon.
- accounts of Cleabourn Lomax
administrator of John Blee.

Robert Jones (g, QA) exhibited:
- bond of Mary Ayler administratrix of Henry Ayler. Sureties: Stephen Rich, Henry Holdson. Date: 28 April 1720.

25:11
- bond of Edward Wrighte administrator of Patrick Cavinah. Sureties: Ernault Hawkins, James Knowles. Date: 25 April 1721.
- bond of Notley Wright administrator of Charles Wright. Sureties: Edward Goodwin, Thomas Godwin. Date: 22 May 1721.
- bond of Mary Gwinn administratrix of John Gwin. Sureties: William Mason, William Ryon. Date: 29 March 1721.
- bond of Francis Bright administrator of Thomas Bright. Sureties: John Stevens, James Morgin. Date: 29 March 1721.
- bond of Edmund Thomas executor of Elisabeth Williams. Sureties: William Turbutt, Trustram Thomas, Jr. Date: 25 November 1720.
- bond of Nathaniel Scott executor of Abraham Oldson. Sureties: Edm. Thomas, John Tillotson. Date: 28 April 1721.
- will of Abraham Oldson.
- will of Henry Ayler.
- will of Elisabeth Williams.
- inventory of John Hays.
- inventory of John Gwinn.
- inventory of Charles Meloyd.
- inventory of Barbary Jackson.
- inventory of John Spry.
- inventory of John Burdin.
- additional accounts of Edward Harris executor of Edward Harris.
- additional accounts of Samuel Neale & his wife administratrix of John Webb.
- accounts of John Wilson administrator of Robert Reddick.
- accounts of John Clements administrator of John Clements.
- accounts of Katharine Williams executrix of James Williams.

25:12
- accounts of William Shield administrator of Bryant Shield.
- accounts of Nicholas Massey administrator of James Bennett.

Adderton Skinner (g, CV) exhibited:
- inventory of Thomas Howes.
- inventory of Robert Heigh.
- accounts of Nathaniel Giles & his wife administratrix of Richard Harris.

Samuel Hopkins (g, SO) exhibited:
- will of Nathaniel Ennis, constituting William Ennis & his wife Elisabeth executors. Said executors were granted administration. Sureties: Christ. Glass, Hugh Nilson. Date: 6 June 1721.
- bond of John Williams & Margaret Rich administrators of Jane Rich. Sureties: Christ. Glass, John Bishop. Date: 7 June 1721.
- bond of Ebenezar Franklin administrator of Jeremiah Veney. Sureties: John Franklin, Abraham Smith. Date: 3 June 1721.
- bond of Thomas Robinson administrator of Joseph Morris. Sureties: Thomas Mumford, William Kennet. Date: 2 June 1721.
- will of William Collins, constituting Mary Collins executrix. Said Mary was granted administration. Sureties: Ebenezar Franklin, Henry Alexander. Date: 1 June 1721.

25:13
- will of Richard Woodcraft, constituting Mary Woodcraft executrix. Said Mary was granted administration. Sureties: James Hogg, Abraham Smith. Date: 2 June 1721.
- bond of Elisabeth Bishop administratrix of William Bishop. Sureties: Thomas Timmons, Nicholas Warren. Date: 1 June 1721.
- will of John Faucit, constituting Tabitha Faucit executrix. Said Tabitha was granted administration. Sureties: Ebenezar Franklin, William Walton. Date: 1 June 1721.
- bond of William Kennet & his wife Catharine administratrix of Trewitt Jarman. Sureties: Thomas Mumford, Richard Webb. Date: 1 June 1721.

- will of Walter Evans, constituting Mary Evans executrix. Said Mary was granted administration. Sureties: Isaiah Bredell, Williams Evans. Date: 2 June 1721.
- will of Parthenia Morris, constituting Nathaniel Rackliffe & William Read executors. Said Rackliffe & Read were granted administration. Sureties: William Kennet, Walter Taylor. Date: 2 June 1721.
- will of Alice Miles, constituting Henry Miles executor. Said Henry was granted administration. Sureties: John Tull, John Gibbins. Date: 22 June 1721.
- will of Robert Twilly, constituting Elisabeth Twilley executrix. Said Elisabeth was granted administration. Sureties: Robert Givan, Thomas Relph. Date: 1 July 1721.
- bond of Elisabeth Crouch administratrix of Robert Crouch. Sureties: Thomas Collier, Richard Phillips. Date: 1 July 1721.
- will of Thomas Studd, constituting John Gibbins executor. Said Gibbins was granted administration. Sureties: John Jones, George Martin. Date: 28 June 1721.

25:14
- will of Thomas Moore, constituting Mary More & John More executors. Said Mary & John were granted administration. Sureties: John Williams, John Sterling. Date: 20 June 1721.
- will of Job Pope, constituting Elisabeth Pope executrix. Said Elisabeth was granted administration. Sureties: John Pope, Thomas Owlen. Date: 26 June 1721.
- will of Wonney Macklemy, constituting William Macklemy executor. Said William was granted administration. Sureties: Christ. Glass, Hugh Porter. Date: 22 June 1721.
- inventory of Darby Kennerly.
- inventory of William Puissey.

- inventory of John Broughton.
- inventory of Margaret Towers.
- inventory of William Ratcliff.
- inventory of Charles Wharton.
- inventory of William Henderson.
- inventory of Richard Waters.
- inventory of Nathaniel Roach.
- inventory of David Lensey.
- inventory of Samuel Powell.
- inventory of William Powell.
- inventory of John Kennett.
- inventory of Robert Johnson.
- inventory of Mark Webb.
- inventory of Job Pope.
- inventory of Robert Anderson.
- inventory of David Jones.

25:15 19 July. Deputy Commissary (SO) to examine accounts of:
- Katherine Porter <torn> Hugh Porter (SO).

Deputy Commissary (BA) to examine accounts of:
- Edward Tippar administrator of William Pritchard (BA).

21 July. Deputy Commissary (SO) to examine accounts of:
- Elisabeth Pope executrix of Job Pope (SO).

Deputy Commissary (PG) to examine accounts of:
- James Reid & his wife Elisabeth executrix of John Burch (PG).

James Harris, Esq. (KE) exhibited:
- bond of James Harris administrator of Charles Hutton. Sureties: Charles Hynson, Thomas Hynson. Date: 7 June 1721.
- bond of John Hebron administrator of John Caslick. Sureties: Roger Hales, William Course. Date: 21 June 1721.
- bond of Katharine Johnson administratrix of William Johnson. Sureties: Edward Holman, George Sanders. Date: 21 June 1721.
- bond of Anne Carey administratrix of Robert Carey. Sureties: Henry

Davis, William Yearly. Date: 24
April 1720.

25:16
- will of Anne Heyden.
- inventory of William Redding.
- inventory of Joseph Hartloe.
- inventory of Robert Carey.
- inventory of Thomas Tilliard.
- additional inventory of William Scott.
- inventory of Isaac England.
- accounts of Agnes MacDaniel administratrix of John MackDaniel.
- accounts of William Early administrator of Thomas Tiller.
- additional accounts of Richard & Sarah Fulston administrators of William Scott.
- accounts of Hannah Page administratrix of Jonathon Page.
- accounts of James Wilson & Peter Jones executors of William Jones.
- accounts of Abigall Ackman administratrix of Grills Ackman.

Exhibited:
- inventory of Douglas Gifford (CH).

Samuel Turbutt (g, TA) exhibited:
- will of Richard Ratcliff, constituting Margaret, James, & John Ratcliff executors. Said executors were granted administration. Sureties: Thomas Atkinson, Isaac Dixon. Date: 1 July 1721.

25:17
- bond of George Sailes administrator of James Hill. Sureties: Mark Noble, Hezekiah Maccotter. Date: 23 May 1721.
- bond of Elisabeth Ross administratrix of John Ross. Sureties: George Shaunahan, John Naylor. Date: 20 June 1721.
- will of Rebecca Brumwell, constituting Richard Andrew executor. Said Andrew was granted administration. Sureties: Benjamin Pemberton, John Oldham. Date: 15 May 1721.
- will of Henry Withgott, constituting Mary Withgott executrix. Said Mary was granted administration. Sureties: George Shannahawn, Walter

Quinton. Date: 16 May 1721.
- inventory of Henry Martindale.
- bond of William Finney administrator of Mary Thornton. Sureties: William Cole, Roger Clayland. Date: 6 June 1721.
- bond of Arthur Conner administrator of William Sheppard. Sureties: Walter Quinton, Jonathon Taylor. Date: 29 May 1721.
- additional inventory of Robert Fellows.
- additional inventory of Richard Webb.
- inventory of Peter Hoskins.
- additional inventory of Henry King.
- accounts of Sarah Webb executrix of Henry King.
- accounts of Rachel Mackway administratrix of Patrick Mackway.
- accounts of Solomon Robinson & his wife Jane administratrix of Thomas Martin.
- accounts of George Cooper & his wife administratrix of Ambros Ford.
- accounts of Elisabeth Rippeth administratrix of James Rippeth.
- accounts of Elisabeth Smith administratrix of Daniel Smith.
- accounts of Judith Lord executrix of James Lord.
- accounts of David Robinson & William Aires administrators of Sarah Collins.

25:18 22 July. Abraham Clark administrator of Robert Anderson (PG) vs. John Mason. Defendant summoned to testify regarding will of dec'd.

Exhibited bond of John Pitts as Deputy Commissary. Sureties: Thomas Hicks, William Ennalls. Date: 2 February 1720.

24 July. Deputy Commissary (CE) to examine accounts of:
- Hugh Mathews administrator of Dennis Sullivant (CE).

25 July. Deputy Commissary (PG) to examine accounts of:
- Elisabeth Brooke administratrix of

Court Session: 1721

Roger Brooke (PG).

Deputy Commissary (DO) to examine accounts of:
• Mary Harper executor of William Harper (DO).

27 July. Roger Woolford (g) to examine accounts of:
• Mary Warner administratrix of Stephen Warner (DO).

Walter Quinton (g, TA) vs.
25:19 Dennis Conoway (DO). Defendant summoned to answer questions regarding estate of Daniel Clark (of said county).

Deputy Commissary (DO) to examine accounts of:
• Thomas Smith who married Rosannah Brown widow & administratrix of Thomas Browne (DO).

28 July. John Jones (g) to examine accounts of:
• Blandinah Bozman executrix of John Bozman (SO).

Attachment rendered to John Ireland (SM) to answer questions regarding the will of Thomas Reeves (SM). Said Ireland is a witness thereto.

Exhibited:
• accounts of James Mouat, Stephen Warman, John Beale, & James Nicholson executors of William Nicholson (AA).

29 July. Deputy Commissary (SO) to examine accounts of:
• Charles Revil executor of Randolph Revell (SO).

25:20 31 July. Samuel Turbut (g, TA) exhibited:
• inventory of Alexander Kinnimont.
• inventory of Joseph Gregory.
• accounts of Thomas Eaton executor of Peter Anderton.
• accounts of Cornelius Flinn & his wife administratrix of Alexander

Maccotter.
- accounts of Cornelius Arrington administrator of Prudence Woolman.
- accounts of Thomas Turner & his wife administratrix of Robert Register.
- accounts of Isabella Taylor executrix of James Taylor.

1 August. Exhibited oath of Mordecai Hammond (g, AA) that he delivered to Carp. Lillingston (g, QA) a copy of the decree & subpoena for compliance.

25:21   2 August. Exhibited:
- 2nd additional accounts of James Wildman on estate of his father Cornelius Wildman.

4 August. Deputy Commissary (SO) to examine accounts of:
- Elisabeth Waters executrix of Richard Waters.
- Susannah Jones administratrix of Daniel Jones.

Deputy Commissary (DO) to examine accounts of:
- Mary Saldsbury executrix of Alexander Fisher (DO).

Deputy Commissary (CV) to examine accounts of:
- Sarah Day executrix of Robert Day (CV).

5 August. Deputy Commissary (BA) to examine accounts of:
- Roger Mathews executor of Thomas Cord.
- Rowland Kimborough executor of Samuel Jackson.

Deputy Commissary (SO) to examine accounts of:
- Margaret Tilman executrix of Gideon Tilman (SO).

Exhibited:
- 2nd additional inventory of James Coursey (QA).

Court Session: 1721

7 August. Exhibited:
- accounts of William Turbut surviving administrator of James Coursey.

11 August. Exhibited:
- inventory of Samuel Burrill.

12 August. Exhibited:
- additional inventory of Robert Gorsuch.

25:22 John Israel (g, BA) exhibited:
- will of William Marshall, constituting Mary Marshall executrix. Said Mary was granted administration. Sureties: John Hall, Esq., Edward Hall. Date: 7 June 1721.
- will of George Hope, constituting Judith Hope executrix. Said Judith was granted administration. Sureties: William Slade, Thomas Taylor. Date: 22 July 1721.
- will of Thomas Cord, constituting Roger Mathews executor. Said Mathews was granted administration. Sureties: Francis Holland, John Clark. Date: 7 June 1721.
- will of Edward Cantwell, constituting Hannah Cantwell executrix. Said Hannah was granted administration. Sureties: Peter Lester, John Bayly. Date: 7 June 1721.
- will of Thomas Newsam constituting Peter Lester executor. Said Lester was granted administration. Sureties: John Durbin, John Stokes. Date: 11 April 1721.
- bond of Mary Bradshaw administratrix of John Bradshaw. Sureties: Archibald Polle, Robert Cutchin. Date: 7 June 1721.
- bond of Elinor Jackson administratrix of Robert Jackson. Sureties: Michael Gormathon, Thomas Hatchman. Date: 8 June 1721.
- bond of Middleston Derumple administratrix of Robert Derumple. Sureties: Mary Marshall, Thomas Birchfield. Date: & June 1721.
- bond of Sarah Taylor administratrix

of Martin Taylor. Sureties: Isaac
Butterworth, John Sumner. Date: 7
June 1721.

25:23   • bond of George York administrator of
William Doddridge. Sureties: John
Elliot, Richard Thrift. Date: 7
June 1721.
• inventory of Henry Shield.
• inventory of John Webster, Jr.
• inventory of Jabez Peirpoint.
• inventory of Walter Pumphry.
• inventory of Edward Carney.
• inventory of Clark Hollis.
• additional accounts of John Taylor
executor of Abraham Taylor.
• additional accounts of Phillip
Sindall executor of Jane Peacock.

14 August. Exhibited:
• accounts of John Gorsuch executor of
Robert Gorsuch (BA).
• accounts of Mary Jones
administratrix of Joshua Jones (AA).

19 August. Exhibited:
• 2nd additional accounts of Mary
Weeks executrix of Benjamin Weeks
(QA).

21 August. Exhibited:
• inventory of Thomas Long (BA).

22 August. Summons rendered to Francis
Whitehead administrator of Edward
Sweeting (BA) to complete accounts.

Alexander Contee (g) vs. Mary Hemsley
(widow). Summons to render accounts on
estate of John Contee, Esq.

25:24   27 August. Patrick Hepburne (g, PG)
exhibited:
• bond of George Busey & his wife Mary
Ann administrators in trust duing
minority of orphans of Francis
Collier. Sureties: Samuel Magruder,
Ninian Magruder. Date: 19 July
1721.
• inventory of David Patten.
• inventory of Samuel Westley.
• inventory of Richard Lambeth.
• additional accounts of Elisabeth

Brook administratrix of Roger Brook.
- additional accounts of Sarah Busey executrix of Paul Busey.
- additional accounts of Elisabeth Wildman (formerly Elisabeth Johnstone) executrix of Stephen Johnston.
- accounts of Robert Gordon & his wife administratrix of William Downes.
- accounts of James Haddock & Weldone Jefferson executors of Robert Hall.
- accounts of John Modesly administrator of Richard Lambeth.

28 August. Exhibited from CH:
- inventory of Edward Williams.
- inventory of Giles Thompkins.

Deputy Commissary (BA) to examine accounts of:
Frances Dorsey executrix of Nicholas Dorsey (BA).

31 August. Exhibited:
- accounts of John Cornelius & his wife administratrix of Stephen White (BA).

25:25 2 September. Samuel Hanson (g, CH) exhibited:
- bond of William Stone administrator of William Elliott. Sureties: William Stone, Jr. Date: 11 August 1721.
- inventory of Thomas Annis.
- additional inventory of John Wilson.
- accounts of William Milstead administrator of Henry Blankshott.
- accounts of Hudson Wathen executor of John Brayfield.

4 September. Richard Tilghman, Esq. to examine accounts of:
- Robert Jones executor of William Sweatnam (QA).

Deputy Commissary (QA) to examine accounts of:
- Thomas Bannan administrator of John Bannan.
- Francis Nicholson executor of John Nicholson.

Court Session: 1721

- John & Francis Jackson executors of Barbara Jackson.
- Ernault Hawkins executor of John Hawkins.
- Joanna Wyat executrix of James Wyat.
- Rachel Meloyd administratrix of Edward Cash.

Summons to QA, to take LoA or to show cause by why not:
- John, Joseph, & William Harris executors of William Harris.
- Thomas Phillips executor of George Phillips.
- Susannah Griffen executrix of Bernard Griffen.
- George Holliday & his wife administratrix of Richard Chapman.

25:26 Robert Jones (g, QA) exhibited:
- bond of William Clayton administrator of Edward Tomlin. Sureties: William Turbutt, Richard Cotton. Date: 29 June 1721.
- bond of William Turner administrator of Robert Parvis. Sureties: Charles Lemar, William Dudding. Date: 24 August 1721.
- will of George Golt, constituting Mary Golt executrix. Said Mary was granted administration. Sureties: Andrew Price, Thomas Silvester. Date: 28 June 1721.
- inventory of Abraham Oldson.
- inventory of Henry Ayler.
- inventory of Charles Wright.
- inventory of Samuel Parsons.
- accounts of John Wright administrator of Thomas Tillotson.

8 September. Exhibited from AA:
- accounts of Daniel Mariartee administrator of Edward Mariartee.
- accounts of John Talbot & his wife administratrix of Richard Bickerdicke.

11 September. Deputy Commissary (CE) to examine accounts of:
- Mary Smith executrix of Thomas Smith (CE).

Page 188

25:27 Mathias Vanderheyden (g, CE) exhibited:
- will of Phillip Edwards, constituting Nicholas Rennolds executor. Said Rennolds was granted administration. Sureties: Walter Rennolds, John Rennols. Date: 12 June 1721.
- will of Robert Wood, constituting Catharine Wood executrix. Said Catharine was granted administration. Sureties: Charles Rumsey, William Rumsey. Date: 18 August 1721.
- will of Edward Lewis, constituting Mary Lewis executrix. Said Mary was granted administration. Sureties: Francis Davis, Darby Nowland. Date: 25 August 1721.
- bond of Gwenllyan Reece administratrix of Evan Reas. Sureties: Gavin Hutchison, Adam Wallace. Date: 1 August 1721.
- bond of Edward Nevile administrator of William Gouldens. Sureties: Jonathon Collins, Thomas Nevill. Date: 28 April 1721.
- bond of Sarah Rose administratrix of Thomas Rose. Sureties: John Camble, James Numbers. Date: 18 August 1721.
- bond of Benjamin Pearce administrator of Edward Williams. Sureties: Mathias Vanderheyden, John Breede, Jr. Date: 31 May 1721.
- will of Thomas Browning.
- inventory of Philip Edwards.
- inventory of Henry D'hoof.
- inventory of William Goulding.
- inventory of William Price, Sr.
- inventory of Dennis Sullivant.
- inventory of Thomas Smith.
- additional inventory of Nicholas Hyland.

25:28
- accounts of Joseph Young administrator of Jacob Young.
- accounts of Henry Price on estate of Francis Smith.
- accounts of Mellice Hyland administratrix of Nicholas Hyland.
- accounts of Hugh Mathews administrator of Dennis Sullivan.

12 September. Exhibited:
* accounts of Lancelot Todd administrator of John Locket (BA).

John Beale (g, AA) exhibited:
* will of John Slatter, constituting Margaret Slatter executrix. Said Margaret was granted administration. Sureties: Alexander Frazer, James Batterson. Date: 11 August 1721.
* will of William Disney, constituting Mary Disney executrix. Said Mary was granted administration. Sureties: Thomas Lewis, Thomas Aldridge, James Disney. Date: 20 June 1721.
* bond of Elisabeth Leek administratrix of Henry Leek. Sureties: Thomas Stocket, William Brewer. Date: 17 July 1721.
* will of Thomas Holmas, constituting Thomas Jobson executor. Said Jobson was granted administration. Sureties: Vachel Denton, Richard Evans. Date: 6 June 1721.

25:29
* inventory of Francis Vison.
* inventory of Robert Thomas.
* inventory of Leonard Wayman.
* inventory of Thomas Holmas.

Exhibited:
* inventory of Hannah Goodhand (QA).

William Cumming & his wife Elisabeth vs. Elisabeth Coursey (QA) widow & administratrix of Henry Coursey (g, QA). Said Elisabeth Cumming is a daughter of said Henry. Summons to defendant to render answer.

Exhibited bond of Vachel Denton (g, AA), John Beale (g, AA) & Thomas Larkin (g, AA) to Thomas Bordley, Esq.
25:30 Date: 28 December 1719. Appointment of said Denton as Register. Witnesses: John Talbot, Henry Ward, William Cumming.

Exhibited letter to Thomas Bordley, Esq., delivered on 14 September 1721 by the Governor's servant. Dismissal of said Bordley.

Court Session: 1721

25:31 Signed: Cha. Calvert.

25:32 Appointment of William Holland, Esq. (AA) as Commissary General by Charles Calvert, Esq. (Governor). Date: 1 September 1721.

25:33 Said Holland took oath on 19 September 1721.

25:34 Appointment of Vachel Denton (Annapolis) as Register. Date: 20 September 1721.

25:35 Bond of said Denton. Signed: John Beale (g), John Baldwin (g).

Court Session: 12 September 1721

Docket:

- T.L. for Thomas Brannock vs. W.C. & D.D. for Nehemiah Beckwith. Libel, answer, replication, duplication.

25:36
- T.L. for Vestry of St. Michaell's Parish vs. D.D. for Michael Fletcher. Libel, answer.
- D.D. & T.L. for Aquila Paca & his wife vs. R.T. for Aquila Hall & his wife executrix of James Phillips. Libel, answer. Abated by death of plaintiff.
- Attachment to Cuthbert Sawell (SM) & Mary Green (CH) to prove will of their brother John Sawell. Leonard Green husband of said Mary deposed that she is lately delivered of a child & is incapable of travelling. Will proved by other witnesses.
- R.T. for Henry Costin, Jr. vs. W.C. for Roger Murphey administrator of Thomas Jones. Libel. Said Murphey deposed that he was held in custody of sheriff (QA) by virtue of a suit against him & could not reply.
- W.C. for Daniel of St. Thomas Jenifer vs. P.K. for Martha Dansey executrix of Charles Ashcom. Libel, plea. Attachment for answer.

25:37
- R.T. for David Robinson vs. P.K. & W.C. for Nicholas Lowe executor of Elisabeth Lowe. Attachment for answer.
- W.C. for Vitus Herbet vs. D.D. for William Thompson administrator of William Herbett. Libel.

Page 191

Court Session: 12 September 1721

- W.C. for the same vs. D.D. for the same. Libel.
- Attachment to Charles Carroll (g) executor of Charles Carroll, Esq. to render accounts on estate of Thomas Docwra & on estate of John Dodd.
- Abraham Clark administrator of Robert Anderson vs. John Mason. Said Mason summoned to testify regarding will of dec'd.
- Walter Quinton vs. Dennis Conoway. Sheriff (DO) to summon defendant regarding estate of David Clark.

25:38
- estate of Thomas Reeves (SM) vs. John Ireland (SM). Mentions: regarding the will of John Hoskins, said Ireland deposed that he saw the dec'd sign his will.
- Mordecai Hammond & his wife vs. Carpender Lillingston executor, etc. Sheriff (QA) to render attachment to defendant.
- Sheriff (BA) to summon Francis Whitehead administrator of Edward Sweeting to complete accounts.

25:39
- Summons to Mary Hemsley to render accounts on estate of John Contee, Esq.
- Thomas Reeves & William Hoskins & his wife Ann vs. Ubgate Reeves executor of Thomas Reeves. Libel.

Court Session: 1721

4 September. Exhibited:
- nuncupative will of Richard Chapman (QA).

20 September. James Harris, Esq. (KE) exhibited:
- will of Edward Sammon, constituting Francis Collens executor. Said Collens was granted administration. Sureties: Richard Davis, Darby Shawn. Date: 8 September 1721.
- bond of Solomon Breward executrix of Ann Heyden. Sureties: William Smathers, Hopton Williams. Date: 30 June 1721.
- bond of William Comegys administrator of John Buttler. Sureties: Samuel Wallis, Abraham

Redgrave. Date: 30 June 1721.
- inventory of Ann Hiden.
- inventory of William Pearce.
- inventory of John Kersly.
- inventory of John Buttler.
- LoD of William Pope.
- inventory of Daniel Dunahaw.

25:40
- inventory of James Ray.
- LoD of James Ray.
- inventory of Thomas Maslin.
- inventory of Sarah Jues.
- accounts of Mathew Pope administrator of William Pope.
- accounts of Andrew Norwell administrator of Phillip Hissett.

21 September. Mr. John Baker (SM) exhibited:
- will of Audry Taylard, constituting Morris Quades executor. Said Quades was granted administration. Sureties: William Cole, Owen Smithson. Date: 16 September 1721.
- bond of Simon Sinnott administrator of John Sinnott. Sureties: Vitus Herbet, John Carmichaell. Date: 14 August 1721.
- inventory of Elisabeth Burrell.
- inventory of Robert Thomas.
- inventory of Elisabeth Brady.
- accounts of William Langly & his wife on estate of Richard Baxter.

22 September. Samuell Hopkins (SO) exhibited:
- will of Francis Joyce. Bond of John Pope & his wife Ann executrix. Sureties: John Purnell, Robert Davis. Date: 11 August 1721.
- will of Thomas Warrington, constituting Mary Warrington & Benjamin Fooke executors. Said executors were granted administration. Sureties: Benjamin Aydolett, Samuel Taylor. Date: 17 August 1721.

25:41
- will of James Townsend, constituting Elisabeth Townsend executrix. Said Elisabeth was granted administration. Sureties: Charles Townsend, Thomas Beivan. Date: 7 July 1721.

- will of Jeremiah Pointer, constituting Elioner Pointer executrix. Said Elioner was granted administration. Sureties: John Trewitt, George Trewitt. Date: 17 July 1721.
- will of John Gosling, constituting James Gosling executor. Said James was granted administration. Sureties: Joseph Venible, John Gosling. Date: 13 July 1721.
- bond of Abigall Waite administratrix of Nathaniel Waite. Sureties: Patrick Guttery, Samuel Ball. Date: 21 August 1721.
- inventory of John Pope.
- inventory of James Curtis.
- inventory of Nathaniel Racklife, Jr.
- inventory of Francis Joyce.
- inventory of Nathaniel Racklife, Sr.
- inventory of Thomas Oxford.
- inventory of Jane Rich.
- inventory of Moses Owen.
- inventory of Thomas Moor.
- inventory of Nehemiah Holland.
- inventory of John Fawsett, Sr.
- accounts of John Hampton administrator of Patrick Dunnock.
- accounts of John Hampton administrator of John Chevous.
- accounts of John Phillips administrator of William Gullett.
- accounts of Thomas Holbrook administrator of Thomas Holbrook.
- accounts of John Williams administrator of Dogett Beaucham.
- accounts of Mercie Fountain administrator of John Brown.
- accounts of Sarah Wheatly administratrix of William Wheatly.

14 September. William Innis who married heiress at law of Daniel Bell (SM) vs. Francis Hopewell. Summons to defendant.

25:42 9 October. Deputy Commissary (DO) to examine accounts of:
- Elisabeth Bartington executrix of Enock Bartington (DO).
- Mary Bradshaw administratrix of Thomas Bradshaw (DO).

Court Session: 1721

4 October. Nath. Hynson (g) to examine accounts of:
- Ariana Frisby executrix of James Frisby (CE).

30 September. Mr. John Pitt (DO) exhibited:
- will of Thomas Heathers, constituting Mary Heathers & William Lowe executors. Said executors were granted administration. Sureties: John Dawson, William Hatfield. Date: 9 August 1721.
- bond of Rebecca Bounds administratrix of John Bounds. Sureties: Edward Biletor, William Clifton. Date: 9 August 1721.
- inventory of Thomas Bradshaw.
- inventory of Moses Lecompt.
- additional accounts of Summer Adams & his wife administratrix of James Staple.
- accounts of Robert Johnson, Jr. executor of Robert Johnson, Sr.
- accounts of Mary Salsbery executrix of Petegrew Salsbery.
- accounts of Mary Harper executrix of William Harper.

25:43 2 October. Exhibited:
- accounts of Benjamin Kerby & his wife Elisabeth executrix of Jacob Blangy (QA).

Adderton Skinner (CV) exhibited:
- will of Gregory Manning, constituting John Manning executor.
- bond of Mary Beacham administratrix of James Beacham. Sureties: John Wilkinson, Brient MackDonell. Date: 9 September 1721.
- inventory of Hugh William.
- inventory of Henry Johnson.
- inventory of Robert Day.
- inventory of Elisabeth Malden.
- inventory of Thomas Gilley.
- accounts of William Young administrator of Francis Young.
- accounts of Jane Meed executrix of William Meed, Sr.
- accounts of Priscilla Johns executrix of Richard Johns, Jr.

Page 195

- accounts of William Young administrator of George Young.
- bond of Darby Henly & his wife Mary administratrix of William Shackers. Sureties: Darby Henly, Sr., Benony Pardo. Date: 5 September 1721.

4 October. Exhibited bond of John Israel (g, BA) as Deputy Commissary (BA).

25:44 Exhibited:
- Charles Carroll (g, Annapolis) executor of Charles Carroll, Esq. (Annapolis). Appraisers (g, BA): Richard Gist, Henry Ridgley, John Dorsey. John Israel to administer oath.

Exhibited bond of Dr. Patrick Hepburn (g, PG) as Deputy Commissary (PG). Mr. Joseph Belt to administer oath.

5 October. Exhibited bond of Nicholas Benson (g, TA) as Deputy Commissary (TA). Surety: Edmond Benson.

10 October. Exhibited bond of John Pitt (g, DO) as Deputy Commissary (DO). Sureties: William Ennalls, LEvin Hicks.

Mr. Samuel Hanson (CH) exhibited:
- will of Michael Martin, constituting John Martin executor. Said John was granted administration. Sureties: Henry Hawkins, Thomas Hawkins. Date: 5 September 1721.

25:45
- inventory of Ledia Ocane.

11 October. Exhibited accounts of Mary Vansweringen administratrix of Joseph Vansweringen (SM) executor of Mrs. Mary Vansweringen.
- receipt by John Parkes who married Teresa from Mr. Joseph Vansweringen on estate of her father Garrett Vansweringen & her mother Mary Vansweringen. Witnesses: Garrard Slye, William Griffen.
- receipt of D. Vansweringen from his brother Mr. Joseph Vansweringen from estate of Mary Vansweringen.

Court Session: 1721

Exhibited:
- 4th additional accounts of William Ringold one of executors of Thomas Ringold (KE).
- accounts of Darius Wayman administratrix of Leonard Wayman (AA).

10 October. Mr. Samuel Turbutt (TA) exhibited:
- inventory of George Bowes.
- inventory of Richard Ratcliff.
- inventory of James Hill.
- inventory of Rebecca Bromwell.
- inventory of Henry Withgart.
- additional inventory of Michaell Russell.
- inventory of John Ross.
- additional accounts of Perry Benson & his wife Rebecca executrix of Michaell Russell.
- accounts of Thomas Turner administrator of John Turner.
- accounts of Benjamin Parrott executor of John Parrott.
- accounts of Ann Turner administratrix of Edward Turner.

12 October. Dr. Patrick Hepburn to examine accounts of:
- Jane Prather administratrix of Jonathon Prather (PG).
- Henry Williams who married executrix of Benjamin Hall (PG).

13 October. Frances King administrator of David James (PG) vs. Margaret James widow of said David. Summons to deliver goods from said estate.

Mary Lowe administratrix of Henry Lowe, Esq. (CE) was granted administration on his estate.

16 October. Samuell Hopkins (SO) exhibited:
- will of Samuel Handy, constituting Ebenezar Handy & Priscilla Handy executors. Said executors were granted administration. Sureties: William Planner, Solomon Coleburn. Date: 13 September 1721.

25:46

25:47

- will of Robert Hill, constituting David Hazard executor. Said Hazard was granted administration. Sureties: Daniel Wharton, John Tull. Date: 16 September 1721.
- bond of Ann Faucitt administratrix of John Faucitt. Sureties: John Tull, William Kennett. Date: 16 September 1721.
- bond of John Jarman administrator of William Jarmin. Sureties: Phillip Trewitt, Roger Hook. Date: 15 September 1721.
- bond of Mary Patrick administratrix of Daniel Patrick. Sureties: William Whittington, Henry Alexander. Date: 19 September 1721.
- inventory of Jeremiah Poynter.
- inventory of Richard Woodcraft.
- inventory of Jonathon Noble.
- coletterall inventory of Jeremiah Poynter.
- inventory of Nathaniel Waite.
- inventory of Joseph Morris.
- inventory of William Collins.
- inventory of Edward Martin.
- inventory of Peirce Reed.
- inventory of Leonard Johnson.
- inventory of Alice Miles.

25:48
- accounts of Levin Denwood administrator of Samuel Groom.
- accounts of Elisabeth Pope administratrix of Job Pope.

17 October. Deputy Commissary (SO) to examine accounts of:
- William Richard administrator of Robert Johnson (SO).
- Mary Pope administratrix of John Pope (SO).
- Elisabeth Bratten administratrix of John Bratten (SO).

Deputy Commissary (CV) to examine accounts of:
- William Dawkins executor of Thomas Gilley administrator of William Gilley (CV).
- John Cox administrator of Henry Cox (CV).

Court Session: 1721

18 October. Sheriff (DO) to summon
James Garrard (DO) to take LoA on estate
of Edward Gerrard or to show cause why
not.

25:49   20 October. Deputy Commissary (KE) to
examine accounts of:
- Samuel Clark & his wife Mary
  administratrix of Dennis Clarke
  (KE).

27 October. George Busey administrator
of Francis Collier (PG) vs. John Evans.
Summons to defendant.

George Busey administrator of Francis
Collier (PG) vs. Henry Smith. Summons
to defendant.

28 October. Thomas Edmondson & his wife
Mary vs. James Lloyd & his wife Ann &
John Pemberton & his wife Deborah
executrices of Robert Grundy (TA). Mary
is a relation & legatee of said Grundy.
Summons to defendants.

31 October. Exhibited:
- accounts of William Clayton
  administrator of William Turlo (QA).
- accounts of William Clayton &
  Katherine Hammond executors of Maj.
  Thomas Emmerson (TA).

Exhibited from TA:
- additional inventory of Maj. Thomas
  Emmerson.

25:50   Exhibited:
- list of expenses of Katherine
  Emerson one of executors of Maj.
  Thomas Emmerson (TA).

1 November. Mr. John Baker (SM)
exhibited:
- will of Margaret Buttler,
  constituting Cecill Buttler
  executor. Said Cecill was granted
  administration. Sureties: William
  Kerby, John Leigh. Date: 5 October
  1721.
- will of Cornelius Manning,
  constituting Elisabeth Manning &

John Miles executors. Said
executors were granted
administration. Sureties: Thomas
Waughop, Robert Wiseman. Date: 6
September 1721.
- bond of Charles Ashcom administrator
of John Ashcom. Sureties: James
Keech, Charles Smith. Date: 3
October 1721.
- bond of Elisabeth Shucoushes
administratrix of Darby Shucoushes.
Sureties: John Horn, Darby Carter.
Date: 20 October 1721.
- inventory of James Thompson.
- additional inventory of Joseph
Vansweringen.
- inventory of George Beveridge.
- inventory of Simon Combes.
- accounts of Rachell Wright
administratrix of William Wright.

25:51   Dr. Patrick Hepburne (PG) exhibited:
- will of Gabrill Burnham.
- will of John Craycroft, constituting
Jane Craycroft executrix. Said Jane
was granted administration.
Sureties: Leonard Brooke, John
Boone. Date: 25 August 1721.
- inventory of Francis Collier.

3 November. Exhibited:
- 2nd additional accounts of Margaret
Rattenberry administratrix of John
Rattenberry (BA).
- accounts of Hannah Cross
administratrix of Robert Cross (AA).

4 November. Mr. Samuell Hopkins (SO)
exhibited:
- will of John Whorton. Also bond of
Boman Townsend & his wife Susannah
executrix. Sureties: William
Pepper, John Woodcraft. Date: 5
October 1721.
- will of John Morris. Also bond of
Sarah Morris administratrix.
Sureties: William Pepper, William
Freeman. Date: 5 October 1721.
- will of Thomas Paynter, constituting
John Paynter executor. Said John
was granted administration.
Sureties: William Pepper, William

Court Session: 1721

25:52

Freeman. Date: 5 October 1721.
- will of Daniel Selby, constituting Mary Selby executrix. Said Mary was granted administration. Sureties: William Selby, Thomas Outten. Date: 7 October 1721.
- bond of Sarah Tingle administratrix of Samuel Tingle. Sureties: Joseph Wyatt, Jonas Smith. Date: 5 October 1721.
- inventory of William Jarman.
- accounts of Ann Renshaw administratrix of John Renshaw.
- accounts of Ann Renshaw administratrix of Francis Roberts.
- accounts of William Kennet administrator of John Kennet.

Exhibited:
- accounts of Benjamin Tasker administrator of William Bladen, Esq. (AA).
- will of Robert Morton (TA).
- accounts of Blandina Bozman executrix of John Bozman (SO).

Exhibited some proceedings from BA in the time of Col. Holland. [See f. 57.]

25:53 Charles Calvert, Esq. (Governor) appointed Col. William Holland (AA), Thomas Addison (PG), & Daniel Dullany, Esq. (AA) as Commissaries General.

25:54 ...

25:55 Appointment of Vachel Denton (Annapolis) as Register.

25:56 ...

25:57 John Israel (BA) exhibited [see f. 52]:
- bond of Sarah Cockey executrix of Joshua Cockey. Sureties: Benjamin Hanson, Joshua Meriken. Date: 8 September 1721.
- bond of James Powell administrator dbn of Edward Talbott. Sureties: John Gordan, Henry Ridgley. Date: 2 September 1721.
- inventory of John Wills.
- inventory of William Jenkins.
- inventory of Thomas Newsam.
- LoD on estate of Thomas Newsam.

- inventory of Benjamin Laurence.
- accounts of Frances Dorsey executrix
  of Nathaniell Dorsey.

25:58 11 November. Richard Moore executor of
Dr. Mordica Moore (AA) was granted
continuance.

15 November. John Gresham (g, AA) vs.
William Selman & his wife Ann executrix
of Thomas Sparrow (AA). Summons to
render answer.

28 November. Mr. Mathias Vanderheyden
(CE) exhibited:
- will of Patrick Killy, constituting
  Judith Killy executrix. Said Judith
  was granted administration.
  Sureties: Cornelius Maccormack, John
  Killy. Date: 17 October 1721.
- will of Henry Gilder, constituting
  Mary Gilder executrix. Said Mary
  was granted administration.
  Sureties: Daniel & Richard Hewhen.
  Date: 4 October 1721.
- bond of William Dare executor of
  Roger Larramore. Sureties: Thomas
  Wamsley, James Husband. Date: 27
  October 1721.
- additional inventory of Jonathon
  Bicks.
- inventory of Edward Lewis.
- inventory of Charles Hatton.
- inventory of Thomas Rose.

25:59

- accounts of Peter Ellrod & his wife
  Sarah on estate of John Smith.
- accounts of Mary Price executrix of
  William Price.
- accounts of Sarah Rose
  administratrix of Thomas Rose.

12 December. Deputy Commissary (KE) to
examine accounts of:
- Nathaniel Hynson administrator of
  William Glanvill (KE).

7 December. Exhibited:
- inventory of William Elliott (CH).

14 December. Dr. Patrick Hepburn (PG)
exhibited:

Court Session: 1721

- accounts of James Read & his wife Elisabeth executrix of John Burch.
- John Evans (p), age 45, deposed on 16 November 1721 that he delivered all goods, etc., from the estate of Francis Collier

25:60

to George Busey (PG) administrator of said Collier, during minority of orphans of Charles Collier.
- Henry Smith (PG), age 47, deposed on 16 November 1721.

4 December. Exhibited from CE:
- accounts of Ariana Frisby executrix of James Frisby (CE).

Court Session: 12 December 1721

25:61 Docket:
- T.L. for Thomas Brannock vs. W.C. for Nehemiah Beckwith. Libel, answer, replication.
- T.L. for Vestry of St. Michaell's Parish vs. Michael Fletcher. Libel, answer.
- R.T. for Henry Costin vs. W.C. for Roger Murphey administrator of Thomas Jones. Libel, answer.
- W.C. for Daniel of St. Thomas Jenifer vs. P.K. for Martha Dansey executrix of Charles Ashcom. Libel, plea.
- R.T. for David Robinson vs. P.K. & W.C. for Nicholas Lowe executor of Elisabeth Lowe. Attachment render for answer.
- W.C. for Vitus Herbert vs. William Thompson administrator of William Herbert. Agreed.
- W.C. for the same vs. the same. Agreed.

25:62
- T.L. for Thomas Reeves, & William Hoskins & his wife Ann vs. Ubgate Reeves executor of Thomas Reeves. Libel, answer.
- William Innes who married heiress at law of Daniel Bell vs. Francis Hopewell. Sheriff (SM) to summon defendant to answer for estate of said Bell.
- Sheriff (DO) to summon James Gerrard to take LoA on estate of Edward

Garrard or show cause why not.

- Thomas Edmondson & his wife vs.
  James Lloyd & his wife & John
  Pemberton & his wife executrices of
  Robert Grundy. Libel.

- Petition of Samuel Thomas (KE).
  Henry Staples (TA) made his will in
  25:63   October 1686, devising to his wife
  Ann Staples. Said Ann, by her will,
  bequeathed lands, etc., part of
  which are possessed by the
  petitioner. Petitioner requested a
  search for will of said Henry, which
  was not found.

  25:64   Petition is that the attested copy
  of the will be recorded. Signed:
  Joshua George for petitioner.
  Summons to the heirs of Henry
  Staples, posed on door of St. Paul's
  Parish (KE).

  25:65   Gideon Pearce (sheriff) summoned:
  Rice Jones, John Fanning, Mathias
  Piner, Mr. John Johnson & his wife.

  25:66   Samuel Thomas (g, KE) deposed.
  25:67   Ruling: said copy of the will is to
  be recorded.

  25:68 • William Offut (p, PG) & James Beall
  (p, PG) to appraise the estate of
  Charles Carroll, Esq. in PG.

- Notice: Thomas Larkin & William
  Cumming, proctors of this court, are
  very much indisposed. Mr. Richard
  Trensam is also indisposed.

Court Session: 1721

15 December. Mr. Adderton Skinner (CV)
exhibited:

- will of Edmond Hungerford,
  constituting Penelope Hungerford
  executrix. Said Penelope was
  granted administration. Sureties:
  John Greeves, Samuell Abbott, John
  Hellen, Peter Hellon. Date: 22
  November 1721.

  25:69 • bond of Elisabeth Meads executrix of
  William Meads. Sureties: William
  Harrison, Francis Hollingshead.
  Date: 16 November 1721.

- bond of John Manning executor of
  Gregory Manning. Surety: William
  Dawkins, Sr. Date: 18 November

1721.
- bond of Gillian Laughlan administratrix of John Laughlan. Sureties: Henry Hanson, James Dorsey. Date: 16 November 1721.
- bond of Winifred Chittam administratrix of John Chittam. Surety: Jeremiah Sheridine. Date: 14 November 1721.
- bond of Sarah Dyer administratrix of Cornelius Dyer. Sureties: Derby Henly, John Hues. Date: 21 November 1721.
- inventory of Richard Garnam.
- accounts of Elisabeth Williams administratrix of Hugh Williams.
- accounts of Sarah Day executrix of Robert Day.
- accounts of William Dawkins executor of William Gilley.
- accounts of John Cox administrator of Col. Henry Cox.

25:70
- accounts of Elisabeth Deavour executrix of Gilbert Deavour.

19 December. Mr. John Baker (SM) exhibited:
- will of Francis Merritt, constituting John Price executor. Said Price was granted administration. Sureties: Justinian Jordaine, John James. Date: 10 November 1721.
- will of Hector Macklin, constituting Ann Macklaine executrix. Said Ann was granted administration. Sureties: Thomas Cooper, John Mackintosh. Date: 8 November 1721.
- bond of Susannah Peters administratrix of Joseph Peters. Sureties: Joseph Watson, James Crook. Date: 8 November 1721.
- inventory of Cornelius Manning.
- inventory of John Sinnott.
- accounts of Mary Askins administratrix of William Askins.

25:71 Deputy Commissary (SM) to examine accounts of:
- William Jamison & his wife administratrix of Thomas Roberts.
- Coll. Watts & his wife executrix of

John Tanny.
- Dryden Jowles executrix of Col. Henry Peregrine Jowles.
- Elisabeth Smith executrix of Daniel Smith.
- Mary Dean administratrix of John Dean.
- Joseph Wheetly administrator of James Wheatly.
- Ann Reed administratrix of James Makin.
- Mary Howard administratrix of Nathaniell Howard.
- Mary Biscoe administratrix of George Biscoe.
- Elisabeth Dillicoate administratrix of James Dillicoate.

8 January. Capt. John Tunstall (SO) exhibited:
- accounts of James Truett executor of James Truett.
- accounts of Tabitha Killam administratrix of William Killam.
- accounts of Mary Owens administratrix of Moses Owens.
- accounts of Robert Atkinson administrator of Jacob Highway.
- accounts of John Brotten executor of David Carsey.

Deputy Commissary (SO) to examine accounts of:
- Thomas Collins executor of Thomas Collins.
- Elisabeth Walton administratrix of Elisha Walton.
- Price Collins executor of John Crapper.
- Elisabeth Holland executrix of Nehemiah Holland.
- John Pope executor of Francis Joyce.
- Brigett Kirk executrix of John Kirk.
- William McClemy executor of Woney McClemy.
- Sarah Perkins administratrix of John Perkins.
- Charles Revell executor of Randolph Revell.
- Booz Walston executor of James Curtis.
- Thomas Banister executor of William

25:72

Banister.
- Francis Martain & his wife Catherine executrix of Thomas Tull, Sr.
- Elisabeth Roach executrix of Nathaniell Roach.
- Alice Pusey administratrix of William Pusey.
- Mary Milburn executrix of Ra. Milburn.
- Thomas Williams executor of Thomas Williams.
- Elisabeth Crouch administratrix of Robert Crouch.
- Mary Selby executrix of Samuell Selby.
- Winifred Driskill administratrix of Dennis Diskill.
- Winifred Driskill administratrix of ditto executor of Edward Hammond.
- Sarah Tull administratrix of Thomas Tull, Jr.
- Denis Hudson executor of Henry Hudson, Sr.
- Joyce Johnson executrix of Leonard Johnson.
- John Painter executor of John Painter.
- Sarah Woolford administratrix of Levin Woolford.

6 January. Deputy Commissary (BA) to examine accounts of:
- Hanah Teal administratrix of Edward Teele (BA).

25:73 9 January. Mr. Samuel Turbutt (TA) exhibited:
- renunciation of Martha Bullock widow of Francis Bullock, recommending her son John Kersey.
- will of Francis Bullock. Also bond of John Kersey. Sureties: Dennis Hopkins, George Shanahawn. Date: 7 December 1721.
- bond of Francis Pickerin & Henry Burgess executors of Robert Morton. Sureties: Fran. Armstrong, William Finney. Date: 8 December 1721.
- bond of Joseph James executor of Joseph James. Sureties: Thomas Martin, Sr., Loftus Bowdle. Date: 13 December 1721.

- will of Robert Pearson.
- will of Richard Swift.
- accounts of James Dauson administrator of James Wright.
- accounts of John Bartlett & Thomas Attkinson administrator of Timothy Mackdaniel.

25:74 10 January. Deputy Commissary (QA) to examine accounts of:
- William Hemsley & Robert Noble executors of Phillimon Hemsley (AA).

12 January. Exhibited:
- accounts of Thomas Price administrator of Phillimon Hemsley (AA).

18 January. Mr. John Israel (BA) exhibited:
- will of Robert Smith, constituting Mary Smith executrix. Said Mary was granted administration. Sureties: Edward Smith, John Weasly. Date: 9 November 1721.
- will of James Barlowe, Sr., constituting Johanna Barlow & Jacob Barlow executors. Said Johanna & Jacob were granted administration. Sureties: Christopher Randall, Maurice Baker. Date: 2 December 1721.
- will of Anthony Arnold, constituting Sarah Arnold executrix. Said Sarah was granted administration. Sureties: Patrick Murphey, Thomas Taylor. Date: 9 December 1721.

25:75
- bond of Stephen Gill administrator of Stephen Gill, Jr. Sureties: William Barney, Richard Deavor. Date: 8 November 1721.
- bond of Barbary Fitzredmond administratrix of John Fitzredmond. Sureties: Robert Chapman, Darby Regan. Date: 2 December 1721.
- will of James Barlow, Jr.
- inventory of Robert Jackson.
- inventory of Martin Taylor.
- LoD of Martin Taylor.
- inventory of John Petit.

Court Session: 1721

19 January. Exhibited:
- bond of Nathaniell Horsey executor of Nathaniell Horsey, Sr. Surety: Benjamin King. Date: 29 December 1721.

23 January. Exhibited:
- inventory of William Thacker (CV).

(N) Emerson vs. (N) Loyd & (N) Pemberton who married executrix of Robert Grundy (TA). Summons renewed.

25:76 25 January. Deputy Commissary (SO) to examine accounts of:
- John Grundy & his wife Sarah administratrix of James Bound (SO).

27 January. Mr. John Baker (SM) exhibited:
- bond of Lancelott Pockley administrator of John Brassey. Surety: George Gillispie. Date: 2 January 1721.
- bond of Patrick Burne administrator of John Burne. Sureties: William White, Henry Attwood. Date: 20 November 1721.
- inventory of Margarett Buttler.
- inventory of Audry Taylor.
- accounts of William Able & his wife administratrix of John Dean.
- accounts of John Millman & his wife Mary executrix of Robert Thomas.
- accounts of Elisabeth Smith executrix of Daniel Smith.
- accounts of Elisabeth Dellicoat administratrix of James Dellicoat.
- accounts of Elisabeth Dafft executrix of Charles Dafft.
25:77 - accounts of Dryden Jowles executrix of Col. Henry Peregrine Jowles.

29 January. Col. William Holland to administer oath to:
- Elisabeth Eastwood widow & administratrix of John Eastwood (AA).

30 January. Exhibited:
- bond of Jane Lewellin administratrix of Thomas Orrell (CH). Sureties:

William Hook, George Brett. Date:
18 December 1721.
* additional accounts of Hudson Wotton
executor of John Brayfield.

31 January. Summons to Thomas Macormick
& his wife Mary administratrix of John
Ching (CH) to render inventory.

1 February. John Pitts (DO) exhibited:
* will of Michael Dean, constituting
Elisabeth Dean executrix. Said
Elisabeth was granted
administration. Sureties: John
Dean, William Spencer. Date: 17
November 1721.

25:78
* will of Mary Molahane, constituting
Abraham Griffith executor. Said
Griffith was granted administration.
Sureties: George Andrews, John
Griffith. Date: 21 October <no year
given>.
* bond of Sarah Potts administratrix
of Thomas Potts. Sureties: Anthony
Rawlings, Sr., Anthony Rawlings, Jr.
Date: 16 January 1721.
* bond of Susannah Dawson
administratrix of Richard Dawson.
Sureties: John Dawson, Henry
Wheeler. Date: 30 November 1721.
* inventory of Thomas Heather.
* inventory of Mary Mollahane.
* accounts of Cornelia Mackall
executrix of David Mackall.
* accounts of William Cullins & his
wife Sarah administratrix of Edward
Bryan.
* accounts of Elisabeth Bartington
administratrix of Enock Bartington.

Deputy Commissary (KE) to examine
accounts of:
* Samuell Wicks administrator of
Michael Willson (KE).

25:79 9 February. Deputy Commissary (DO) to
examine accounts of:
* Mary Lecompt, Phillip, Samuell, &
Joseph Lecompt executors of Moses
Lecompt (DO).

Court Session: 1721

10 February. Deputy Commissary (CE) to examine accounts of:
- Ann Lewis executrix of Richard Lewis (CE).

Exhibited:
- additional accounts of Daniel Jenifer & his wife Elisabeth executrix of John Rogers.

Daniel Dulany, Esq. vs. Stephen Gill (BA). Summons to defendant to show cause why the will of Stephen Gill should not be recorded.

Court Session: 13 February 1721

25:80 Docket:
- T.L. for Thomas Brannock vs. W.C. for Nehemiah Beckwith. Agreed.
- T.L. for Vestry of St. Michaell's Parish vs. Michael Fletcher. Libel, answer.
- R.T. for Henry Costin vs. W.C. for Roger Murphey. Libel, answer.
- W.C. for Daniel of St. Thomas Jenifer vs. P.K. & J.G. for Martha Dansey executrix of Charles Ashcom. Libel, plea.
- R.T. & J.G. for David Robinson vs. P.K. & W.C. for Nicholas Lowe executor of Elisabeth Lowe. Libel; attachment for answer.

25:81
- T.L. for Thomas Reeves, & William Hoskins & his wife Ann vs. J.G. for Ubgate Reeves executor of Thomas Reeves. Libel, answer. Samuell Williamson, Justinian Jordan, Gerrard Slye, & Mathew Mason to examine witnesses.
- Joshua George for Thomas Edmondson & his wife vs. James Loyd & his wife & John Pemberton & his wife executrices of Robert Grundy. T. Bozman (sheriff, TA) to render attachment to defendants. Joshua George exhibited that said Thomas Edmondson is dec'd.

25:82
- Summons to Thomas Maccormick & his wife Mary administratrix of John Ching (CH) to render inventory.
- Summons to Stephen Gill executor of

Court Session: 13 February 1721

Stephen Gill (BA) to show cause why
the will should not be recorded.
- J.G. for Gideon Pearce executor of
William Potts vs. St. Ledger Codd
attorney for John Potts. Petition
for execution of decree.
- W.C. for Mordecai Hammond & his wife
vs. Carpender Lillingston & his
wife executrix, etc. Val. Carter
(sheriff, QA) rendered attachment to
defendant. He is so sick &
languishing.

Court Session: 1721

25:83

15 February. Exhibited:
- bond of Edmund Benson & William
Chapman administrators of William
Dare (CE). Sureties: John Stokes,
Vachel Denton. Date: 15 February
1721. Also, deposition by said
Benson.

17 February. Deputy Commissary (SM) to
examine accounts of:
- Richard Keen administrator of
William Cretchett.
- Mary Thomas executrix of Robert
Thomas.

20 February. Exhibited:
- 2 inventories of John Dawson
(chyrurgeon, AA).

25:84

Deputy Commissary to examine accounts
of:
- Elinor Rigby administratrix of
Arthur Rigby (TA).

Exhibited:
- will of Oswald Hoskins, constituting
Bennet Hoskins executor. Said
Bennet was granted administration.
Sureties: John Courts, Ralph
Falkner. Date: 3 February 1721.

Deputy Commissary (TA) to examine
accounts of:
- William Austin & Jacob Falkenar
administrators of Joseph Gregory.
- John Spriggnall executor of Anthony
Wise.

21 February. Deputy Commissary (TA) to examine accounts of:
- Anne Dawson widow of John Dawson (TA).

Thomas Brook (g, PG) exhibited:
- bond of John Clarvo administrator of John Clarvo. Sureties: John Middleton, John Howell. Date: 23 January 1721.
- bond of Robert Levet administrator of Mary Biddle. Surety: John Docwra. Date: 16 February 1721.

25:85
- bond of Aaron Lomus administrator of Walter King. Sureties: Thomas Buckannan, Richard Buckley. Date: 9 February 1721.
- will of Francis Clarvo.
- renunciation of Bridget Clarvo widow of Francis Clarvo, recommending her son John Clarvo. She is very ill & weak. Date: 21 January 1721/2. Witnesses: James Bramell, Thomas Lowden. Attested on 23 January 1721.

Mr. John Israell (BA) exhibited:
- will of Anthony Johnson.
- inventory of Joseph Coale.

John Tunstall (g, SO) exhibited:
- will of Ralph Milburne.
- will of George Truitt.
- will of Nathaniel Horsey.
- will of Dennis Driskill.
- will of James Atkinson.

25:86
- inventory of Robert Twille.
- inventory of James Townsend.
- inventory of Jane Elsey.
- inventory of Hugh Porter.
- inventory of Thomas Paynter.
- accounts of William Richardson administrator of Robert Johnson.
- accounts of Francis Irving administratrix of Robert Anderson.
- accounts of Sarah Tull administratrix of Thomas Tull.
- accounts of Robert Martin administrator of James Emanuell.
- accounts of John Woodcraft administrator of Thomas Wildgoos.
- accounts of John Murrow

Court Session: 1721

administrator of Hugh Porter.

Sheriff (QA) to summon:
* Susannah Griffen executrix of Bernard Griffen.
* John, Joseph, & William Harris executors of William Harris.
* Thomas Phillips executor of George Phillips.

Deputy Commissary (QA) to examine accounts of:
* Roger Murphey administrator of Thomas Jones.
* Robert Bessuet administrator of John Barron.

23 February. Deputy Commissary (PG) to examine additional accounts of:
* Katherine Boteler executrix of Henry Boteler (PG).

25:87   26 February. Deputy Commissary (CH) to examine accounts of:
* Elinor Sanders executrix of Mathew Sanders.
* executrix or administratrix of Elisabeth Hayden.

27 February. Deputy Commissary (PG) to examine accounts of:
* Thomas Dorset executor of Anne Dorset (PG).

Exhibited from QA:
* inventory of Thomas Williams.
* inventory of Elisabeth Williams.
* accounts of Edm. Thomas executor of Elisabeth Williams.

Deputy Commissary (QA) to examine accounts of:
* Edm. Thomas executor of Thomas Williams (QA).

Mr. Walter Smith (CV) exhibited:
* inventory of John Laughlan.
* inventory of Gregory Manning.

28 February. Deputy Commissary (SM) to examine accounts of:
* James Thompson (Newtown) executor of

Court Session: 1721

Elisabeth Burrell.
- James Thompson (St. Inegoes)
  executor of James Thompson.
- William Thompson administrator of
  William Herbert.
- James Baker administrator of William
  Hebb.
- Vitus Herbert executor of Gilbert
  Turbevile.

Deputy Commissary (PG) to examine
accounts of:
- Anne Giddings executrix of Philip
  Giddings (PG).

GENERAL INDEX

Ralph 41
Sarah 208
William 58
Arnoldy
    John 24, 74, 116,
      164
Arrington
    Christ. 152
    Christo. 24
    Cornelius 184
Arthuron
    John 22
Ashcom
    Charles 131, 144,
      174, 191, 200,
      203, 211
    John 200
    Margaret 107, 147
    Nathaniel 107, 130,
      147, 170
    Samuel 130
Ashley
    John 70
Ashman
    John 51, 86, 140
    Richard 140
Askins
    Mary 205
    William 205
Atkinson
    James 213
    Robert 206
    Thomas 53, 181
Attkinson
    Thomas 208
Attwick
    John 23
Attwood
    Henry 4, 209
Atwick
    John 155
Austin
    Joseph 14
    William 108, 212
Aydelot
    William 166
Aydolett
    Benjamin 193
Ayler
    Henry 177, 188
    Mary 177
Ayres
    Henry 79
    William 11

Baggs
    John 157
Bagly
    Ralph 140
Bailey
    Elisabeth 89
    Henry 89
Baily
    Ann 52
    Henry 85
    John 173
Baimon
    John 22
Baker
    James 16, 42, 215
    John 6, 28, 39, 42,
      48, 51, 52, 62,
      63, 72, 78, 81,
      83, 84, 86, 89,
      107, 111, 115,
      116, 122, 123,
      128, 158, 161,
      168, 170, 193,
      199, 205, 209
    Maurice 86, 208
    Mr. 28
    Thomas 80
    William 131
Balch
    Hezekiah 126
Baldwin
    John 18, 24, 38,
      191
Bale
    Anthony 65
Ball
    Samuel 194
Ballard
    Charles 78, 96, 149
Banister
    Thomas 206
    William 207
Bannan
    John 153, 187
    Thomas 153, 187
Bannister
    Thomas 104
    William 104, 105,
      135
Bannon
    John 99
    Thomas 99

Beanes
  Lidia 168
Beans
  John 39
Beard
  John 18, 73, 74,
    88, 146
Beather
  William 95, 149
Beathers
  Mary 95
  Richard 95, 149
  William 149
Beaucham
  Dogett 194
  Edmon 79
  Thomas 162
Beauman
  John 61
Beaumans
  John 101
Beavan
  Charles 119
Beck
  John 175
  Jonathon 20, 29, 33
  Mary 29
Beckwith
  Henry 30, 54, 71
  Nehemiah 30, 48,
    54, 65, 71, 76,
    91, 115, 120,
    129, 141, 143,
    173, 191, 203,
    211
Becraft
  Rebecca 2, 19
Becwith
  Henry 10, 13
  Nehemiah 10, 13
Bedford
  Gunning 135
  Running 61
Beivan
  Thomas 193
Bell
  Adam 7, 34, 42, 52
  Ann 52
  Anne 7, 42
  Daniel 194, 203
Bellin
  Thomas 50
Belt
  Joseph 9, 17, 30,

  76, 196
Bennet
  James 154
  John 173
  Richard 114
Bennett
  James 49, 100, 109,
    177
  Richard 49
Benney
  James 156
Bennit
  Richard 22
Bennitt
  Richard 38
  William 36
Benson
  Edmond 196
  Edmund 212
  Nicholas 196
  Perry 11, 165, 197
  Rebecca 197
  William 140
Benton
  Francis 109
  Mary 109
Berroughs
  John 34
Berry
  Andrew 1
  Benjamin 44, 76,
    128
  John 69, 103
  Mary 45, 128
  Samuel 84
  Tamer 69
Bessuet
  Robert 214
Beswick
  Thomas 14, 24, 42,
    54, 69, 77, 98,
    152, 157, 158
  William 77
Beswik
  Thomas 24
Beveridge
  George 128, 200
Beverly
  George 89
Bexley
  William 103
Bickerdicke
  Richard 188
Bickerdike

Boone
   Jane 147
   John 91, 93, 147,
      200
   Robert 163
Borden
   John 136
Bordley
   Rachel 73, 145
   Thomas 38, 39, 73,
      190
Bordon
   John 136
   Margaret 136
Borroughs
   John 29
Bosman
   Frances 11
   Risdon 11
   Thomas 11
Boston
   Esau 50, 56, 149,
      167
   Isaac 50
Boteler
   Edward 68
   Henry 214
   Katherine 214
Botfield
   John 88
Boult
   Thomas 128
Bound
   James 15, 209
   William 15
Bounds
   James 104, 138
   John 195
   Rebecca 195
   Sarah 104
Bourk
   Cesely 10
Bourn
   Elisabeth 74, 107
Bourne
   Elisabeth 75
   Thomas 74
Bowdle
   Loftus 207
Bowen
   Abraham 112, 139,
      170
   Charles 112, 139,
      170

David 11, 12, 68,
   107
   Edward 79
   Elisabeth 79
   Isaac 112
   Jonas 1
Bowers
   James 85
Bowes
   Frances 132, 144,
      157
   George 132, 144,
      157, 197
Bowin
   Edward 105
   William 79
Bowles
   Mary 85
Boy
   Jane 55
Boyce
   Roger 64, 76
Boye
   Jane 77, 118
   John 20
   Pidgeon 77, 118
   Pigeon 20
Boyer
   John 107
Boyl
   Mary 37
Boyle
   Mary 64
Boyston
   Thomas 37
Bozman
   Blandina 201
   Blandinah 183
   John 60, 183, 201
   Risdon 151
   T. 98, 115, 144,
      151, 152, 211
   Thomas 97, 136,
      144, 173
Braburne
   William 81
Brackhon
   John 92
Bradburne
   Elisabeth 72
   William 72
Bradford
   John 45, 90, 93
   Thomas 78

Bradley
  Henry 23, 110
  Mary 65
Bradshaw
  John 69, 185
  Mary 175, 185, 194
  Thomas 175, 194,
    195
Brady
  Charles 72
  Elisabeth 16, 171,
    193
  Owen 16, 171
Bramell
  James 213
Brandt
  Jacob 26, 32, 33
Brannock
  John 141, 173
  Thomas 13, 48, 65,
    74, 76, 91, 115,
    117, 120, 129,
    143, 173, 191,
    203, 211
Branson
  John 39
  Michael 16, 39
Brassey
  John 209
Bratten
  Bruff 134
  Elisabeth 96, 134,
    149, 198
  James 104, 105, 150
  John 14, 96, 134,
    138, 149, 166,
    198
  Quandan 104
  Quantan 150
  Samuel 104
Bratton
  Bruff 167
Brauner
  John 45
  Mary 45
  William 45, 82
Bray
  Edward 96, 150
Brayfield
  John 87, 118, 187,
    210
Bredell
  Isaiah 166, 179
Breede

John 189
Brett
  George 1, 3, 210
  Henry 43, 55, 87,
    118
  Sarah 43, 87, 118
  Thomas 164
  William 1, 3
Brettargh
  Thomas 59, 65, 76,
    82, 91, 115,
    120, 129, 143,
    144, 173
Breward
  James 60
  Solomon 192
Brewer
  James 137
  John 45, 63, 89
  Joseph 45, 89
  William 7, 73, 190
Brian
  John 115
Brice
  John 106
Bright
  Francis 164, 174,
    177
  Thomas 164, 174,
    177
Briney
  Edward 35, 36
Brinney
  Edward 30
Briscoe
  Ann 52
  George 128, 168
  John 52
  Mary 128
  Philip 128
Bristoe
  Anne 29
  John 29
Bristor
  Anne 27
  John 27
Bristow
  John 33
Brogden
  Richard 69, 152,
    157
Brome
  John 37, 74
Bromwell

Rebecca 14, 197
Brook
    Elisabeth 12, 147,
        187
    Grace 46, 80
    Henry 8
    Robert 46, 80
    Roger 147, 187
    Thomas 213
Brooke
    Elisabeth 25, 182
    Henry 8
    Jane 2
    John 2, 12, 107
    Leonard 16, 200
    Richard 16
    Roger 12, 25, 183
Brookes
    John 4
Brooks
    Elisabeth 164
    Leonard 12, 34, 82
    Richard 34, 82
    Robert 64
    Roger 164
Brooksbank
    Abraham 34
    Anne 34
Brooksby
    Cornelius 164
Brotten
    John 206
Broughton
    John 180
Brown
    Adam 20
    Edward 108
    Francis 168
    James 20, 107
    John 14, 44, 49,
        50, 93, 99, 136,
        147, 153, 168,
        170, 194
    Judith 49, 99, 153
    Martha 93
    Rosannah 183
    Signey 56
    Thomas 53
    William 71
Brownbitt
    Henry 138
Browne
    Adam 155
    Elisabeth 116

George 105
John 12, 75, 102,
    149, 159
Martha 147
Mary 137
Thomas 15, 183
Browning
    Anne 119, 135
    Thomas 47, 101,
        119, 135, 165,
        175, 189
Browsbank
    Edward 8
Browsbanks
    Edward 8
    Rachell 8
Bruce
    John 66
    Judith 66
Bruff
    Cathrine 10, 31
    Katharine 46
    Kathe. 57
    Thomas 10, 31, 33,
        46, 57
Bruffett
    John 175
Brumwell
    Rebecca 54, 181
Bryan
    Cornelius 154
    Edward 74, 119,
        176, 210
    Hannah 112, 115,
        154
    John 112, 119
    Sarah 73
    Terence 119
Bryant
    John 119
    Morte 22, 153
Bryarly
    Anne 159
Bryon
    Cor. 32
    Cornelius 100
    Edward 135
    Hanah 32
    Hannah 100
Buck
    John 7
Buckannan
    Mary 163, 174
    Thomas 163, 174,

213
Buckingham
   Katharine 88, 89,
      125
   Thomas 88, 89, 125
Buckley
   Richard 213
Bucknall
   Mary 89
   Thomas 70, 89, 111,
      126
Bucknam
   John 55
Buley
   John 40
Bullen
   Henry 4, 10
   John 121, 173
Bullock
   Anne 98
   Francis 207
   Joseph 55, 88, 89,
      99
   Martha 207
Buly
   John 46
Burch
   John 119, 140, 180,
      203
Burdin
   John 177
Burgess
   Henry 207
Burgin
   Sutton 84
Burk
   John 40
Burle
   John 4
Burne
   John 209
   Patrick 209
Burnell
   William 10
Burnham
   Anne 124
   Gabriel 120, 124
   Gabrill 200
Burnyatt
   John 53
Burrell
   Anne 142
   Elisabeth 159, 193,
      215

Samuel 142
Burrill
   Samuel 185
Burrough
   Elisabeth 44
   Richard 44
Burroughs
   Elisabeth 50
   John 48
   Richard 50
   William 60
Burton
   Anne 139
   Thomas 27
Busey
   George 186, 199,
      203
   Mary Ann 186
   Paul 40, 187
   Sarah 40, 187
Bush
   John 69, 152, 157
Buterworth
   Jane 35
Butler
   Edward 125
Butt
   John 37, 94
Buttenshire
   Thomas 132
Butterworth
   Isaac 186
   Jane 83
   Michael 35, 83
Buttler
   Cecill 199
   John 192, 193
   Margaret 199
   Margarett 209
Button
   John 142, 176
   Mary 142, 176
Butts
   John 110, 111

Cadell
   John 55
Cage
   William 90, 92, 94
Caldwell
   John 22
Callaghace
   Ferdinando 108

Page 224

Callahon
 Darby 41
 Mary 41
Calvert
 Cha. 191
 Charles 191, 201
Camble
 John 61, 135, 189
Cammeron
 John 64
Campbell
 Frances 40, 92
 Francis 146
 James 92, 102, 145,
  146, 162
 John 20
 Walter 59
Canaday
 Daniel 107
 Jane 107
Canida
 Daniel 85
 Jane 85
Caniday
 Daniel 135
Cannon
 James 97, 151, 162
 Rasanna 97
 Rosanna 151, 162
 Thomas 126
Canon
 James 15
Cantwell
 Edward 185
 Hannah 185
Capell
 Isabell 48
Carbery
 John Baptista 7
 John Bta. 128
Carey
 Anne 180
 Robert 180, 181
Carlyle
 Alexander 22
Carmichaell
 John 193
Carney
 Edward 126, 186
Carr
 Thomas 160
Carrington
 Henry 161
Carroll

Charles 18, 32,
  105, 112, 116,
  146, 163, 174,
  192, 196, 204
 Daniel 18, 116, 146
 James 105, 116,
  130, 146, 163
 John 73, 145, 146,
  168
 Mary 73, 145, 146
Carsey
 David 206
Carslake
 John 54
Carter
 Daniel 5, 19
 Darby 200
 John 63
 Ruth 5
 Val. 212
 Valentine 63
Casey
 Philip 24, 103
Cash
 Edward 188
Caslick
 John 180
Catling
 William 79
Catnor
 Elinor 97
Catton
 William 19, 38, 91
Caudry
 Daniel 78, 104, 167
Caulk
 Jacob 135
Causeen
 John 2, 118
 William 2
Caval
 Christopher 35
Cavenah
 Elisabeth 26, 153
Cavener
 Elisabeth 109
Cavinah
 Patrick 177
Cay
 John 52
 Jonathon 102, 117,
  162
Cecill
 James 35

Cermichell
  John 35
Chaires
  John 108, 109, 163
Chairs
  John 163
  Katharine 163
Chandler
  John 2, 87
  Thomas 70
Chaplin
  William 127
Chapman
  Anne 26
  Edward 140
  Richard 6, 12, 37,
    188, 192
  Robert 208
  William 24, 212
Chares
  John 43
  Kathe. 43
Charlescraft
  John 82
Chatham
  Edward 129
Cheattell
  William 71
Cheeny
  Edward 127
Cheseldyne
  Kenelm 121
  Kenelmn 34
  Kenlem 148
  Kennelmn 6
  Mary 6, 121, 148
Cheshire
  John 164
Chetham
  Edward 44, 143,
    171, 172
Chevous
  John 194
Chew
  Elisabeth 48, 92,
    103
  Henry 12
  John 48, 92, 103
  Joseph 76
  Samuel 36, 48, 92,
    103, 116, 142,
    146
  Samuell 92
  William 116, 124,

    165
Chillcutt
  Anthony 117
Ching
  John 126, 210, 211
  Mary 126
Chinton
  Elinor 19
Chittam
  John 205
  Winifred 205
Chonvo
  John 150
Chouvo
  John 79
Chove
  John 167
Christian
  Thomas 59
Chuvly
  Samuel 127
Clagett
  Charles 132
  Thomas 93, 130
Claggett
  Thomas 147
Clark vs. Mason
  192 1
Clark
  Abraham 182, 192
  Anne 147
  Daniel 183
  David 141, 192
  Dennis 17, 41, 60
  Edward 69
  John 1, 15, 33, 39,
    57, 126, 185
  Joshua 6
  Mary 39, 41, 66,
    90, 199
  Samuel 9, 17, 41,
    60, 199
  Tabitha 15
  Thomas 39, 66, 75,
    87, 90, 140,
    147, 161
  William 92, 132,
    147
Clarke
  Caleb 156
  Dennis 9, 199
  Edward 6, 133
  George 16
  John 21, 25

Thomas 11, 143,
152, 153, 156,
157, 179
Collings
Thomas 134
Collins
Andrew 133
Arabella 95, 149
Cornelius 91, 97
John 95, 108, 109,
149
Jonathon 189
Mary 162, 178
Price 162, 206
Samuel 50
Sarah 97, 145, 152,
182
Thomas 133, 166,
206
William 178, 198
Collter
Thomas 98
Colt
Dorothy 9
Comb
Simon 16
Combes
Enoch 128
Simon 200
Comegeys
Guybertus 23
Comegys
William 192
Comerford
George 25, 28, 31,
38
Compton
John 2
Conally
Daniel 34, 35
Condon
James 109
Connar
Arthur 126
Conner
Arthur 53, 182
Darby 59
John 134
Nathaniel 26
Philip 134
Conoway
Dennis 183, 192
Contee
Alexander 1, 3, 6,

8, 20, 43, 45,
46, 55, 66, 67,
75, 77, 87, 110,
117, 171, 186
John 186, 192
Conyer
Henry 71
Conyers
Henry 57
Sarah 57
Cood
John 34, 83
William 168
Coode
Anne 34, 80, 83
John 80
William 52
Cook
William 64, 111
Cooks
John 98
Cookson
John 137
Cooley
George 53
Cooly
Daniel 16
Coombes
Mary 123
Thomas 123
Cooper
Edward 21, 111
George 182
John 1, 18, 55, 75
Jonathon 56, 139
Mary 56
Nathaniel 52
Nathaniell 81
Thomas 34, 205
Corbes
Samuel 123
Corbesly
Samuel 51, 52
Corbeslye
Samuel 78
Cord
Thomas 64, 70, 184,
185
Corne
Thomas 29, 102,
155, 156
Cornelius
John 5, 187
Sarah 5

Mary 92, 106
Patrick 92, 106
Creatchett
  William 16, 90
Creed
  Kathe. 71
Cretchet
  William 42
Cretchett
  William 212
Cromwell
  John 22, 36, 51
Crook
  James 205
Cropper
  John 162
Cross
  Elinor 24, 38, 40,
    74, 116
  Hannah 116, 200
  Mary 38
  Robert 116, 164,
    200
  Thomas 24
Crouch
  Anne 7
  Elisabeth 179, 207
  James 7
  Josiah 127
  Josias 158
  Robert 179, 207
  Thomas 58
Crowley
  Daniel 6
  Elinor 6
Crudgenton
  Roger 106
Crump
  Heneritta 98, 152
  Henrietta 30
  Walter 30, 98, 152,
    157
Crundwell
  Joseph 104
Crutchley
  Thomas 106
Cullen
  James 57
  John 38, 162
  Mary 97, 126
  Peter 97, 126
  Sarah 135
  William 135, 176
Cullins

Sarah 210
William 210
Cumbton
  John 55
  Mathew 55
Cumin
  William 28
Cuming
  William 39
Cumming
  Elisabeth 125, 129,
    190
  William 41, 88,
    118, 125, 129,
    143, 144, 171,
    173, 174, 175,
    190, 204
Cunclift
  Henry 123
Cundlift
  Henry 78
Cunliffe
  Henry 51
Curtis
  James 134, 194, 206
Cusack
  George 34
Cutchin
  Alice 76
  Robert 185
Cutler
  William 63, 158

D'hoof
  Henry 189
Dafft
  Charles 158, 171,
    209
  Elisabeth 158, 209
Dahley
  John 32
Daines
  John 162
Dallicoat
  James 94
Dalton
  William 78
Damper
  Daniel 101
  Johana 101
Dampier
  Daniel 29, 112
  Johanna 29, 112

Dancy
    Peter 100
    Sarah 100
Dansey
    Martha 130, 144,
        174, 191, 203,
        211
Darby
    Susanah 101
    William 60, 83, 101
Dare
    William 20, 33, 61,
        101, 135, 155,
        202, 212
Darick
    John 106
Darnall
    Henry 116, 146, 163
    Juliana 26
Dash
    Oswald 34
Dashiel
    Robert 95
    Sarah 95
Dashield
    Robert 105
    Sarah 105
Dashiell
    George 21, 25, 57,
        78
    James 25
    Robert 21
    Sarah 21
Dauson
    James 208
Davis
    Edward 9, 23, 70,
        137, 155, 158
    Francis 189
    Henry 181
    John 8, 54, 74
    Mary 70, 155, 158
    Nicholas 2, 3
    Richard 8, 192
    Robert 193
    Samuel 79, 96, 150,
        167
    Sarah 162
    Thomas 7, 90, 162
    William 170
Davison
    John 50
Dawkins
    William 74, 132,

198, 204, 205
Dawson
    Anne 15, 54, 97,
        122, 151, 152,
        213
    James 11, 58, 59,
        69, 88
    John 54, 82, 97,
        122, 151, 152,
        195, 210, 212,
        213
    Richard 210
    Susannah 210
    Thomas 73
Day
    Mathew 3
    Robert 169, 170,
        184, 195, 205
    Sarah 169, 170,
        184, 205
Dayle
    James 50
Dean
    Elisabeth 210
    John 123, 206, 209,
        210
    Mary 39, 123, 206
    Michael 210
    William 100, 155
Deane
    William 8
Deavers
    Elisabeth 11
    James 11
Deavor
    Antle 70
    Gilbert 74
    Richard 208
Deavour
    Elisabeth 74, 205
    Gilbert 75, 205
    James 107
Debruler
    Peter 70
Decrego
    William 168
Delahunt
    Daniel 113
Delhoser
    Daniel 82
Dellicoat
    Elisabeth 209
    James 209
Delliose

Egan
  Charles 141, 145,
    171
  Elinor 141, 145
Elbert
  Frances 54
  William 54
Elder
  John 38
Elles
  William 176
Ellidge
  Joseph 160
Elliot
  John 186
  William 128
Elliott
  William 187, 202
Ellis
  John 60, 84
  Mary 141
  William 60, 141
Ellott
  William 45
Ellrod
  Peter 202
  Sarah 202
Elsey
  Jane 213
Elzey
  Peter 105
Emanuell
  James 213
Emerson
  (N) 209
  Anne 29
  Katherine 199
  Thomas 29
Emmerson
  Anne 98, 152
  Katharine 88
  Thomas 58, 71, 88,
    98, 112, 152,
    199
Emmery
  Daniel 64
Emms
  Thomas 124
Emory
  Arthur 99, 102,
    154, 163
  John 49
Empey
  George 99

Emry
  Daniel 12
England
  Elisabeth 119, 169
  Isaac 119, 169, 181
Ennalls
  Elisabeth 10, 97
  Henry 59, 97, 110,
    140, 144, 151
  John 97, 110, 140,
    151
  Thomas 10, 97, 115
  William 115, 182,
    196
Ennis
  Elisabeth 178
  Nathaniel 178
  William 56, 178
Ensor
  Abraham 111
  Elisabeth 111
Ereckson
  Charles 25
  Elisheba 25
Erreckson
  Charles 153, 170
  Elishabe 170
  Elisheba 153
Eruin
  William 162
Ervin
  Francis 114
  George 117, 162
  John 114
Erwing
  Frances 56
  Francis 135, 166
  John 56, 135
Esam
  Benjamin 104
Eskridge
  Abigall 80
  William 80
Eton
  Thomas 143
Eubank
  Thomas 9
  William 9
Eubanks
  Richard 100, 152
  Thomas 100, 152
Evans
  Elisabeth 79
  John 79, 80, 199,

203
Mary 179
Richard 73, 190
Walter 14, 179
Weighborough 148
William 95, 148
Williams 179
Wyborough 95
Eyre
Robert 135

Fairbank
David 24
Fairbanks
David 88, 103
Fairbrother
Oliver 141
Falcom
Peter 31, 100, 154
Falconar
Gilbert 112
Falkenar
Jacob 212
Falkner
Ralph 212
Fall
Abraham 14, 96, 149
Mary 14, 96, 149
Fanning
John 40, 113, 204
Farrow
John 100
Robert 26, 32, 154
Farthing
William Maria 62,
117
Faucit
John 178
Tabitha 178
William 79, 96,
149, 167
Faucitt
Ann 198
John 198
Faulkner
Jacob 156
Fausit
William 134
Fawset
John 79
Fawsett
John 194
Fearson

Percival 168
Feddeman
Phil. 10, 57
Philip 65, 71, 82,
109, 117, 122
Phillip 46
Fedeman
Philip 13
Fee
George 10, 30, 99
Feilder
Barbary 52
William 52
Felk
Ann 131
Fellows
John 98, 143, 152
Robert 98, 143,
152, 182
Fendall
John 87
Fenton
Moses 79
Fenwick
Cuthbert 72, 84,
117, 162
Enoch 72, 117, 162
Ignatius 72, 84,
117, 162
John 72, 84, 117,
162
Richard 72, 84,
117, 162
Ferguson
Elisabeth 23
George 23
Ferrell
Mathew 2, 20
Ferrill
Daniel 113
Ferson
Percivall 12
Field
Christ. 54, 151
Christo. 98
Christopher 30
Elisabeth 30, 98,
151
Filleman
Joseph 14
Fillingham
Martha 100, 155
Richard 100, 155
Finch

John 201
Gorden
  Mary 160
  Robert 50, 160
Gordon
  Robert 187
Gormathon
  Michael 185
Gorsuch
  Charles 72
  John 113, 186
  Robert 72, 103,
    185, 186
  Thomas 72, 121
Goslin
  John 150
  Peter 116
Gosling
  James 194
  John 194
Got
  Richard 92
Gott
  Richard 92, 146
Gouldens
  William 189
Gouldesborough
  Robert 58, 144
  William 95, 148
Goulding
  William 189
Goule
  Christopher 22
Gover
  Ephraim 169
Grace
  Thomas 16
Granger
  Christo. 26
Grasly
  Samuel 86
Grastey
  Samuell 62
Grasty
  Anne 62
Graven
  Christo. 26
Graves
  William 47
Gray
  Johana 102
  John 3, 4, 9, 13,
    14, 19, 27, 41,
    47, 65, 74, 76,

96, 149, 167
  Margaret 74, 75,
    96, 112, 150
  Miles 96, 150
  Thomas 4, 9, 13,
    27, 41, 47, 65,
    76
  Zachry 3, 19
Green
  Agnus 162
  J. 41, 47, 65
  James 162, 176
  John 28, 98, 153
  Leonard 191
  Mary 124, 129, 143,
    174, 191
  Philip 3
  Robert 158
Greenberry
  Charles 127
Greenfield
  James 114
  T. T. 94, 144, 148,
    174
  Thomas 114
  Thomas Truman 81,
    83, 95, 114
Greening
  Albertus 116, 164
Greenwell
  John 63
Greenwood
  Thomas 103, 121
Greeves
  John 204
Gregory
  Jacob 156
  Joseph 183, 212
Gresham
  John 202
Greves
  John 169
Grienfield
  James 2
  Thomas 2
Griffen
  Bernard 188, 214
  Lewis 141
  Susannah 188, 214
  William 196
Griffin
  Francis 110
  John 104, 110
  Lewis 176

Mary 104
Richard 28, 52
Thomas 86
Griffith
Abraham 210
Benjamin 137
Edward 130
Elisabeth 12
John 138, 210
Samuel 12, 107, 169
Griggs
George 63
John 51
Grinin
Albert 24
Groom
Samuel 198
Groome
Samuel 135
Groves
William 20
Grundy
Issabell 103
John 209
Margarett 18
Robert 18, 24, 65,
91, 98, 115,
121, 127, 129,
144, 157, 174,
199, 204, 209,
211
Sarah 209
Thomas 103
Guichard
Samuel 106
Guilshiott
Lawrence 112
Gullett
William 194
Gunby
John 104
Gutherick
William 29
Gutherie
William 34
Guthrick
William 94
Guthrie
William 145, 148,
157
Gutridge
Henry 2
Guttery
Patrick 194

Guy
William 162
Guybert
Thomas 7
Guyther
John 72
Mary 52
Gwin
John 177
Gwinn
John 177
Mary 177
Gyant
Anne 70
John 70

Hacket
Hester 109
John 108
Hackett
John 154
Michael 85
William 108, 109,
154
Hadder
Warren 96, 130, 149
Haddock
James 40, 50, 81,
119, 120, 147,
187
Hader
Warren 14
Hagan
Dr. 147
Thomas 67, 75
Hague
Elisabeth 18, 27,
55
Haines
John 52, 83
Joyce 52, 83
Hale
Christopher 106
Diana 131
Mathew 68, 131
Hales
Roger 180
Haley
Elisabeth 2, 111,
118
John 2
Hall
Acquila 129, 143,

160, 174
Alexander 104
Aquila 125, 126,
   191
Benjamin 105, 139,
   159, 197
Christ. 155
Christopher 169
Edward 9, 29, 34,
   65, 93, 126,
   146, 185
Johanna 126
John 70, 125, 126,
   146, 185
Joseph 18
Mary 139
Mat. 22
Richard 6
Robert 40, 62, 81,
   104, 147, 187
Halpen
   Elisabeth 176
Halpin
   Elisabeth 82, 141,
      151
Hambleton
   Andrew 36, 81
   John 17, 122
   William 116
Hamett
   Robert 16, 52
Hamilton
   Andrew 11, 119
   John 93
   William 113, 131
Hammett
   Cathrine 16, 52
   Robert 16
Hammilton
   John 173
Hammond
   Charles 127
   Edward 95, 148, 207
   Frances 43, 171
   John 39
   Katherine 199
   Mary 142
   Mord. 136, 173
   Mordecai 43, 47,
      49, 65, 90, 115,
      120, 129, 143,
      160, 171, 184,
      192, 212
   Phil. 17, 18, 19

Phillip 39
Rachel 127
Thomas 113, 173
Hammott
   Katherine 42
   Robert 42
Hamond
   Phil. 7, 24
   Philip 5
   Thomas 4
Hampton
   John 5, 23, 79,
      150, 194
   Mary 5
   Thomas 6
Hancock
   Edward 124
   John 40, 59
Hancok
   John 40
Handy
   Ebenezar 197
   Jane 25
   John 130
   Priscilla 197
   Samuel 79, 197
   William 23
Hanson
   Benjamin 20, 55,
      125, 201
   Dorothy 61, 127,
      137
   Frederick 40
   Fredrick 106
   George 84
   Hans 84
   Henry 205
   Jonathon 161
   Robert 43, 55, 61,
      118, 127, 137
   Samuel 27, 32, 126,
      140, 160, 168,
      175, 187, 196
Harbert
   Ann 89
   John 89
   Vitus 158
   William 158
Harcom
   John 67
   William 46, 60, 67
Harcum
   John 84
   William 1, 83, 84

Harden
    Edward 63
Hardin
    Edward 37, 103
    Joseph 28
    Thomas 23
Harding
    Edward 152
    John 62
    Thomas 9
Hardisty
    Thomas 122
Hardy
    Elisabeth 94, 148
    William 81, 94, 148
Hardyn
    John 137
    Joseph 115
Hardyne
    Joan 52
    Joseph 52
Hargesson
    Elisabeth 10
    George 10
Hargis
    Thomas 148
Harison
    Richard 20
Harney
    Philip 16
Harper
    Mary 110, 183, 195
    William 71, 110,
        117, 176, 183,
        195
Harrahan
    John 72
Harrard
    Pheby 83
    William 83
Harris
    Daniel 153
    Edward 177
    George 170
    Issaac 22, 35
    James 1, 17, 23,
        33, 40, 41, 46,
        59, 68, 70, 77,
        78, 81, 83, 84,
        106, 107, 113,
        118, 137, 157,
        180, 192
    John 4, 47, 188,
        214

    Joseph 188, 214
    Richard 118, 178
    Sarah 48, 130
    Thomas 48, 106, 130
    William 28, 30, 33,
        75, 90, 170,
        171, 188, 214
Harrison
    Francis 54
    John 36, 53, 152
    Joseph 2, 18, 20,
        27, 32, 43, 55,
        82, 94, 148
    Priscilla 75
    Richard 43, 55, 67,
        82, 148
    Robert 36
    Samuel 51, 67, 83,
        116
    Sarah 53, 152
    William 36, 54, 62,
        63, 75, 87, 115,
        122, 152, 157,
        158, 159, 204
Harry
    Edward 63, 146
Hart
    Arthur 57, 82, 97,
        110, 122
    Richard 57, 97,
        110, 122
Hartley
    Jos. 137
Hartloe
    Joseph 181
Harvey
    Thomas 17, 26, 32,
        93
    William 99, 109
Harvie
    Thomas 110
Harwood
    John 3, 110
    Peter 53, 54, 69
    Pheby 51
    Richard 7
    William 51
Hasler
    William 95, 148
Hatcher
    Thomas 140
Hatchman
    Thomas 185
Hatfield

Page 243

George 131
John 29, 33
Hitherington
Elisabeth 29
Thomas 29, 156
Hithrington
Thomas 101
Hix
Roger 1
Hockens
John 73
Hodson
John 97
Hogg
James 138, 178
Hoggin
John 167
Hoggins
John 151
Holbrook
Thomas 14, 194
Holdbrook
John 95
Thomas 95, 149
Holden
Joshua 94
Holdson
Henry 177
Holdsworth
Thomas 54, 62, 80
Holeadger
Philip 59, 60
Holebrook
Thomas 149
Holladay
George 49
Holland
Col. 201
Elisabeth 166, 206
Fran. 1
Francis 19, 63, 65,
68, 70, 83, 89,
111, 185
Jacob 4
John 14, 62, 74,
133, 159
Nehemiah 166, 167,
194, 206
Otho 71
Richard 14, 50, 149
Thomas 3, 4, 39,
65, 83, 126
William 39, 40, 65,
73, 83, 92, 134,

142, 146, 161,
191, 201, 209
Winifred 62
Winifret 159
Holliday
George 136, 188
James 131
Jonathon 43
Thomas 114
Hollingshead
Francis 204
Hollingsworth
Robert 136
Hollins
Robert 108
William 109
Hollis
Clark 125, 186
William 125
Hollyday
Jonathon 75
Holman
Edward 84, 180
Holmas
Thomas 164, 190
Holmes
Thomas 38
Holsteen
Andrew 54
Holstien
Andrew 24
Frances 24
Holston
Joseph 149
Holtam
John 85
Hood
Thomas 91, 92
Hook
Roger 198
William 210
Hooper
Anne 36, 97, 151
Henry 109, 110, 127
Mary 109
Richard 36, 97,
110, 151
Hope
George 185
Judith 185
Hopewell
Francis 194, 203
Hugh 52, 72, 107
John 37

Richard 7, 63, 81,
   116
Hopkins
   Ann 22
   Dennis 53, 207
   Elisabeth 30, 42,
     69
   Johanna 88
   John 22, 42, 47,
     68, 83, 93, 146,
     166
   Jonathon 4, 9, 13,
     27, 41, 47, 65,
     76, 88, 129
   Joseph 53, 55
   Nathaniel 79
   Phil. 23
   Philip 4, 88
   Robert 6, 30, 35,
     42
   Samuel 14, 21, 47,
     49, 56, 57, 77,
     78, 104, 130,
     132, 135, 138,
     166, 178
   Samuell 193, 197,
     200
   Thomas 6
Hopper
   David 43
Hore
   John 61
Horn
   John 200
Horne
   Henry 39, 63, 86,
     117, 123
   John 63
   Sarah 63, 117, 123
Horney
   Philip 23, 69
Horsey
   Nathaniel 213
   Nathaniell 209
   Stephen 14
Hoskins
   Ann 192, 203, 211
   Bennet 212
   Charles 123
   John 62, 171, 192
   Oswald 212
   Peter 98, 152, 182
   Philip 118
   William 118, 192,

     203, 211
Houlton
   William 57
Housekin
   Peter 29
Houston
   Robert 79, 80
   Thomas 79
How
   Thomas 26
Howard
   Benjamin 67, 86,
     116, 121
   Charles 71
   Cornelius 176
   Elisabeth 119
   John 94, 113, 116,
     121, 160
   Mary 128, 206
   Michael 59
   Mordecai 76
   Nathaniel 128, 171
   Nathaniell 206
   Thomas 32, 33, 38
   William 119, 137
Howe
   Sarah 132
   Thomas 132
Howel
   Francis 90
Howell
   Evan 16, 84, 90, 95
   Frances 16, 95
   John 213
   Philip 5
   Samuell 170
   Thomas 71
   William 11
Howes
   Thomas 178
Howston
   Robert 138
Huddlestone
   George 33
Hudson
   Denis 207
   Dennis 133
   Ellis 133
   Henry 133, 134,
     166, 207
   John 110, 151
   Jonathon 166
   Richard 166
   Robert 166

Hues
    John 205
Huff
    John 157
Huggins
    Turlo 69
Hughs
    Hu. 113
    Thomas 72
Hungerford
    Edmond 204
    Penelope 204
Hunt
    John 22
    William 40, 84, 85,
      101
Hunter
    Samuel 31, 100, 154
    William 111, 161
Hurlock
    James 37
Husband
    James 202
    John 112
    William 6
Husitt
    Philip 70
Huskins
    Peter 145, 157
Hutchin
    Franc. 35
Hutchins
    Francis 33, 72
    James 73
    Robert 5, 34, 72,
      116
    William 34
Hutchison
    Gavin 189
Huthins
    William 5
Hutton
    Charles 120, 180
Hyland
    Mellice 61, 77, 189
    Nicholas 5, 61, 77,
      85, 189
Hynson
    Charles 40, 180
    John 84, 103, 141,
      155
    Nath. 195
    Nathaniel 40, 84,
      101, 155, 202

    Thomas 68, 180

Iago
    Richard 26
Ibettson
    Francis 147
Impey
    George 99
    Joanna 31
    Johanna 154
    William 31, 154
Impy
    Johanna 100
    William 100
Inch
    John 25, 70, 125
Ingram
    John 7, 44, 67
Innes
    William 203
Innis
    William 194
Insley
    James 36
    William 15, 36
Ireland
    John 62, 183, 192
    Thomas 20
Irvan
    George 102
Irvin
    George 52
Irving
    Francis 213
    John 80
Israel
    John 102, 113, 116,
      121, 124, 125,
      126, 130, 185,
      196, 201, 208
Israell
    John 86, 131, 160,
      213

Jack
    John 137
Jackson
    Barbara 31, 154,
      188
    Barbary 49, 100,
      154, 177
    Barbery 100

Kellam
  John 56, 80
  Tabitha 96, 149
  William 96, 149
Kelly
  James 16
  John 28, 39
Kemball
  John 98, 152
Kemble
  John 29
Kemp
  Shadreck 58, 59
  William 123
Kendall
  Thomas 166
Kendelo
  Thomas 148
Kendeloe
  Thomas 16
Keneday
  Hugh 24
Kenman
  John 169
Kennard
  Richard 1
Kennerly
  Darby 179
Kennet
  Catharine 178
  John 95, 148, 201
  William 95, 178,
    179, 201
Kennett
  John 180
  William 148, 198
Kennyman
  John 46, 147
Kent
  John 132
  Robert 26
Kerby
  Anne 100, 154
  Benjamin 195
  Elisabeth 195
  William 100, 154,
    199
Kerr
  Robert 32, 94
Kersey
  John 207
Kersly
  John 193
Key

Philip 144, 145
Keys
  John 19
Kibbe
  William 97
Kibble
  William 104, 167
Kidd
  Sarah 64, 75
Killam
  Tabitha 206
  William 206
Killingsworth
  John 21
Killy
  John 202
  Judith 202
  Patrick 202
Kimble
  Rowland 64
Kimborough
  Rowland 184
Kinderick
  Thomas 128
King
  Benjamin 209
  Charles 7, 16, 29,
    34, 45, 90, 94
  Frances 197
  Francis 171
  Henry 23, 37, 98,
    114, 121, 152,
    182
  John 16, 52, 72,
    107
  Julian 99, 102,
    154, 163
  Juliana 26
  Richard 64, 125,
    141, 146
  Robert 104
  Thomas 1, 18, 45,
    55, 75, 94
  Walter 213
Kinimont
  Ambross 136
  Francis 6
Kinnimont
  Alexander 156, 183
  Ambros 156
  John 136
Kirby
  Anne 31
  Thomas 16

William 31, 63
Kirk
   Bridgett 56
   Brigett 206
   John 56, 59, 80,
     162, 206
Knatchbull
   Norton 49, 66, 114
Knight
   Stephen 20, 107
Knowles
   James 177
Knowlman
   Anthony 127, 158

Lackey
   John 40
Lamar
   John 62
Lambert
   Joseph 4, 9, 33,
     43, 117, 171,
     172
Lambeth
   Richard 140, 186,
     187
Lancaster
   Richard 30, 93, 102
Langford
   Vincent 29, 34, 40,
     63
Langley
   John 17
   Moor 17
Langly
   William 168, 193
Lanham
   Josias 8
Lankford
   Joseph 134
Lant
   Laurence 25
Lappidge
   Edward 33
Larey
   Daniel 95, 149
   Mary 95, 96, 149,
     150
Larke
   Daniel 18
Larkin
   Thomas 39, 59, 115,
     129, 145, 171,

190, 204
Larkins
   Thomas 18, 38
Larramore
   Roger 202
Lary
   Daniel 15
   Mary 56, 105
Lashley
   John 30
Lashly
   John 9, 17
Laughlan
   Gillian 205
   John 205, 214
Laurance
   Robert 39
Laurence
   Ann 35
   Benjamin 124, 127,
     129, 160, 202
   Henry 35
   Joseph 16
   Noah 47, 84, 101,
     119
   Rachel 127, 129,
     144, 160
Lawes
   Thomas 166
Lawrence
   Ann 52
   Benjamin 144
   Henry 52
   William 62
Laws
   Robert 56
   Thomas 56
Lawson
   Richard 176
   Robert 22
Lawton
   Thomas 72
Layfield
   Anne 15
   Robert 15
Leakie
   John 74
Leakings
   John 90
Leckie
   John 38, 145
Leckin
   John 36
Lecompt

Loften
    Frances 32, 94
    John 32, 94
Logwood
    Richard 133
Lomax
    Aaron 171
    Cleabourn 176
    Cleborn 140
    Cleborne 87
Lomus
    Aaron 213
Loney
    Arrabello 111
    William 111
Long's Addition
    xx 174
Long
    John 49
    Susannah 163, 174
    Thomas 131, 163,
        174, 186
Longwood
    Richard 56
Loockerman
    Gov. 59
    Govert 117, 141
    Jacob 88
Lord
    James 143, 156, 182
    Judith 143, 156,
        182
Loutherland
    John 169
Love
    John 24, 89, 98
    Rebecca 89, 98
Loveday
    Sarah 63, 103
Low
    Elisabeth 36, 59,
        114
    Elisbeth 53
    Henry 113
    John 22
    Nicholas 121
    William 22, 36
Lowcock
    William 155
Lowcocks
    William 60
Lowden
    Thomas 213
Lowdes

Charles 49
Lowe
    Bennet 55, 113
    Elisabeth 85, 114,
        121, 122, 144,
        174, 191, 203,
        211
    Henry 55, 113, 197
    John 1, 146
    Margaret 114
    Mary 197
    Nicholas 53, 85,
        114, 122, 136,
        144, 162, 174,
        191, 203, 211
    Thomas 148
    William 1, 146, 195
Lowkock
    William 23
Loyall
    William 83
Loyd
    (N) 209
    Col. 47, 48, 57
    James 57, 58, 211
    Madam 48
    Phile. 47
    Philemon 58
    Sarah 57
Lucas
    Thomas 128
Ludingham
    John 69
Ludwell
    William 124
Luke
    Isaac 56, 139
Lukes
    Isaac 96, 150
Lynam
    Ann 74, 80
    John 74, 80, 123

Macbride
    David 60
Maccambly
    Daniel 27
Maccarty
    John 161
Maccentos
    Daniel 64
Macclester
    John 60

124, 130, 145,
157
Timothy 127, 141
Macomus
Alexander 36
William 36
Maconnakin
John 108
Macormick
Mary 210
Thomas 210
Madden
John 23
Maddin
Cathrine 15
John 16, 81, 106
Maddox
Alexander 56
James 2, 37, 94,
111
Lazarus 133
Mary 56
Samuel 51
Maddux
Lazarus 134
Madkin
Theod. 141
Madrin
Peter 46
Madring
Peter 64
Magner
John 119
Magruder
John 21
Ninian 21, 186
Samuel 21, 113,
159, 186
Maham
Edward 131
Mahann
Timothy 140
Mahey
Edward 1
Major
Edm. 3
Makin
James 206
Malden
Elisabeth 132, 195
James 132
William 132
Mallahane
Mary 117

Patrick 117
Man
George 106, 164
Maning
Cornelius 7
John 1, 3, 7
Joseph 1
Mankin
Josias 111
Stephen 110, 176
Manning
Cornelius 199, 205
Elisabeth 199
Gregory 195, 204,
214
John 195, 204
Joseph 3
Mansell
Robert 30
Manuell
James 50, 96, 150,
167
March
John 139, 175
Marchment
Samuel 14
Mariarte
Daniel 92
Edward 92
Mariartee
Daniel 33, 108,
129, 146, 188
Edward 24, 33, 108,
146, 188
Marloe
Edward 140
Marrett
William 15, 117
Marriott
Augustine 48
John 48
Joseph 48
Marrott
Phillis 97
William 97
Marsey
Nicholas 49, 100,
153
Marsh
Thomas 38
Marshall
Mary 55, 185
Thomas 45, 64, 127
William 9, 55, 64,

68, 185

Martain
Catherine 207
Francis 207
William 136

Martin
Edward 138, 198
Elisabeth 43, 76
Francis 162
George 56, 179
James 43, 76
Jane 98, 153
John 7, 196
Katherine 162
Margaret 108, 154
Michael 196
Robert 50, 96, 138,
150, 213
Thomas 54, 89, 98,
125, 143, 153,
156, 182, 207
William 108, 154

Martindale
Elisabeth 6, 98,
151, 153
Henry 6, 30, 98,
151, 153, 182
Samuel 30, 71, 72

Maslin
Thomas 158, 193

Mason
John 34, 40, 182,
192
Mat. 34
Mathew 39, 211
William 49, 177

Massey
Nicholas 177

Mather
George 3, 71, 142
Susanna 142
Susannah 71

Mathews
Hugh 60, 135, 182,
189
Roger 125, 126,
160, 184, 185
Thomas 6, 87, 140

Matthews
Thomas 87

Mattig
Elisabeth 10
Godfrey 10

Mattiggs

Elisabeth 31
Godfrey 31

Maudlin
Francis 61

Maudsley
Anne 10, 97
James 10, 97

Mauldin
Elisabeth 37, 123
Francis 165
William 37

Maxwell
James 160
Samuel 114

McBride
David 33

McClemy
William 206
Woney 206

McLoyd
Charles 26

McWilliams
Thomas 168

Mead
Francis 13
William 13

Meade
William 169

Meads
Elisabeth 204
William 122, 132,
204

Meares
Elisabeth 169

Mears
Elisabeth 132, 157

Medcalf
John 162

Medford
Rachel 81, 155
Rachell 1
Thomas 1, 41, 81,
155

Medley
John 51, 123

Medly
John 72

Meed
Anne 139
Jane 195
William 139, 195

Meeds
Jane 122

Meekins

Mary 210
Mollahane
    Mary 210
Mollen
    Charles 165
Moncaster
    William 55, 75
Montsier
    Margarett 26
    William 22, 26
Montsiere
    Margaret 32
    William 32
Moody
    James 58
Moor
    Thomas 194
Moore
    Deborah 116
    James 113
    Joseph 121
    Judith 31
    Michael 109, 164,
      174
    Mordecai 116
    Mordica 202
    Richard 26, 32, 49,
      116, 202
    Sarah 53
    Thomas 179
More
    Anne 15
    John 15, 179
    Joseph 53, 69
    Mary 179
Morgan
    James 61
    John 69, 90
    William 116
Morgin
    James 177
Morley
    Richard 89
    Sarah 89
Morris
    John 200
    Joseph 178, 198
    Manus 82
    Parthenia 179
    Perthenia 78
    Richard 12, 55, 170
    Samuel 166, 167
    Sarah 200
    Stephen 2, 28, 32

    Thomas 2, 28, 32,
      78
Morton
    Ann 54
    Robert 54, 201, 207
Moss
    Robert 7
Mouat
    James 24, 92, 113,
      183
Moulder
    Thomas 70
Moulen
    Robert 130
Mulcan
    Timothy 84
Mullakin
    James 77
Mullikin
    Daniel 38
    James 5, 12, 21
    John 24
    Patrick 53
Mumford
    James 56
    Thomas 133, 138,
      178
Muncester
    William 1, 18
Munday
    Robert 26
Munkister
    William 2
Munroe
    Dunkin 173
Murfee
    George 118
Murlow
    Mary 19
    William 19
Murphey
    Patrick 208
    Roger 108, 130,
      144, 174, 191,
      203, 211, 214
    Thomas 108
Murrain
    Grace 12
    James 12, 107
Murray
    John 56, 104, 138,
      150
Murrey
    Josephus 35

Murrow
   John 213
Musgrave
   Charles 2, 75
   William 2, 20, 75

Nairn
   Robert 56
Nairne
   Robert 79
Nash
   Charles 12, 46
   Elisabeth 46
Navarr
   John 92
Naylor
   John 181
Neal
   Charles 154
   Francis 72
   James 94
   Jonathon 72
   Raphael 77, 92, 94
Neale
   Charles 35, 108
   James 2, 77, 89, 92
   Jonathon 24
   raphael 89
   Raphaell 12, 34
   Roswell 39
   Samuel 103, 177
Negroes
   Bess 58
   Frank 58
   Joan 58
   Nan 58
   Tom 58
Nevet
   Francis 159
   Thomas 90, 115
Nevett
   Thomas 59, 65, 76,
      120, 129, 143,
      173
Nevile
   Edward 189
Nevill
   Thomas 189
Newbald
   William 80
Newbold
   Abigall 23, 96
   William 23, 96

Newgin
   Mary 15, 20
   Thomas 15, 20
Newman
   John 6, 29, 173
   Mary 29
Newnam
   Daniel 49
   John 54
   Mary 54
Newsam
   Thomas 185, 201
Newsham
   John 63, 146
Newsom
   Thomas 63
Newsome
   Thomas 70
Newton
   Edward 10, 15, 57,
      141
Nicholls
   Anne 74
   Isaac 117, 141
   Mary 74, 75, 123
   Susanna 74
   William 17, 147
Nichols
   William 106
Nicholson
   Charles 138
   Frances 32, 100,
      154
   Francis 187
   James 24, 183
   John 7, 9, 24, 32,
      100, 154, 187
   Rebecca 9, 24
   William 24, 74,
      120, 183
Nilson
   Hugh 178
Noble
   John 81
   Jonathon 50, 167,
      198
   Mark 181
   Robert 58, 73, 85,
      108, 208
   William 78
Noele
   John 15
Noell
   James 110

Pumphary
    Ebenezar 161
    Mercy 161
    Nathan 67
    Walter 67, 161
Pumphry
    Mary 67
    Walter 186
Purnell
    John 134, 166, 193
Purvis
    Thomas 19
Pusey
    Alce 134
    Alice 207
    William 134, 207
Pyper
    Isaac 138
Pypor
    Isaac 138

Quades
    Morris 193
Queen
    John 50
Quinnally
    Elisabeth 175
    Patrick 175
Quinton
    Walter 141, 182,
        183, 192

Rabblin
    Thomas 81
Rablin
    David 163, 170
    Elisabeth 163
    Mary 81
Rabling
    Thomas 90
Racey
    Dorothy 17
    Thomas 17
Racklife
    Nathaniel 194
Rackliffe
    Charles 134
    Nathaniel 134, 179
Raglass
    Margarett 6
Ragon
    John 37

Philip 39
Rakliffe
    Charles 134
Ramsey
    Barnet 80
    Barnett 138
    Charles 103
Ramxy
    Elisabeth 138
Randall
    Christ. 125
    Christopher 208
    Robert 70
    Thomas 67, 72, 125,
        146
Rankin
    Elisabeth 46
    John 32, 37, 46
Ransom
    George 33
    William 28, 30, 36,
        90
Ransome
    George 28
Rash
    Thomas 68
Rashoon
    Ann 89
    Anne 103
    Stephen 89, 103
Rason
    Philip 60
Ratcliff
    Charles 133
    James 53, 181
    John 181
    Margaret 181
    Nathaniel 133, 134
    Richard 181, 197
    William 133, 180
Rathell
    John 69
Rattenberry
    (N) 47
    John 47, 50, 51,
        200
    Margaret 50, 51,
        200
Rattenbury
    (N) 42
    John 42, 72, 131
    Margaret 131
Rawley
    Mary 38, 151, 176

Samuel 38, 151, 176
Rawlings
    Anthony 71, 82, 210
    Richard 124, 145,
        146, 161
Rawlins
    Richard 92
Rawly
    Samuel 57
Ray
    James 157, 193
    Luke 30, 93, 102
    Margaret 157
    William 119
Rayson
    Thomas 60
Read
    Anne 72, 115
    Elisabeth 119, 203
    Frances 23
    George 77
    James 119, 203
    Pierce 14, 149
    Richard 72
    Walter 14, 149
    William 115, 179
Reader
    Benjamin 81, 84,
        165, 168
    Elisabeth 81, 165,
        168
    Simon 81, 165, 168
Reading
    Elinor 137
    William 137
Readish
    Daniel 159
    Mary 159
Reas
    Evan 189
Reason
    Philip 40
Reave
    John 21
Reaves
    John 5, 12
    Thomas 2
Recards
    Thomas 70
Reckcott
    Susannah 112
Reddick
    Robert 177
Redding

William 181
Reddish
    Daniel 176
Redgrave
    Abraham 1, 40, 60,
        157, 193
    Elisabeth 40
Redmond
    Mary 97, 150
    Walter 97, 150
Reead
    John 34
Reece
    Gwenllyan 189
Reed
    Ann 206
    Anne 34
    Elisabeth 166, 167
    George 33
    John 70
    Kath. 84
    Peirce 198
    Pierce 166, 167
    Walter 21
    William 84
Reeves
    John 77
    Mary 102
    Thomas 51, 62, 63,
        66, 102, 120,
        122, 183, 192,
        203, 211
    Ubgat 66
    Ubgate 102, 120,
        192, 203, 211
    Ubgatt 51
Regan
    Darby 208
Register
    Robert 35, 89, 125,
        143, 151, 156,
        184
    Sarah 89, 125, 143,
        151, 156
Reglace
    Margaret 98, 153
Reid
    Elisabeth 180
    James 180
Relph
    Thomas 179
Rennolds
    Nicholas 189
    Walter 189

Rennols
　John 189
Renshaw
　Ann 201
　Anne 7, 96, 150,
　　164
　John 96, 150, 164,
　　165, 201
　Thomas 104, 166
　Underwood 166
　William 45
Revell
　Charles 134, 206
　Randolph 183, 206
Revil
　Charles 183
Reynoulds
　John 37
Riccaud
　Thomas 40
Rich
　David 56, 80
　Henry 21
　Jane 21, 178, 194
　Margaret 178
　Stephen 177
Richant
　Stephen 6
Richard
　William 198
Richards
　Abraham 15, 57
　Anne 86
　David 86
　Jones 14
　William 57
Richardson
　Bridget 42, 48, 80,
　　83
　John 175
　Nathaniel 48
　Nicholas 42, 80, 83
　Simon 175
　Thomas 51
　William 139, 165,
　　166, 213
Rickards
　John 133
Rickcott
　Susannah 112
Ricketts
　Susanna 85
Ridgley
　Henry 196, 201

Jane 72
　William 17, 72
Rigby
　Arthur 69, 114, 212
　Elinor 69, 212
　Elisabeth 105
　Lewis 105
Right
　Joseph 70
Ringgold
　William 139
Ringold
　Thomas 197
　William 175, 197
Rippeth
　Elisabeth 152, 182
　James 54, 152, 182
Rippith
　Elisabeth 23
　James 23
Rix
　John 10, 30, 33
Roach
　Elisabeth 133, 207
　John 105, 133
　Michael 133
　Nathaniel 133, 134,
　　180
　Nathaniell 207
　Sarah 105
Roberts
　Francis 7, 164, 201
　Jacob 169
　James 13, 25, 64
　John 61, 109, 160
　Theodolia 1
　Theodotia 100
　Thomas 205
　William 70
Robeson
　William 138
Robin
　Thomas 17
Robins
　Henry 30
　Thomas 30, 93, 122
Robinson
　Bridget 61, 135,
　　155
　David 11, 38, 53,
　　59, 85, 97, 114,
　　121, 122, 144,
　　145, 152, 174,
　　182, 191, 203,

Semmes
    Marmaduke 87
Serman
    Edward 167
Sermon
    Edward 104, 150
Serogin
    John 37
servant
    Scotch Mogzy 172
Severson
    Cathrine 17
    Thomas 17
Sewell
    Richard 91
Sexton
    Patrick 108
Shackers
    William 196
Shanahan
    George 98
Shanahawn
    George 207
Shanhan
    George 152
Shank
    John 52
Shanks
    John 27
Shannahawn
    George 23, 181
Sharp
    John 57
    Peter 54, 85
    William 57
Sharpe
    William 57
Sharply
    John 141
Shaunahan
    George 181
Shaw
    James 11, 68
    John 55
    Mary 22, 68
    Thomas 23
Shawn
    Darby 192
Shehon
    John 37
Sheild
    William 103
Shekertie
    John 118

Shepard
    John 68, 75, 107
    Mary 64, 107
Shephard
    John 64
Shepherd
    John 64
Sheppard
    William 182
Sheredine
    Jeremiah 46
    Thomas 131, 174
Sheridine
    Jeremiah 205
Sherwood
    Daniel 58
    Frances 121
    John 53, 121
    Philip 11, 35, 151
Shewell
    Charles 14, 149
Shield
    Bryan 99
    Bryant 153, 177
    Edmond 109
    Edward 99
    Henry 186
    William 99, 153,
        177
Shields
    Henry 161
    Laurana 161
Shiles
    Naomy 14, 96, 149,
        167
    Thomas 14, 96, 135,
        149, 167
Shipley
    Peter 116
Shirley
    Kath. 78
    Richard 78, 83
Shore
    John 95, 148
Shores
    Edward 130
Short
    Anne 55, 87, 118
    George 55, 75, 87,
        118
Showell
    Charles 50
Shucoushes
    Darby 200

Elisabeth 200
Shuttleberry
John 101, 156
Silvester
Thomas 188
Simcocks
William 137
Simmonds
Sarah 92
Simmons
Elisabeth 106
George 106, 126
Richard 92
Robert 165
Thomas 74, 165
Simms
Anthony 128
Simpson
William 80, 157
Simson
William 96
Sinclear
Michael 124
Sindall
Philip 132
Phillip 186
Singer
Thomas 28, 52
Sinnot
John 94
Sinnott
John 89, 193, 205
Simon 193
Skidmore
Samuel 7
Skinner
Adderton 11, 13,
    43, 45, 46, 64,
    74, 80, 106,
    112, 122, 132,
    169, 178, 195,
    204
Aderton 19
Andrew 38
Elisabeth 38
William 59, 65, 76,
    91, 115, 120,
    129, 143, 144,
    173
Skirven
Esther 133
William 133, 134
Slade
William 185

Slatter
John 92, 164, 190
Margaret 190
Slayde
William 51
Sly
Gerard 129
Slye
Garrard 196
Gerard 122
Gerrard 211
Smallwood
Ledstone 2
Smart
Capt. 58
John 50, 155
Sarah 50, 155
Smathers
William 192
Smith
Abraham 79, 178
Anne 3, 75
Charles 157, 200
Charles Somersett
    75
Daniel 53, 98, 123,
    153, 157, 171,
    182, 206, 209
Dorothy 44, 124
Edward 38, 142, 208
Elisabeth 53, 98,
    123, 153, 182,
    206, 209
Francis 85, 91,
    158, 189
Henry 199, 203
James 15, 116
John 17, 21, 24,
    27, 44, 64, 75,
    76, 85, 112,
    118, 119, 124,
    135, 156, 202
John Penny 128
Jonas 201
Martha 101, 142,
    155
Mary 165, 188, 208
Matha 15
Peter 117, 128
Renatus 22, 25,
    114, 127, 173
Robert 112, 208
Samuel 119
Sarah 112, 156

Thomas 15, 53, 84,
101, 141, 142,
155, 165, 183,
188, 189
Thomas Dyer 123
Walter 214
William 1, 3, 6,
19, 73, 75, 82,
138, 169
Smithers
Richard 9
Smithson
(N) 41, 65
Ann 52
Mary 98, 153
Owen 51, 52, 128,
193
Owin 52
Thomas 11, 98, 144,
145, 152, 153
William 47
Smock
Henry 133
Smoot
John 87, 88, 168
Thomas 45
Smoott
Thomas 37
Smothers
John 106
William 106
Smyth
Charles 158
Smythson
Mary 35
Smytly
Mary 28
Snowden
Richard 73, 74, 83,
163
Sollers
Sab. 94, 147
Somervell
James 73, 132
Southern
John 40
Southeron
John Johnson 39
Spalding
William 16
Sparrow
Sarah 92
Solomon 92, 145,
146, 157

Thomas 202
Spearman
William 16, 85, 101
Spedden
Hugh 88
Spence
Adam 79, 133, 150
Spencer
Daniel 37
Daniell 12
Edward 60, 61
William 210
Spink
Edward 81
Spinkes
Henry 52
Spinks
Francis 72
Sprigg
Thomas 40, 76
Spriggnal
John 143
Spriggnall
John 58, 97, 152,
156, 212
Sprignal
John 59
Sprignall
John 30
Springall
Charles 157
Heneritta 157
Spry
John 31, 100, 154,
177
Squires
John 162
St. Clare
Robert 127
Stanaway
Joseph 57, 82, 97
Sarah 57, 97
Standford
Charles 82
Standforth
John 8
Standifer
John 126, 131
Margaret 126
Stanford
Mary 31, 36
Richard 10
Stansbury
Luke 35

Thomas 29, 34
William 19
Sumner
John 186
Surman
Edward 167
Suttle
John 37, 118
Suttleberry
John 136
Sutton
John 58, 59
Swann
James 128
John 124
Thomas 140
Sweatnam
Hester 3
Sarah 3
William 3, 26, 109,
153, 187
Sweeting
Edward 186, 192
Sweetlove
James 92, 164
Swift
John 49
Mark 76
Richard 157, 208
Symons
Richard 106
Sympson
Patrick 73, 112

Talbot
John 124, 127, 144,
188, 190
William 43
Talbott
Edward 41, 201
John 129, 145
Thomas 23
William 12
Tall
Anthony 141
Talley
Thomas 131
Taney
John 5, 128, 165
Katharine 116
Tanny
John 206
Tany

John 116
Tarlton
John 17
Tarr
Samuel 49, 57
Tasker
Benjamin 4, 38,
116, 201
Tate
Hannah 54
Thomas 54
Tawney
John 34
Taylard
Audry 193
Taylor
Abraham 8, 19, 22,
42, 47, 65, 68,
76, 91, 93, 111,
161, 186
Ann 52
Anne 28
Audry 209
Henry 81, 94
Isabella 143, 151,
156, 184
Issabell 42
James 24, 42, 143,
151, 156, 184
Jane 76
John 19, 22, 42,
47, 65, 68, 76,
91, 93, 138,
161, 162, 186
Jonathon 136, 182
Martin 186, 208
Samuel 193
Sarah 185
Thomas 28, 37, 52,
53, 86, 88, 131,
140, 144, 160,
185, 208
Walter 179
Teal
Hanah 207
Teale
Edward 131
Hannah 131
Teele
Edward 207
Tennison
Abraham 62
Terrin
Robert 162

Ware
  John 38
Waren
  Basell 11
Warfield
  Alexander 19
  Benjamin 3
  Elisabeth 3
  John 1, 5, 12, 19
  Ruth 1
Warman
  Stephen 4, 9, 24,
    32, 39, 73, 74,
    92, 124, 130,
    142, 145, 174,
    183
Warner
  Charles 172
  Mary 10, 30, 99,
    110, 183
  Stephen 10, 30, 99,
    110, 183
  William 23
Warren
  Arthur 96, 150
  John 66
  Mary 71
  Nicholas 178
  Sampson 113
  Thomas 71
Warring
  Bazel 120
  Sampson 123
Warrington
  Mary 193
  Thomas 193
Warwick
  Arthur 134, 167
  William 134, 167
Wasson
  Francis 130
Wate
  Elias 138
  Sarah 138
Waterman
  Nicholas 137
  thomas 37, 45, 118
Waters
  Anne 92
  Elisabeth 104, 150,
    184
  Henry 83, 86, 92
  Richard 104, 105,
    150, 180, 184

William 104
Wathen
  Hudson 87, 187
Watkins
  John 24, 124, 130,
    144
  Mary 25
Watson
  Joseph 205
Watt
  George 53
Watters
  John 57
Watts
  Alexander 39, 92,
    103, 164
  Anne 138
  Coll. 205
  Elisabeth 16, 42,
    62, 83
  John 135, 138
  Peter 16, 34, 42,
    62, 83
  Stephen 16
  William 103, 165
Waughop
  James 123
  Thomas 90, 95, 123,
    200
Wauhop
  Thomas 16
Wayman
  Darcus 163
  Darius 197
  Edmund 163
  Leonard 38, 163,
    190, 197
Weasly
  John 208
Webb
  Aron 102
  Edgar 122
  Edward 136
  Henry 57
  John 104, 177
  Mark 133, 180
  Martha 102
  Peter 24, 121
  Rebecca 42, 88
  Richard 24, 42, 88,
    133, 178, 182
  Sarah 24, 37, 98,
    152, 182
Webster

John 161, 186
Mary 161
Weeden
   Henry 25
Weeks
   Benjamin 5, 186
   Mary 5, 186
Weers
   Robert 162
Welch
   Joan 52
   John 52, 115
   William 60
Wellman
   Elisabeth 5, 7
   Joseph 5, 67
   Martha 27
   Michael 27, 67
   Michaell 5
   Michell 5
   Thomas 5, 27, 67
Wells
   Frances 90, 93
   George 9, 22, 55,
     56, 68
   John 172, 173
   Martin 45
   Mary 78
   Thomas 11, 65, 90,
     93
Welman
   Michael 7
Welsh
   John 16, 26, 28,
     49, 74, 123
   Jone 28
   Judith 160
   Mary 30
   Pierce 30, 54, 97,
     126
   William 8, 101, 160
West
   John 26, 62
   Joseph 32, 100,
     154, 171
   Kath. 62
   Lotan 53
   Stephen 38
   William 171
Westall
   George 38, 44, 66
Westley
   Samuel 186
Westly

Samuel 128
Wetherall
   Elisabeth 10, 31
   William 10, 31
Wharton
   Charles 22, 167,
     180
   Daniel 198
   Henry 34
   Thomas 120
Wheatly
   James 123, 206
   John 107
   Sarah 14, 149, 159,
     194
   William 14, 56,
     149, 159, 194
Wheeler
   Benjamin 161
   Henry 210
   Roger 46
   William 104, 166
Wheetly
   James 107
   Joseph 206
Wherrett
   William 17
Whitcharly
   David 53
White
   Bernard 2, 19, 39,
     43, 76, 142,
     145, 147, 159,
     171
   Cathrine 10
   David 25
   Elisabeth 53
   Ellinor 76
   James 53
   John 78, 162
   Jonathon 19, 141,
     145, 171
   Josias 124
   Margaret 15
   Richard 53, 54, 121
   Rowland 42, 89
   Sarah 42, 162
   Stephen 5, 95, 149,
     187
   Timothy 10
   William 15, 53, 95,
     107, 209
Whitehead
   Francis 186, 192

William 116
Whittington
   Esther 79, 150
   Hannah 79, 150
   Southy 79, 133, 150
   William 51, 79, 80,
     95, 133, 138,
     149, 150, 198
Whitton
   Richard 165
Whorton
   John 200
Wickes
   Samuel 137
Wicks
   Samuell 210
Wild
   Peter 109
Wildgoes
   Thomas 138
Wildgoos
   Thomas 213
Wildgoose
   Thomas 167
Wildman
   Cornelius 184
   Elisabeth 187
   James 128, 170, 184
Wiles
   Peter 26
Wilkins
   Andrew 58
Wilkinson
   Anthony 8, 100, 155
   John 46, 132, 195
   Mary 8
   William 34
Willcoxen
   Thomas 67
William
   Hugh 195
Williams
   Baruch 45
   Edward 176, 187,
     189
   Elisabeth 169, 177,
     205, 214
   Enion 18, 157
   Henry 26, 197
   Hopton 192
   Hugh 169, 205
   Jacob 128
   James 109, 177
   John 178, 179, 194

   Katharine 109, 177
   Mary 176
   Mathew 26
   Thomas 18, 45, 79,
     80, 207, 214
   William 169
Williamson
   James 73, 106
   Samuel 28
   Samuell 211
   Thomas 7, 44, 124
Willin
   Robert 6
Willis
   John 131
   Richard 13
Willison
   Mary 175
Willmot
   William 75
Willmott
   James 46, 75
   John 22
   William 46, 74
Willotson
   Thomas 22, 32, 99,
     154
Willott
   Edward 45
Wills
   John 160, 201
   Margaret 160
Willson
   John 69
   Mary 168
   Michael 210
   Thamer 69
   Thomas 100
Willymott
   Margaret 132
   William 132, 169
Wilmer
   Lambert 160
   Simon 40, 60, 68,
     88, 113
Wilmore
   Simon 9, 46
Wilmote
   Jane 41
   John 41
Wilmott
   John 48, 146
   William 12
Wilson

Mary 49
Nathaniel 26, 32,
    49, 99
Neriah 32
Notley 177
Rachel 159
Rachell 200
Robert 154
Robert Norris 109
Solomon 26, 49, 108
Thomas Hynson 3,
    17, 49
William 159, 162,
    200
Wrighte
  Edward 177
Wrightson
  John 17
  Mary 17
Wyat
  James 108, 109,
      136, 154, 188
  Joanna 108, 154,
      188
  William 108
Wyatt
  Joseph 201

142, 147, 195
George 3, 142, 196
Jacob 85, 135, 156,
    189
James 140
John 51, 132
Jos. 29
Joseph 61, 155,
    156, 189
Mary 85, 156
Richard 67
William 3, 37, 74,
    142, 147, 195,
    196

Yates
  Charles 124
  Jane 124
  Lydia 11, 19
  Robert 19
Yealdhall
  William 63
Yearly
  William 157, 181
Yiealdhall
  William 18
Yopp
  Charles 6, 18, 88,
      94, 140
  Margaret 148
  Margarett 12
  Roger 12, 37, 148
  Susanna 6, 18, 87,
      94
  Susannah 88
York
  George 186
Young
  David 49, 127, 163
  Francis 37, 77,

INDEX OF EQUITY CASES

Hopkins vs. Schee 9, 13, 27, 41, 47, 65, 76, 88
Howard vs. Lillingston 76

Innes vs. Hopewell 194, 203

Jenifer vs. Dansey 131, 144, 174, 191, 203, 211

King vs. James 197

Laurence vs. Talbot & Watkins 144
Laurence vs. Talbott 129
Lloyd & Lloyd vs. Lloyd 57

Macnemara vs. Henderson 130

Nevett vs. Skinner 59, 65, 76, 91, 115, 120,
   129, 143, 173

Paca vs. Hall 129, 143, 160, 174, 191
Pearce vs. Codd 212
Pemberton & Pemberton vs. Beswick & Blackwell 77
Pemberton vs. Grundy 65, 91
Pemberton vs. Lloyd & Pemberton 127, 129, 144,
   174
Potts vs. Pearce 127

Quinton vs. Conoway 183, 192

Reeves & Hoskins vs. Reeves 192, 203, 211
Reeves vs. Reeves 102
Robinson vs. est. of Lowe 59, 121
Robinson vs. Lowe 85, 114, 144, 174, 191, 203,
   211

Schee vs. Hopkins 129
Slye vs. est. of Vansweringen 122
Smithers & Stokes vs. Marshall 9
Stephens vs. Maccambly 27

Trensam vs. Rattenberry 50

Vestry of St. Michael's Parish vs. Fletcher 115,
   120, 129, 143, 173, 191, 203, 211

Warring vs. est. of Craycroft 120
White vs. Burnham 124

www.ingramcontent.com/pod-product-compliance
Lightning Source LLC
Chambersburg PA
CBHW061004280326
41935CB00009B/824